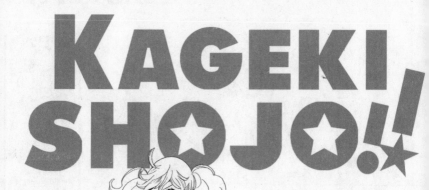

KAGEKI SHOJO!!

story & art by
Kumiko Saiki

6

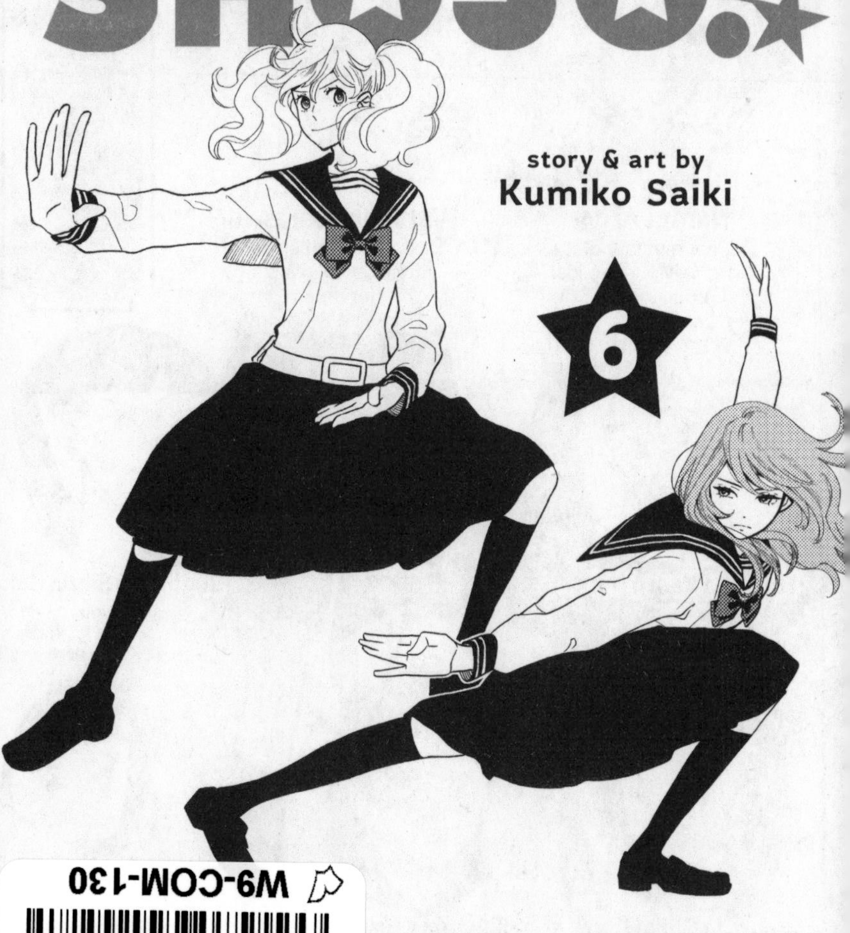

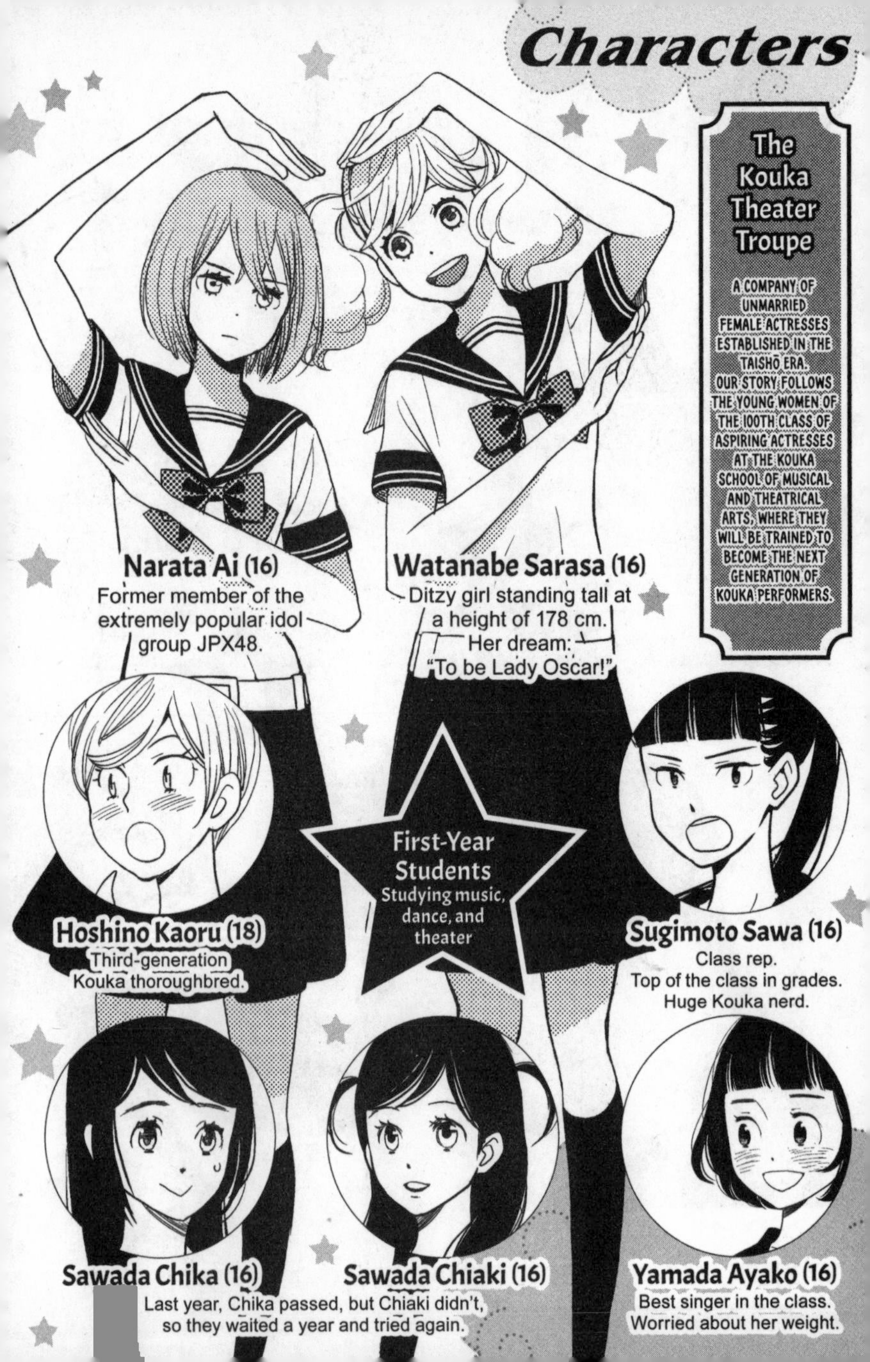

Characters
The Kouka Theater Troupe
A COMPANY OF UNMARRIED FEMALE ACTRESSES ESTABLISHED IN THE TAISHO ERA. OUR STORY FOLLOWS THE YOUNG WOMEN OF THE 100TH CLASS OF ASPIRING ACTRESSES AT THE KOUKA SCHOOL OF MUSICAL AND THEATRICAL ARTS, WHERE THEY WILL BE TRAINED TO BECOME THE NEXT GENERATION OF KOUKA PERFORMERS.
Narata Ai (16)
Former member of the extremely popular idol group JPX48.
Watanabe Sarasa (16)
Ditzy girl standing tall at a height of 178 cm. Her dream: "To be Lady Oscar!"
First-Year Students
Studying music, dance, and theater
Hoshino Kaoru (18)
Third-generation Kouka thoroughbred.
Sugimoto Sawa (16)
Class rep. Top of the class in grades. Huge Kouka nerd.
Sawada Chika (16)
Sawada Chiaki (16)
Last year, Chika passed, but Chiaki didn't, so they waited a year and tried again.
Yamada Ayako (16)
Best singer in the class. Worried about her weight.

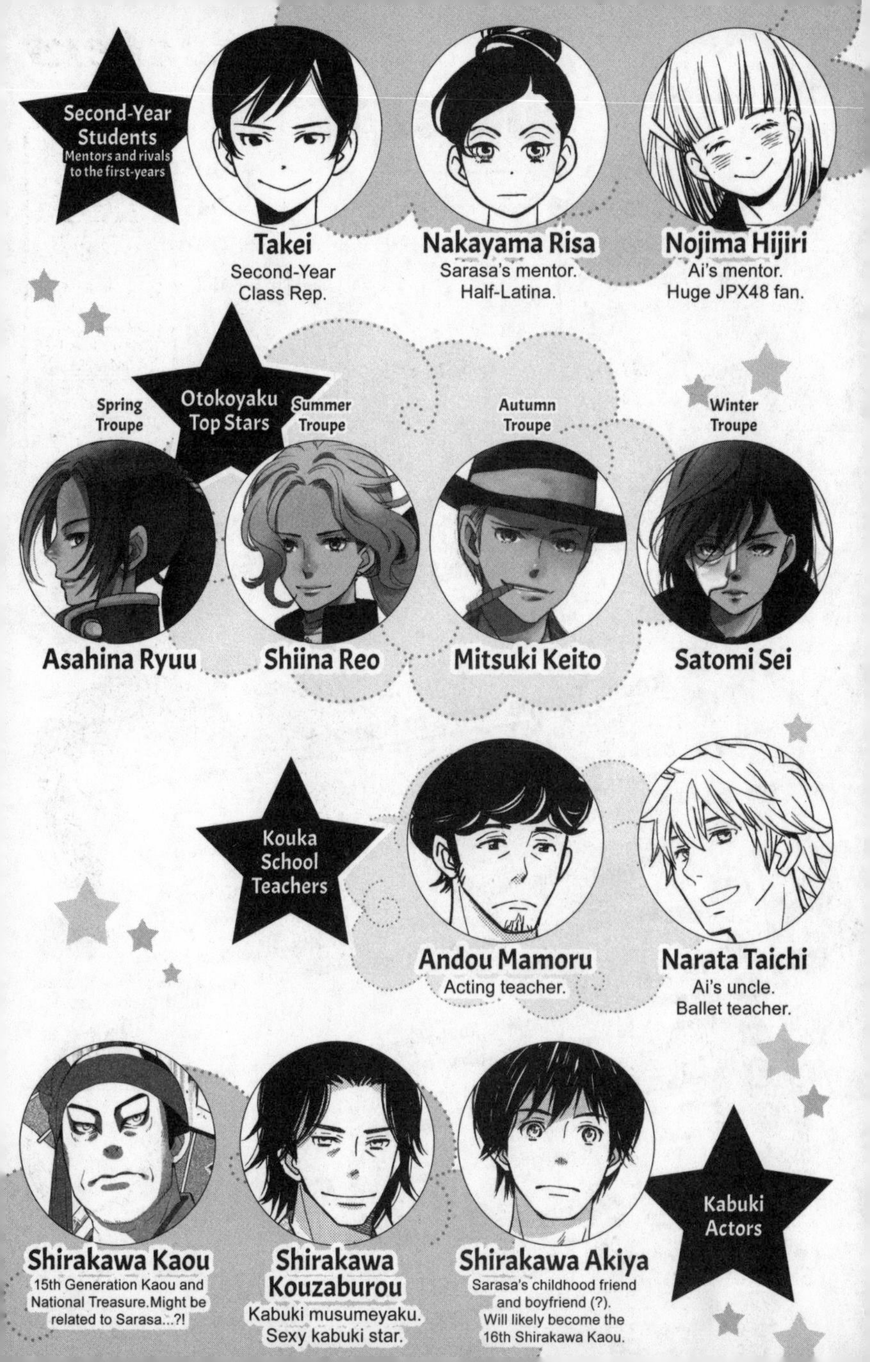
Second-Year Students
Mentors and rivals to the first-years
Takei
Second-Year Class Rep.
Nakayama Risa
Sarasa's mentor. Half-Latina.
Nojima Hijiri
Ai's mentor. Huge JPX48 fan.
Otokoyaku Top Stars
Spring Troupe
Asahina Ryuu
Summer Troupe
Shiina Reo
Autumn Troupe
Mitsuki Keito
Winter Troupe
Satomi Sei
Kouka School Teachers
Andou Mamoru
Acting teacher.
Narata Taichi
Ai's uncle. Ballet teacher.
Kabuki Actors
Shirakawa Kaou
15th Generation Kaou and National Treasure.Might be related to Sarasa...?!
Shirakawa Kouzaburou
Kabuki musumeyaku. Sexy kabuki star.
Shirakawa Akiya
Sarasa's childhood friend and boyfriend (?). Will likely become the 16th Shirakawa Kaou.

CONTENTS

No.

Date

Kouka Troupe Terms to Know! ★

Kouka Theater Troupe
Founded a hundred years ago as a theater troupe comprised of young, unmarried women.
Split into four troupes (Spring/Summer/Autumn/Winter). Main theater is in Kobe.

Otokoyaku / Musumeyaku
Designated roles for the gender of characters actresses play. Otokoyaku actresses play male or
masculine characters, while musumeyaku actresses play female or feminine characters.

Top Star
The actress who heads her troupe. Each troupe has an otokoyaku top star and musumeyaku top star.
Top stars appear in every major production.

Kouka School of Musical and Theatrical Arts
Two-year prep school where the next stars of the Kouka Troupe are forged.
Girls can apply anytime between 9th and 12th grade!

First-Year Students vs. Second-Year Students
While first-year students primarily focus on their studies, second-year students are tasked both
with their studies and mentoring the first-year students, as well as managing their cleaning
schedule and helping them with lifestyle adjustments.

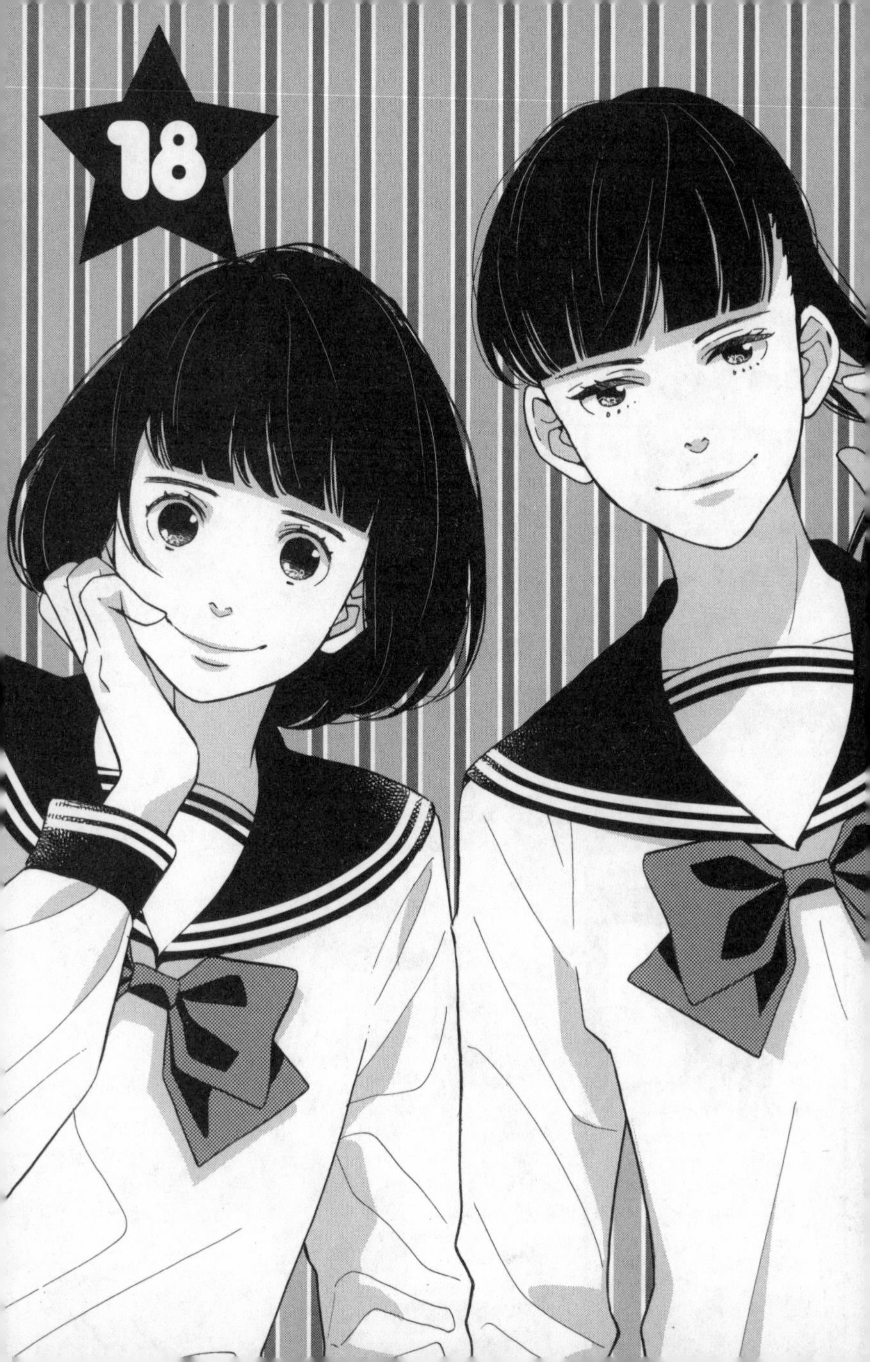
18

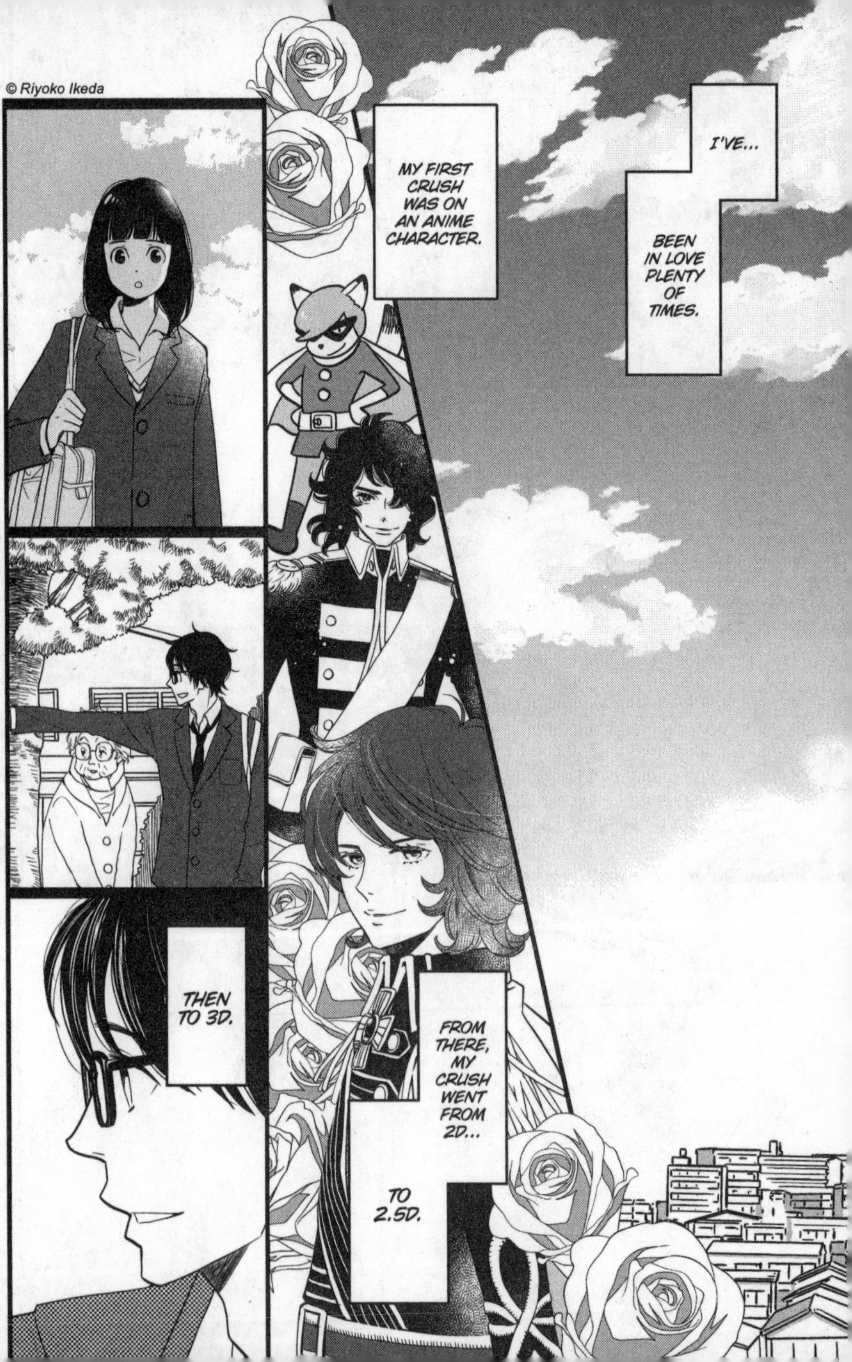
I'VE...
BEEN IN LOVE PLENTY OF TIMES.
MY FIRST CRUSH WAS ON AN ANIME CHARACTER.
FROM THERE, MY CRUSH WENT FROM 2D...
TO 2.5D.
THEN TO 3D.

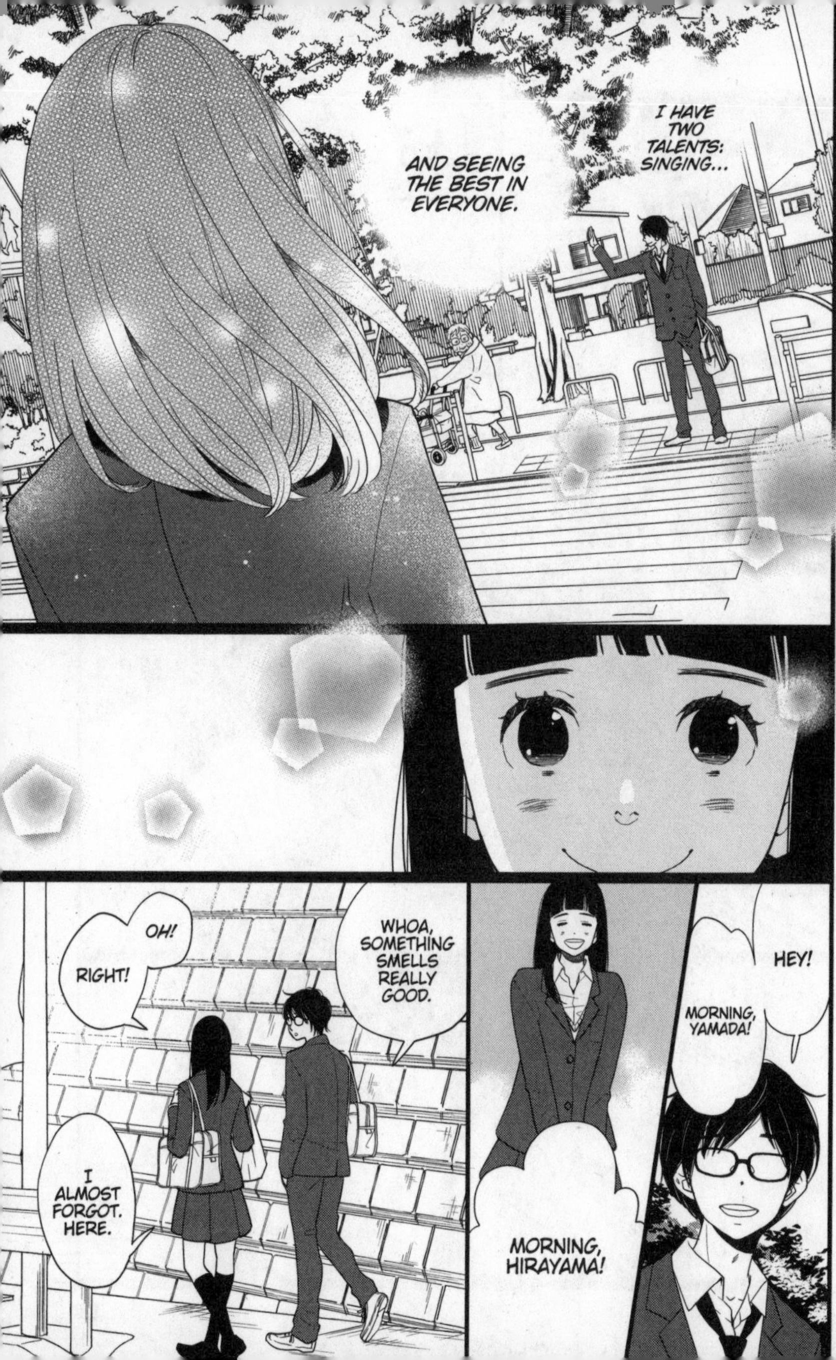
I HAVE TWO TALENTS: SINGING...
AND SEEING THE BEST IN EVERYONE.
HEY!
MORNING, YAMADA!
MORNING, HIRAYAMA!
WHOA, SOMETHING SMELLS REALLY GOOD.
OH!
RIGHT!
I ALMOST FORGOT. HERE.

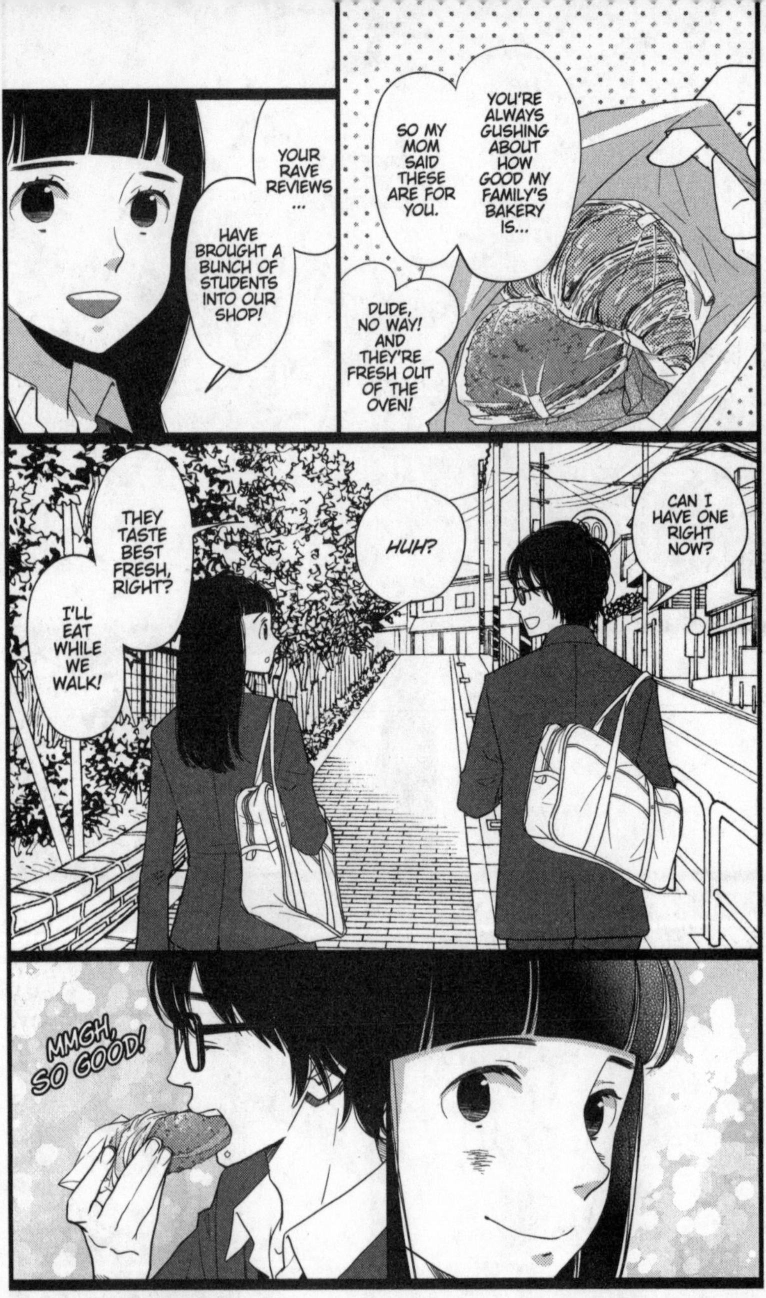
YOU'RE ALWAYS GUSHING ABOUT HOW GOOD MY FAMILY'S BAKERY IS...
SO MY MOM SAID THESE ARE FOR YOU.
DUDE, NO WAY! AND THEY'RE FRESH OUT OF THE OVEN!
YOUR RAVE REVIEWS ...
HAVE BROUGHT A BUNCH OF STUDENTS INTO OUR SHOP!
CAN I HAVE ONE RIGHT NOW?
HUH?
THEY TASTE BEST FRESH, RIGHT?
I'LL EAT WHILE WE WALK!
MMGH, SO GOOD!

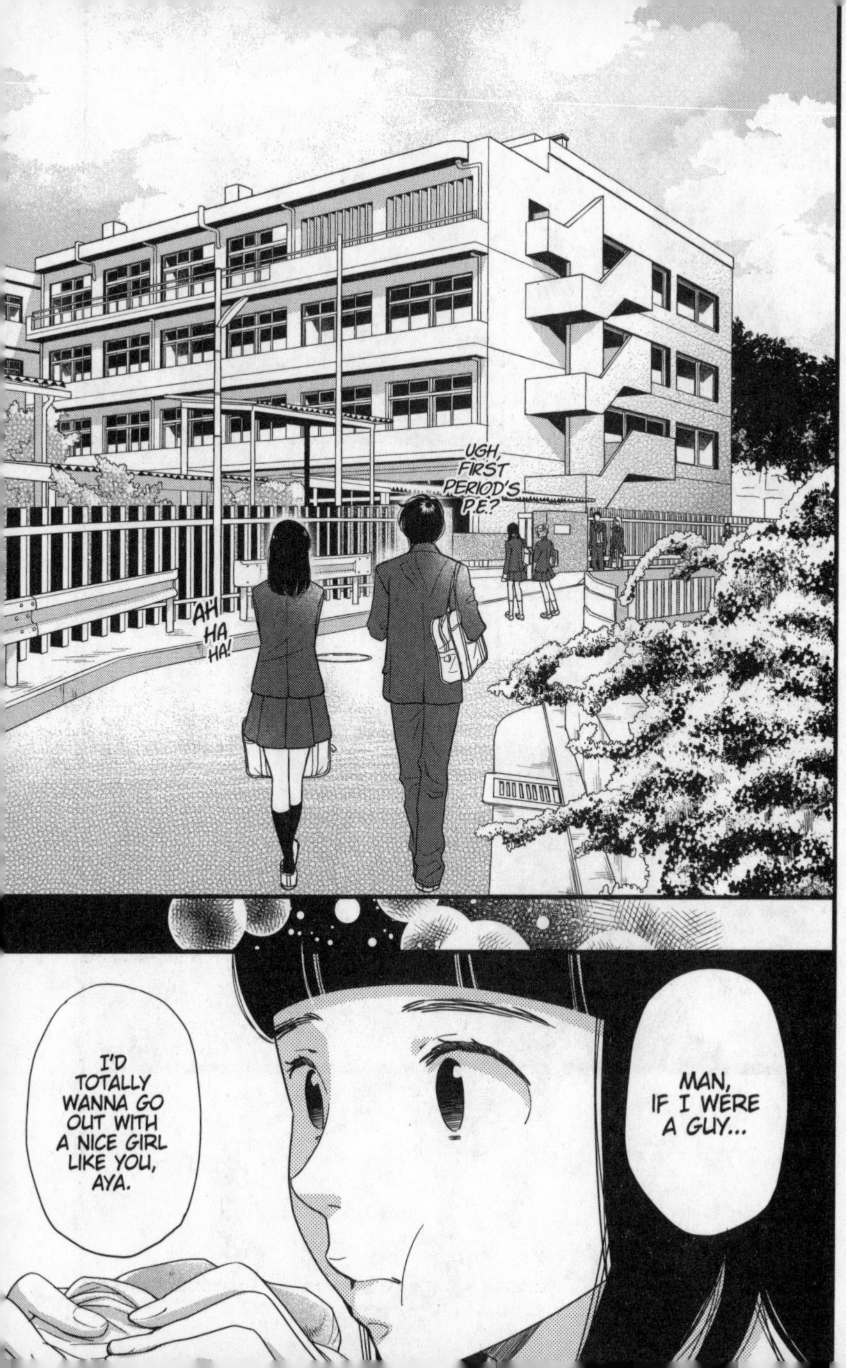
UGH, FIRST PERIOD'S P.E.?
AH HA HA!
MAN, IF I WERE A GUY...
I'D TOTALLY WANNA GO OUT WITH A NICE GIRL LIKE YOU, AYA.

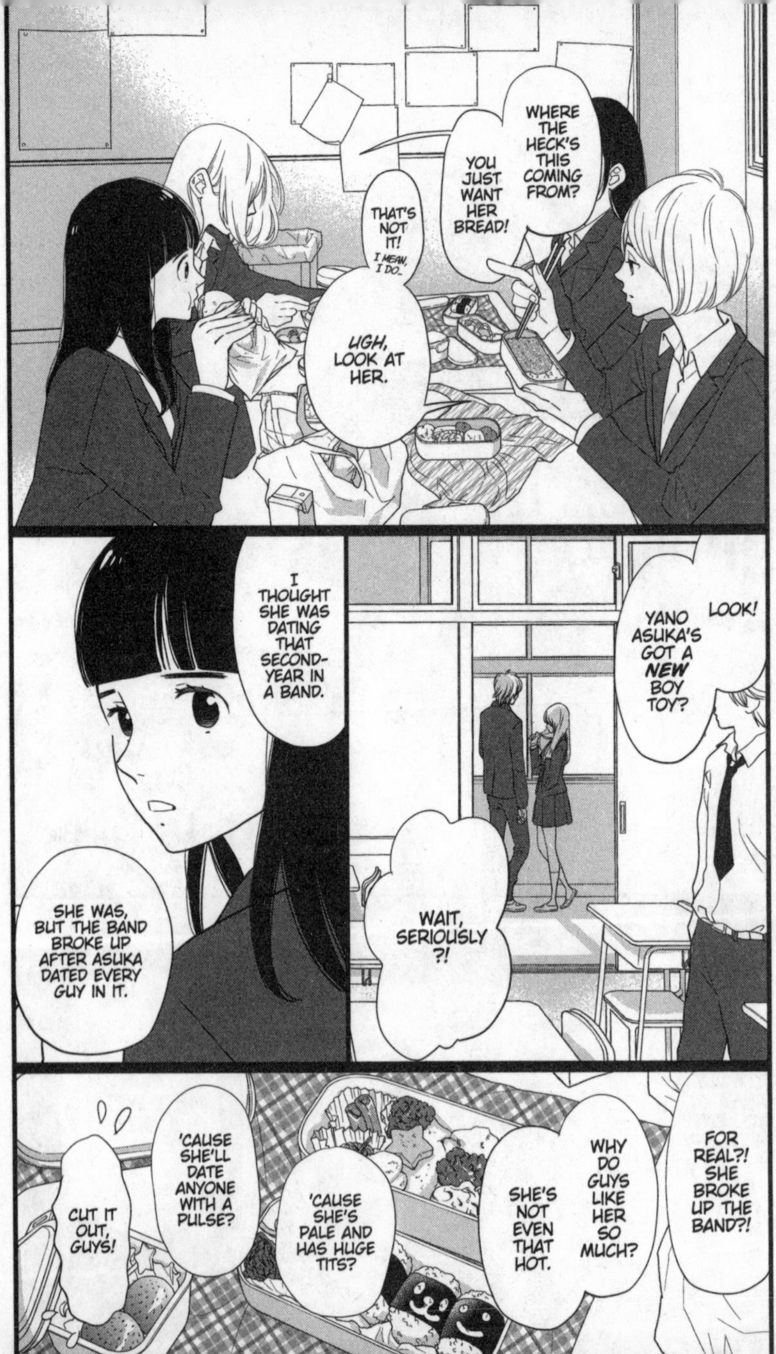
WHERE THE HECK'S THIS COMING FROM?
YOU JUST WANT HER BREAD!
THAT'S NOT IT!
I MEAN, I DO...
UGH, LOOK AT HER.
LOOK!
YANO ASUKA'S GOT A NEW BOY TOY?
WAIT, SERIOUSLY?!
I THOUGHT SHE WAS DATING THAT SECOND-YEAR IN A BAND.
SHE WAS, BUT THE BAND BROKE UP AFTER ASUKA DATED EVERY GUY IN IT.
FOR REAL?! SHE BROKE UP THE BAND?!
WHY DO GUYS LIKE HER SO MUCH?
SHE'S NOT EVEN THAT HOT.
'CAUSE SHE'S PALE AND HAS HUGE TITS?
'CAUSE SHE'LL DATE ANYONE WITH A PULSE?
CUT IT OUT, GUYS!

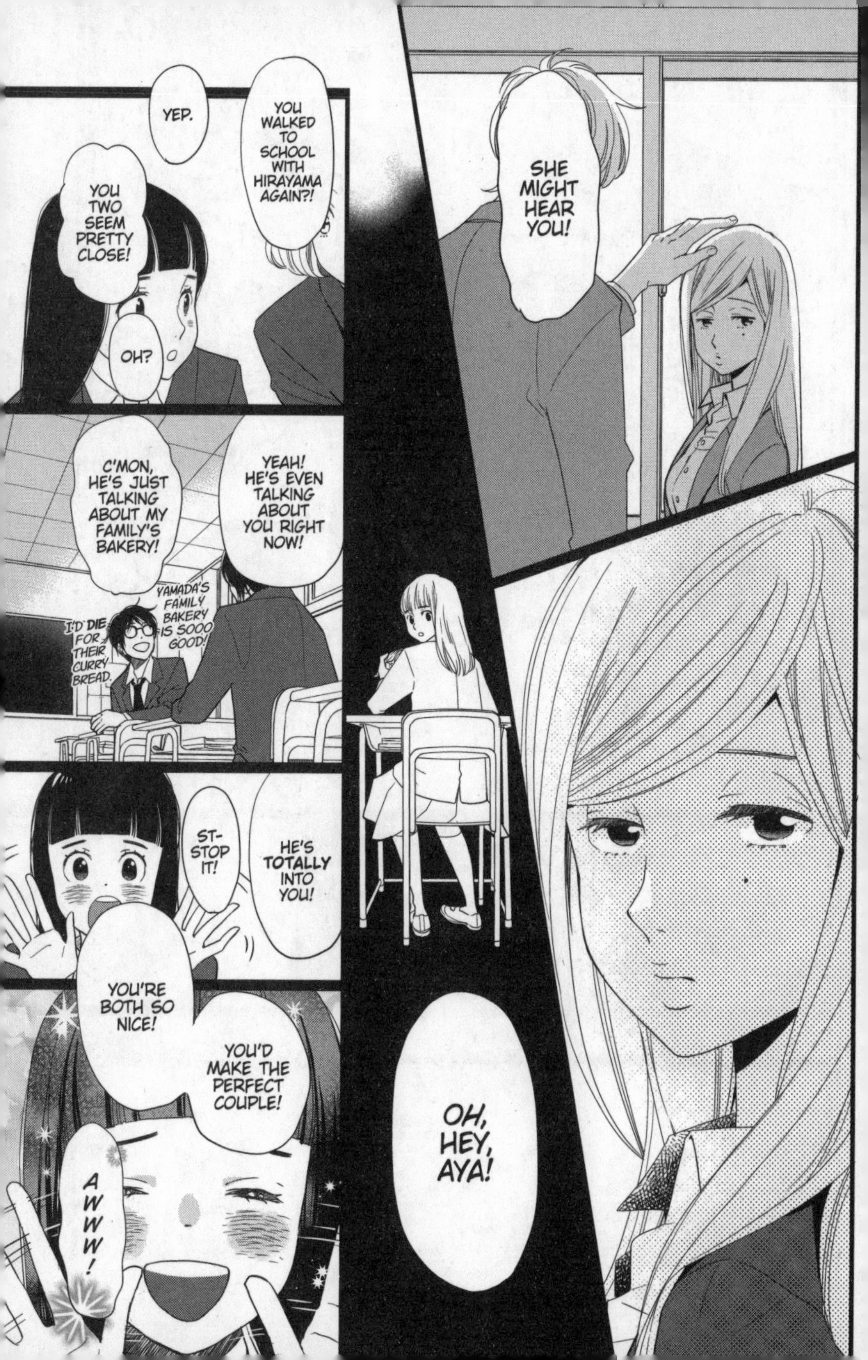
SHE MIGHT HEAR YOU!
OH, HEY, AYA!
YOU WALKED TO SCHOOL WITH HIRAYAMA AGAIN?!
YEP.
YOU TWO SEEM PRETTY CLOSE!
OH?
YEAH! HE'S EVEN TALKING ABOUT YOU RIGHT NOW!
C'MON, HE'S JUST TALKING ABOUT MY FAMILY'S BAKERY!
YAMADA'S FAMILY BAKERY IS SOOO GOOD!
I'D DIE FOR THEIR CURRY BREAD.
HE'S TOTALLY INTO YOU!
ST-STOP IT!
YOU'RE BOTH SO NICE!
YOU'D MAKE THE PERFECT COUPLE!
AWWW!

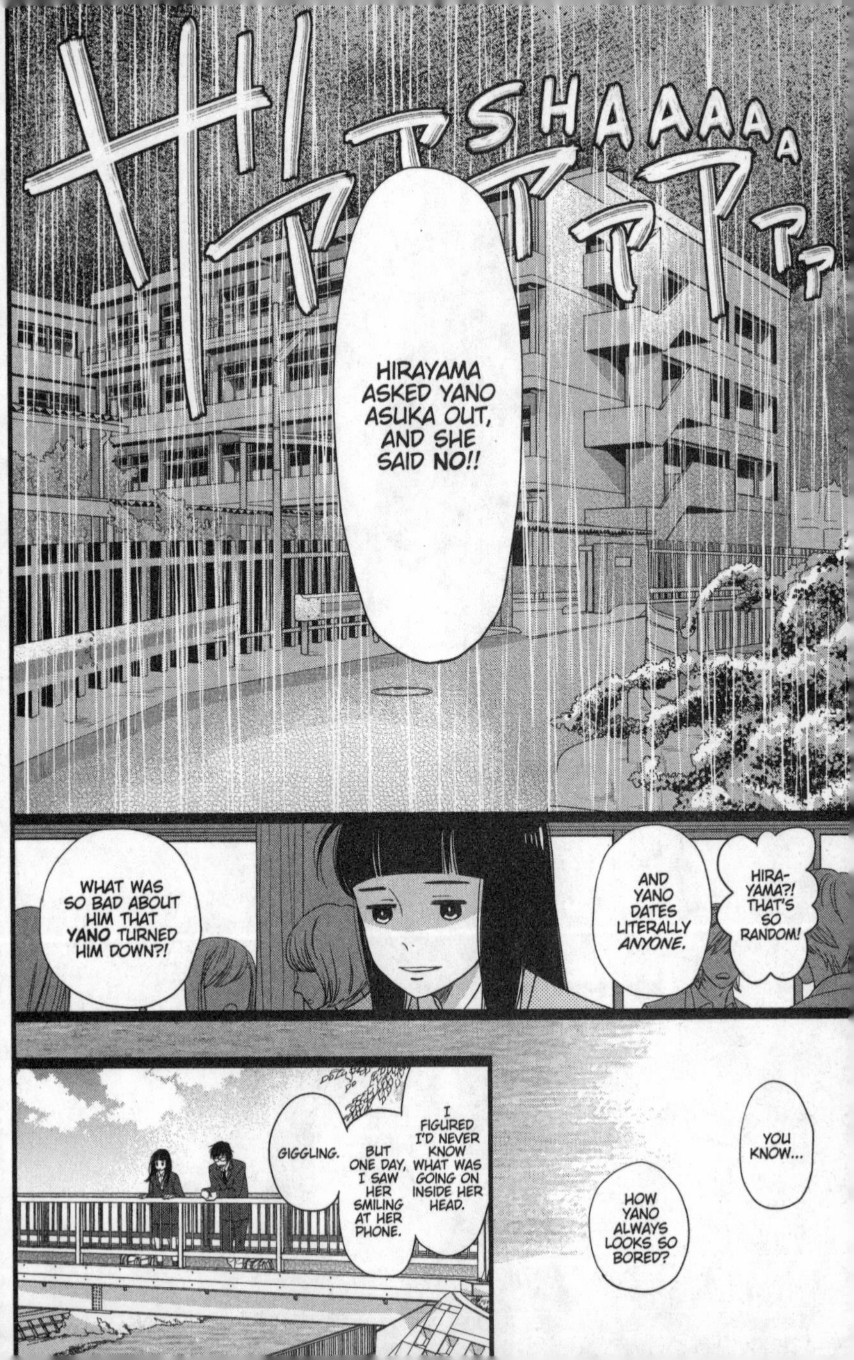
SHAAAAA
HIRAYAMA ASKED YANO ASUKA OUT, AND SHE SAID NO!!
HIRA-YAMA?! THAT'S SO RANDOM!
AND YANO DATES LITERALLY ANYONE.
WHAT WAS SO BAD ABOUT HIM THAT YANO TURNED HIM DOWN?!
YOU KNOW...
HOW YANO ALWAYS LOOKS SO BORED?
I FIGURED I'D NEVER KNOW WHAT WAS GOING ON INSIDE HER HEAD.
BUT ONE DAY, I SAW HER SMILING AT HER PHONE.
GIGGLING.

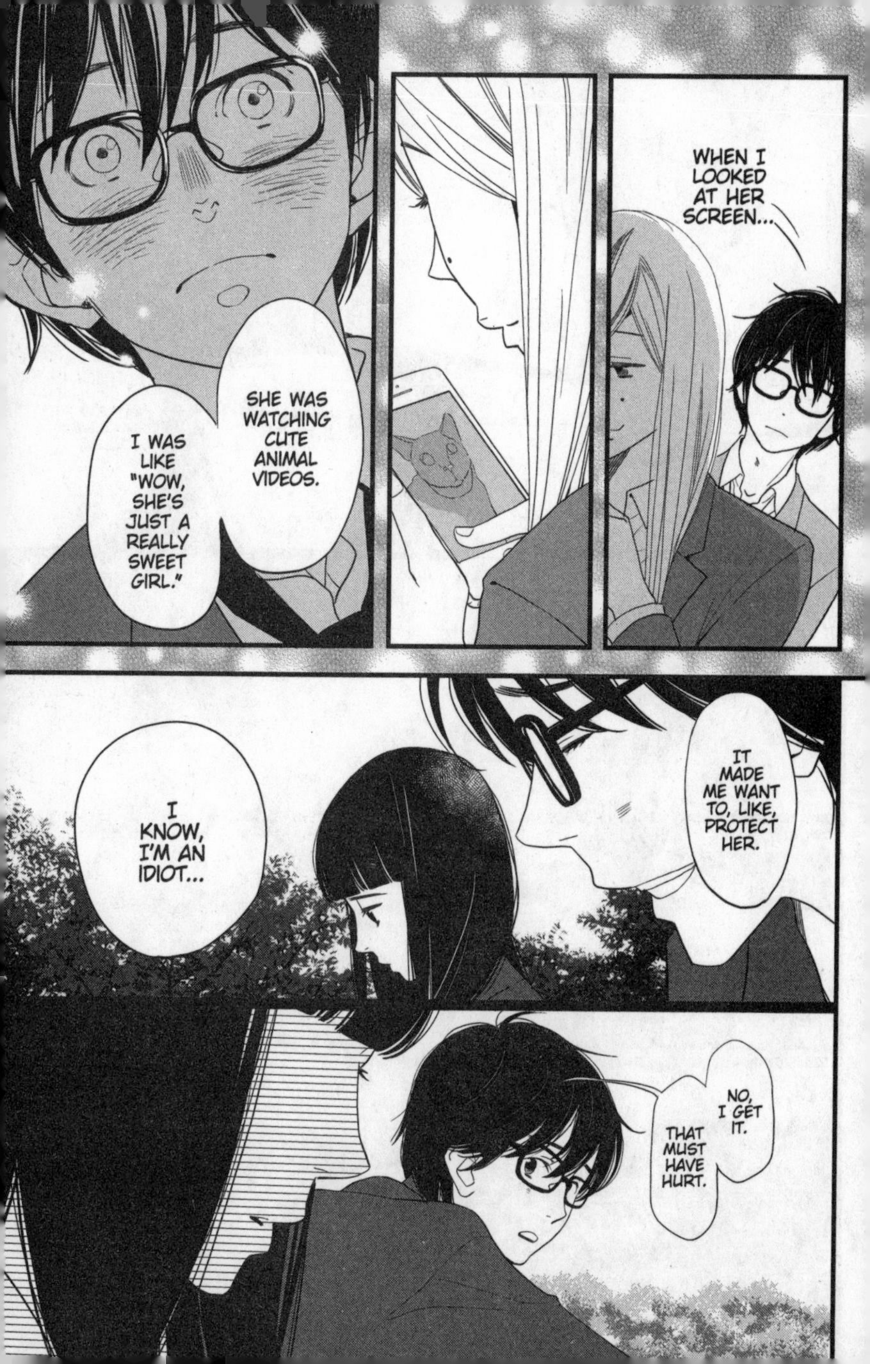
WHEN I LOOKED AT HER SCREEN...
SHE WAS WATCHING CUTE ANIMAL VIDEOS.
I WAS LIKE "WOW, SHE'S JUST A REALLY SWEET GIRL."
IT MADE ME WANT TO, LIKE, PROTECT HER.
I KNOW, I'M AN IDIOT...
NO, I GET IT.
THAT MUST HAVE HURT.

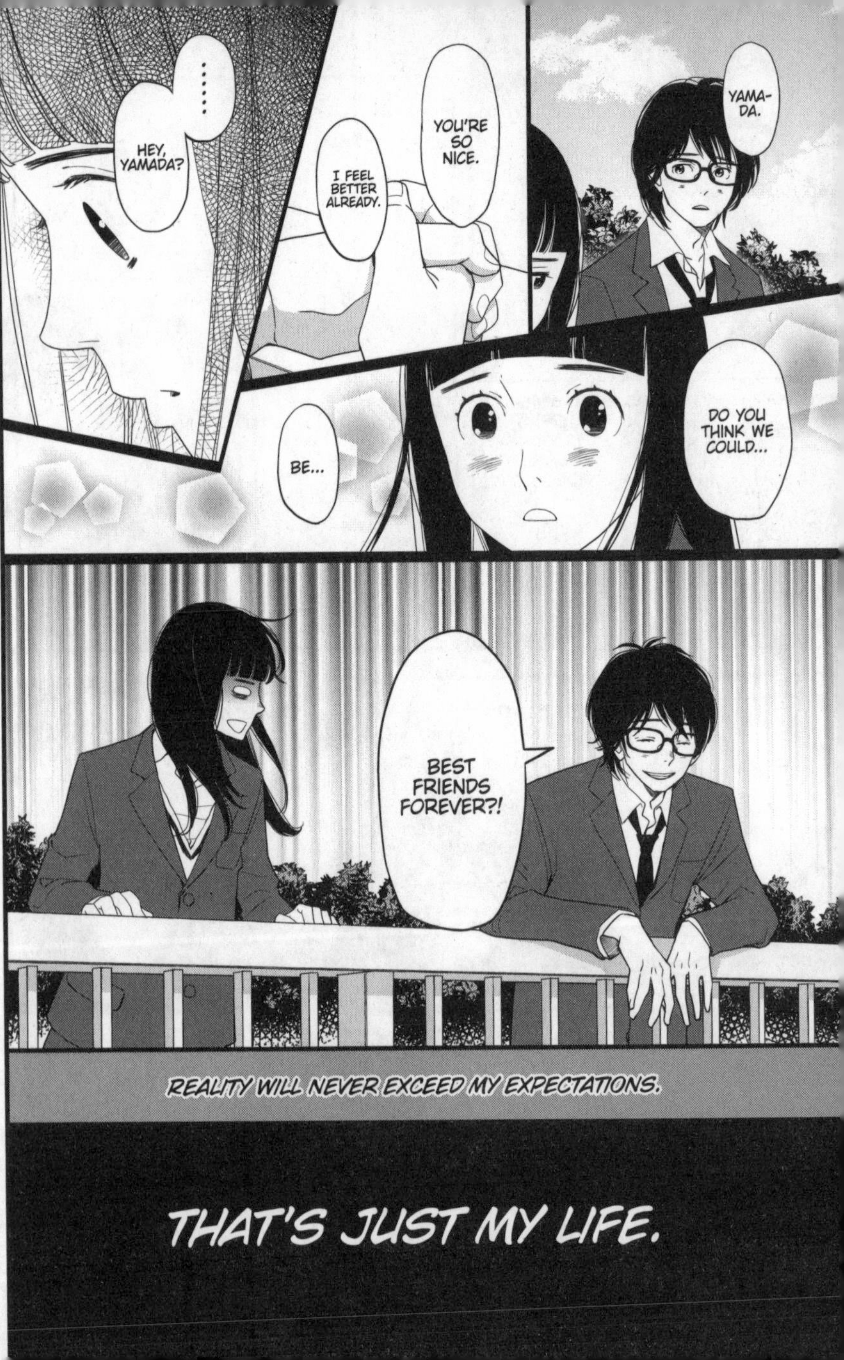
YAMA-DA.
YOU'RE SO NICE.
I FEEL BETTER ALREADY.
......
HEY, YAMADA?
DO YOU THINK WE COULD...
BE...
BEST FRIENDS FOREVER?!
REALITY WILL NEVER EXCEED MY EXPECTATIONS.
THAT'S JUST MY LIFE.

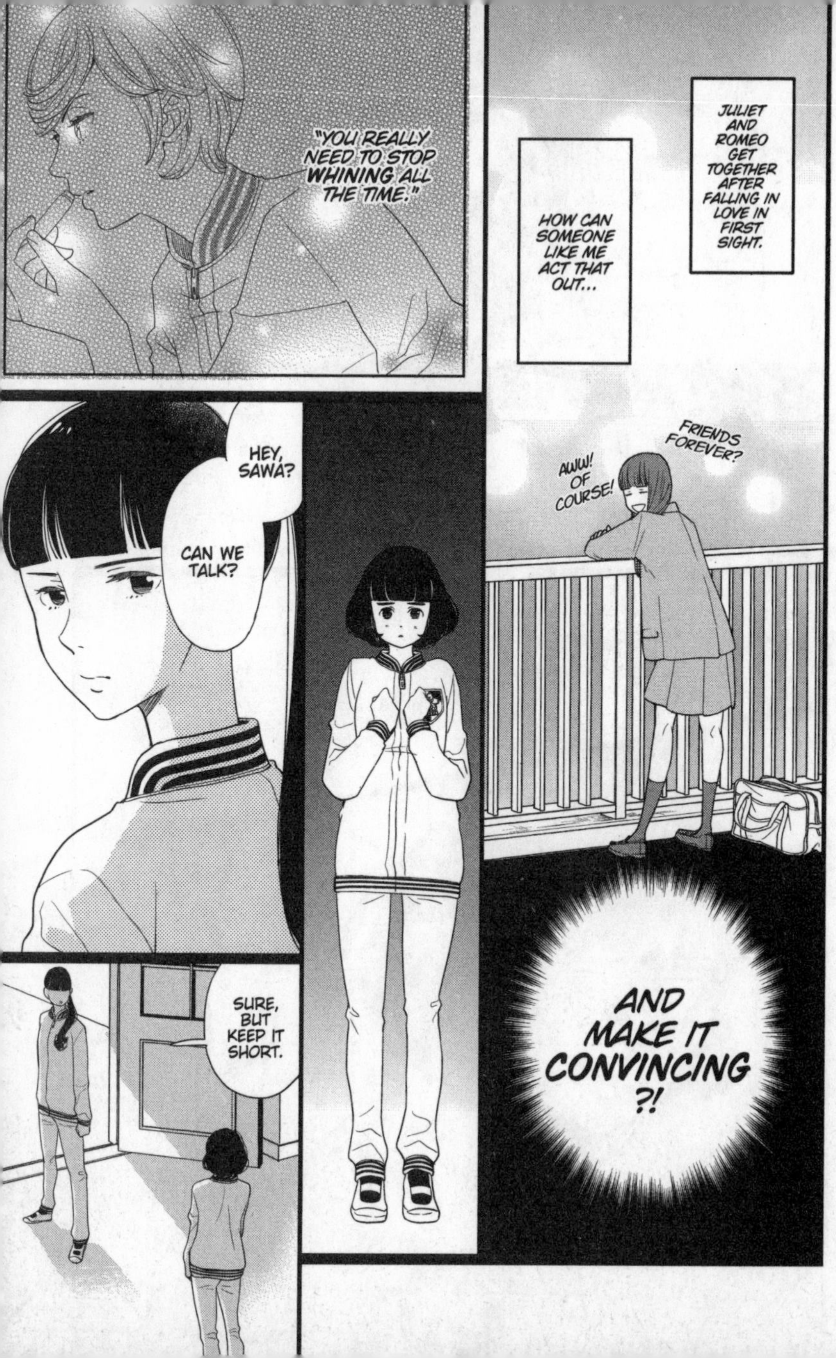
JULIET AND ROMEO GET TOGETHER AFTER FALLING IN LOVE IN FIRST SIGHT.
HOW CAN SOMEONE LIKE ME ACT THAT OUT...
FRIENDS FOREVER?
AWW! OF COURSE!
AND MAKE IT CONVINCING ?!
"YOU REALLY NEED TO STOP WHINING ALL THE TIME."
HEY, SAWA?
CAN WE TALK?
SURE, BUT KEEP IT SHORT.

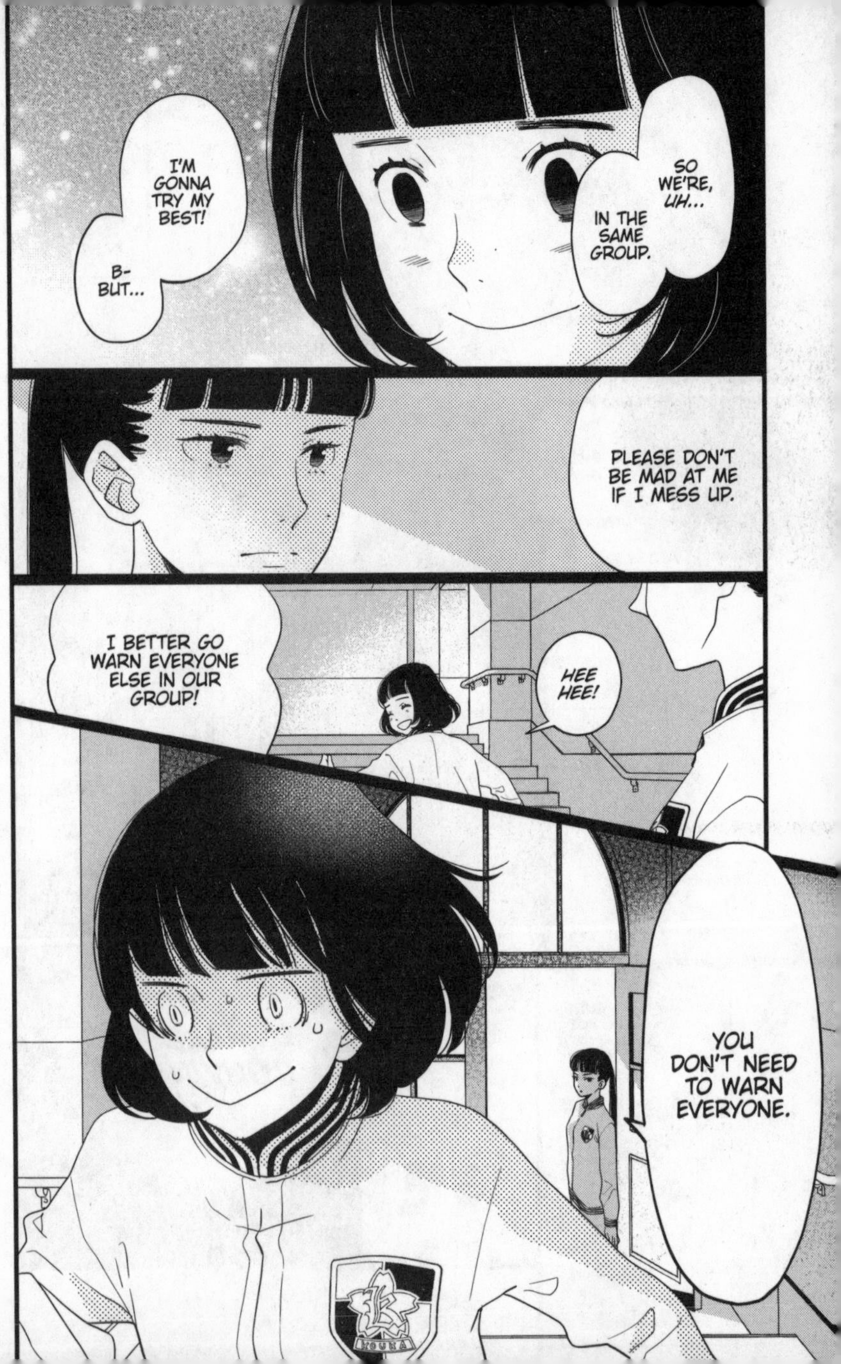
SO WE'RE, UH... IN THE SAME GROUP.
I'M GONNA TRY MY BEST! B-BUT...
PLEASE DON'T BE MAD AT ME IF I MESS UP.
I BETTER GO WARN EVERYONE ELSE IN OUR GROUP!
HEE HEE!
YOU DON'T NEED TO WARN EVERYONE.
KOUNA

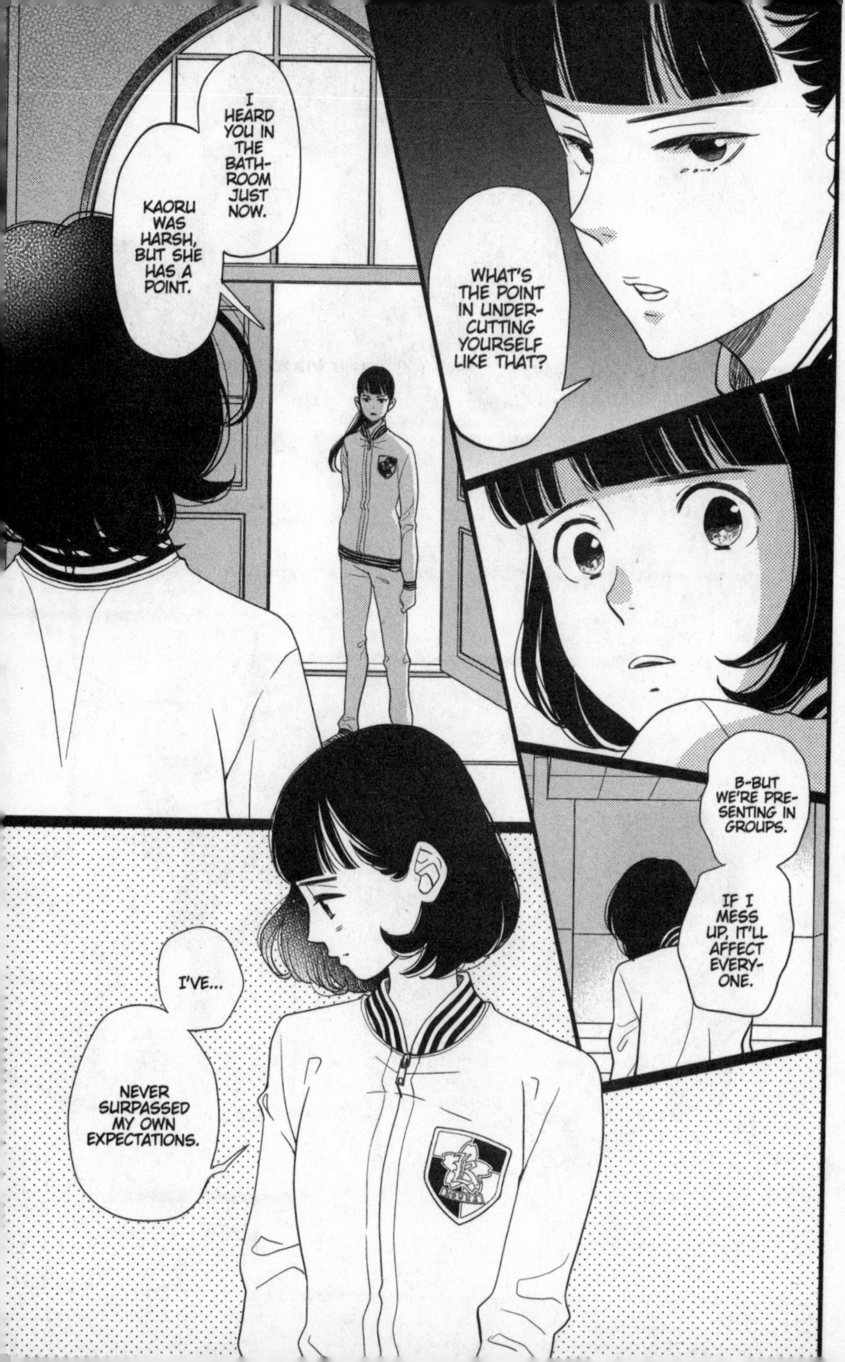
WHAT'S THE POINT IN UNDER-CUTTING YOURSELF LIKE THAT?
B-BUT WE'RE PRE-SENTING IN GROUPS.
IF I MESS UP, IT'LL AFFECT EVERY-ONE.
I HEARD YOU IN THE BATH-ROOM JUST NOW.
KAORU WAS HARSH, BUT SHE HAS A POINT.
I'VE...
NEVER SURPASSED MY OWN EXPECTATIONS.

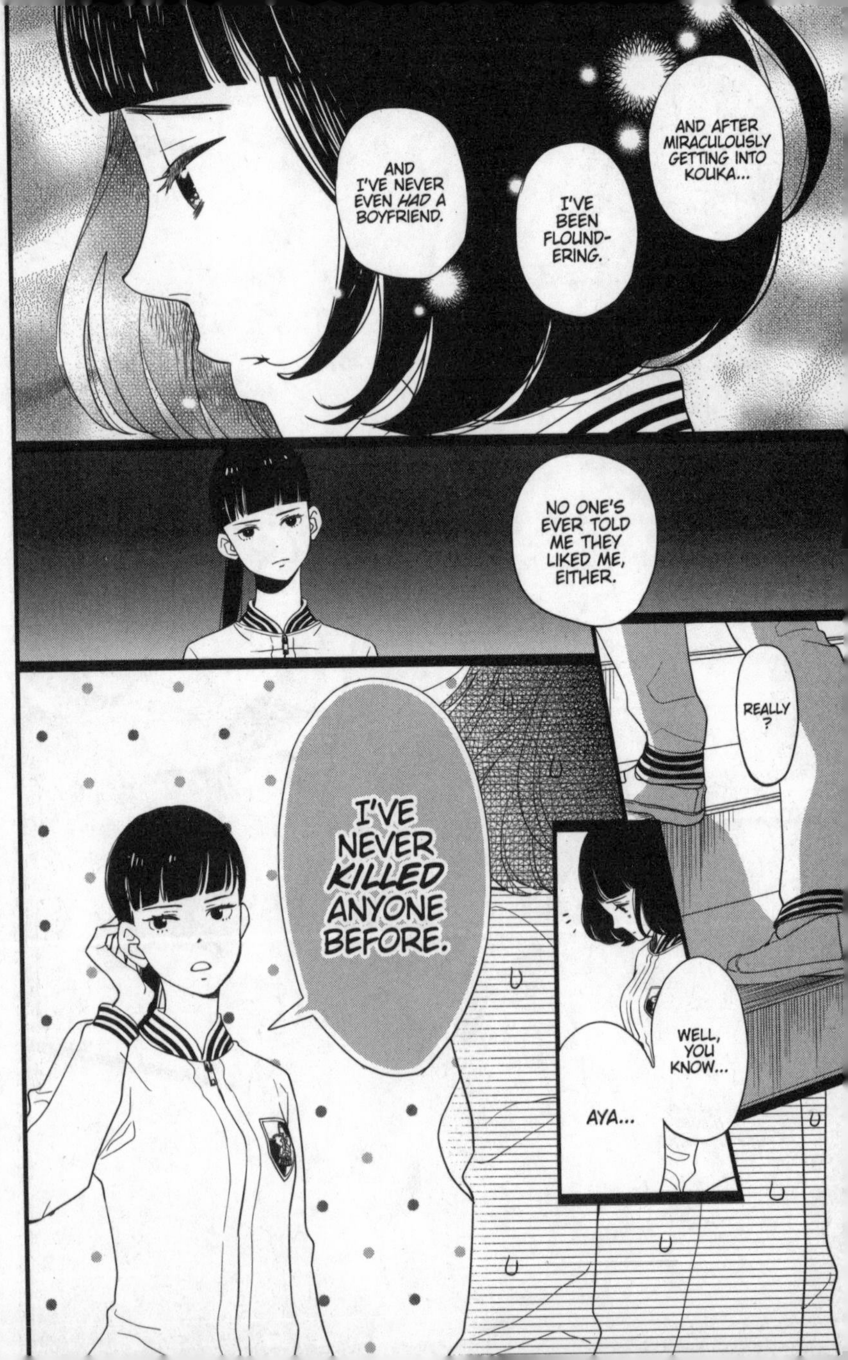
AND AFTER MIRACULOUSLY GETTING INTO KOUKA...
I'VE BEEN FLOUNDERING.
AND I'VE NEVER EVEN *HAD* A BOYFRIEND.
NO ONE'S EVER TOLD ME THEY LIKED ME, EITHER.
REALLY?
WELL, YOU KNOW...
AYA...
I'VE NEVER ***KILLED*** ANYONE BEFORE.

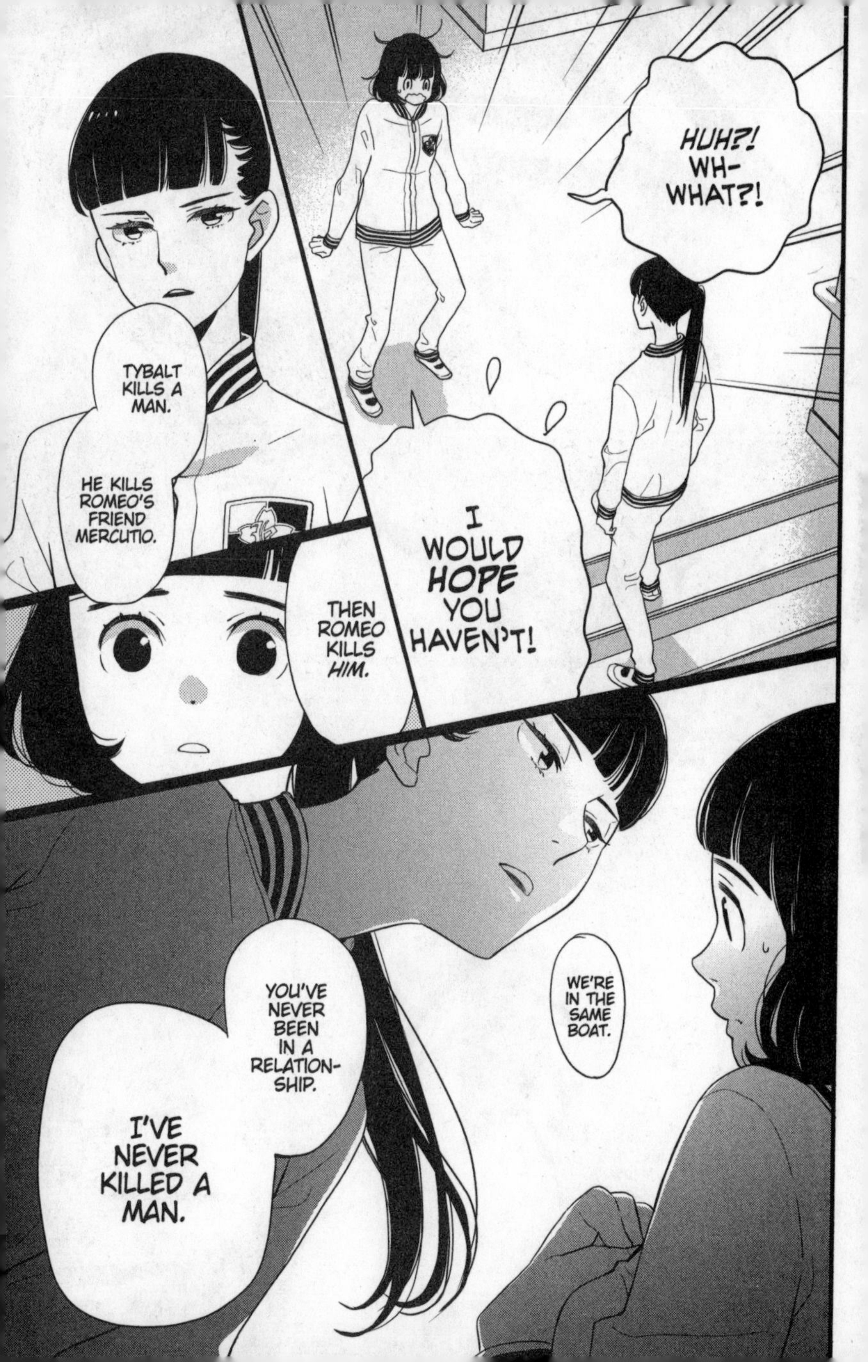
HUH?! WH-WHAT?!
I WOULD *HOPE* YOU HAVEN'T!
TYBALT KILLS A MAN.
HE KILLS ROMEO'S FRIEND MERCUTIO.
THEN ROMEO KILLS *HIM*.
WE'RE IN THE SAME BOAT.
YOU'VE NEVER BEEN IN A RELATION-SHIP.
I'VE NEVER KILLED A MAN.

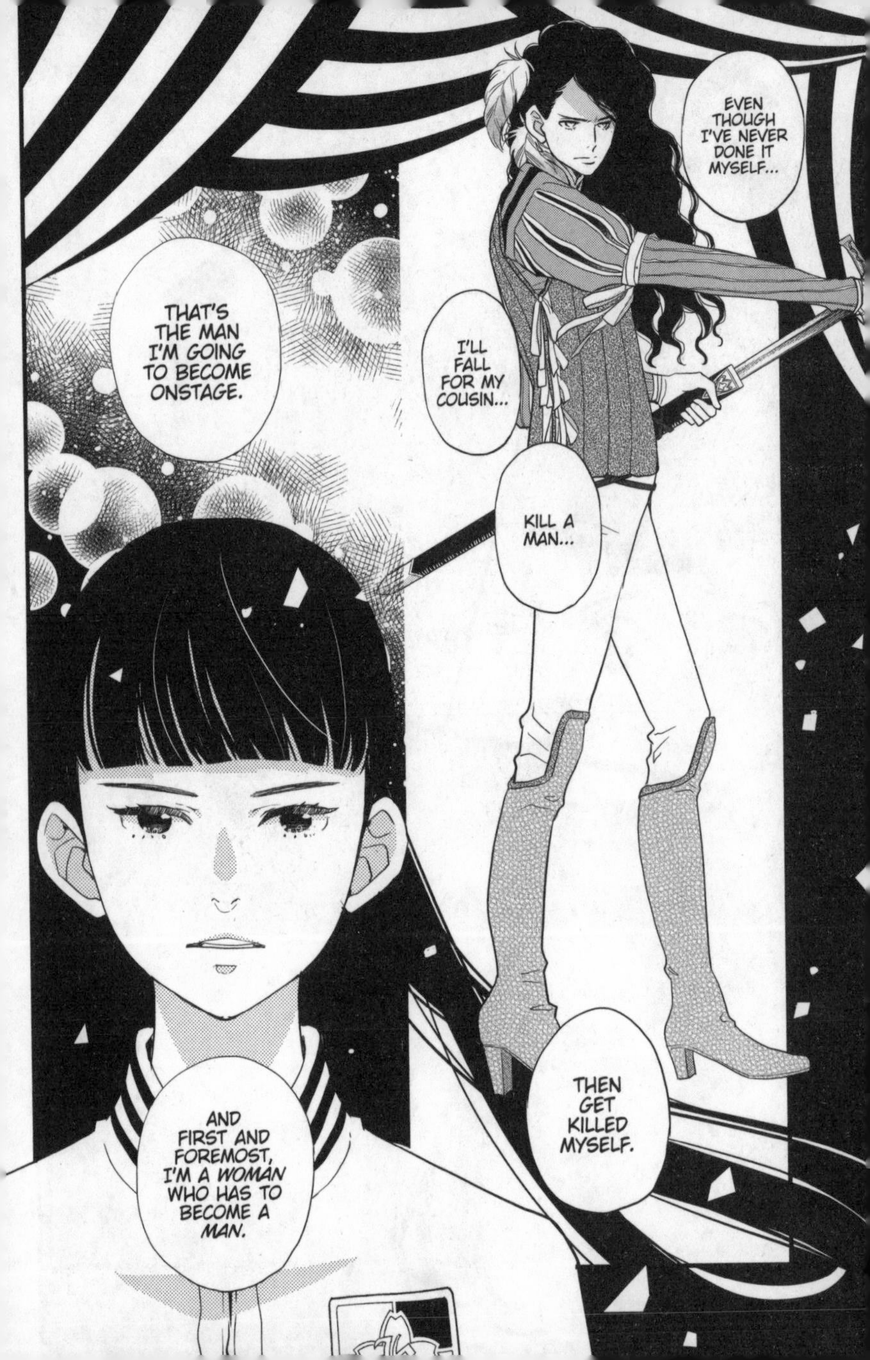
EVEN THOUGH I'VE NEVER DONE IT MYSELF...
I'LL FALL FOR MY COUSIN...
KILL A MAN...
THEN GET KILLED MYSELF.
THAT'S THE MAN I'M GOING TO BECOME ONSTAGE.
AND FIRST AND FOREMOST, I'M A *WOMAN* WHO HAS TO BECOME A *MAN.*

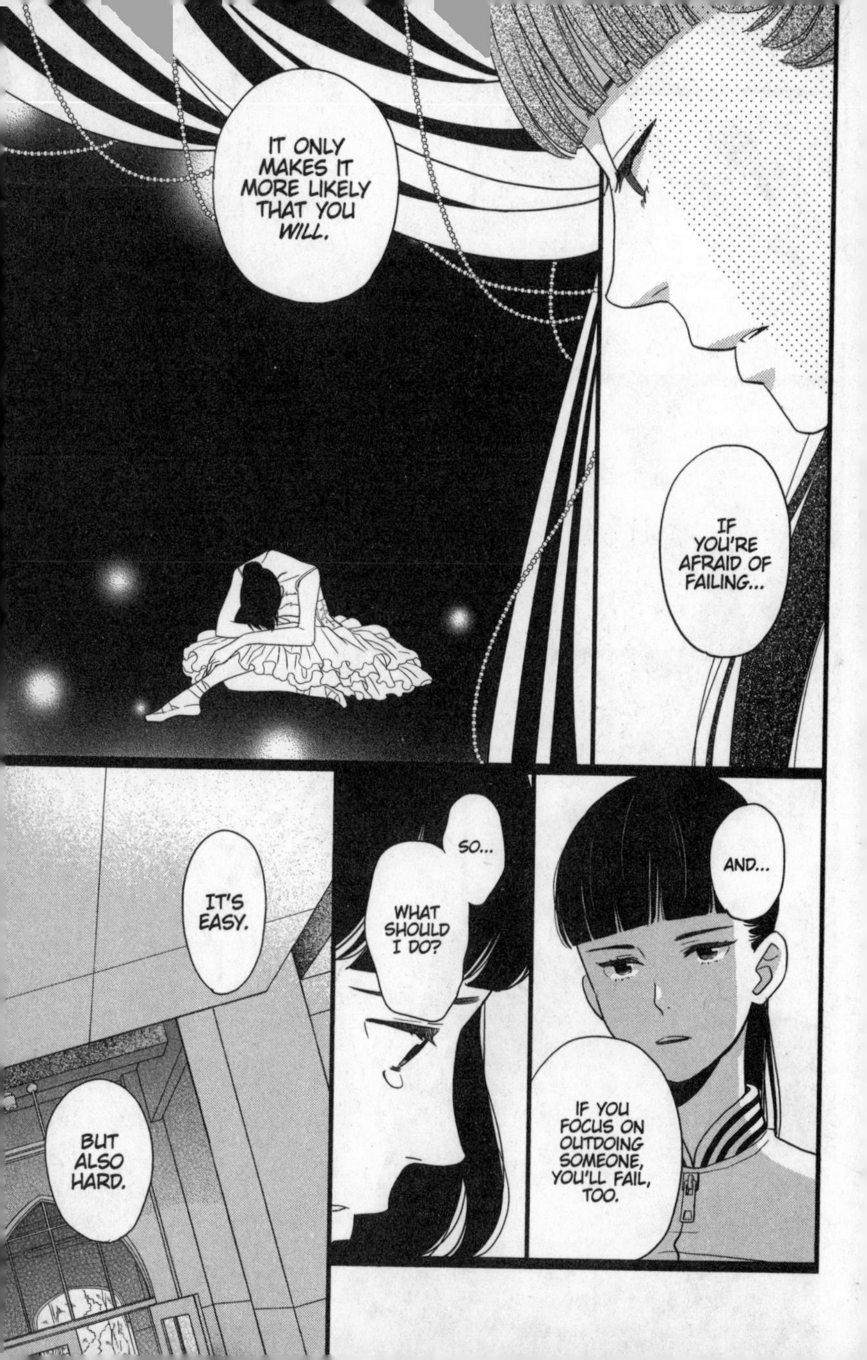
IF YOU'RE AFRAID OF FAILING...
IT ONLY MAKES IT MORE LIKELY THAT YOU WILL.
AND...
IF YOU FOCUS ON OUTDOING SOMEONE, YOU'LL FAIL, TOO.
SO...
WHAT SHOULD I DO?
IT'S EASY.
BUT ALSO HARD.

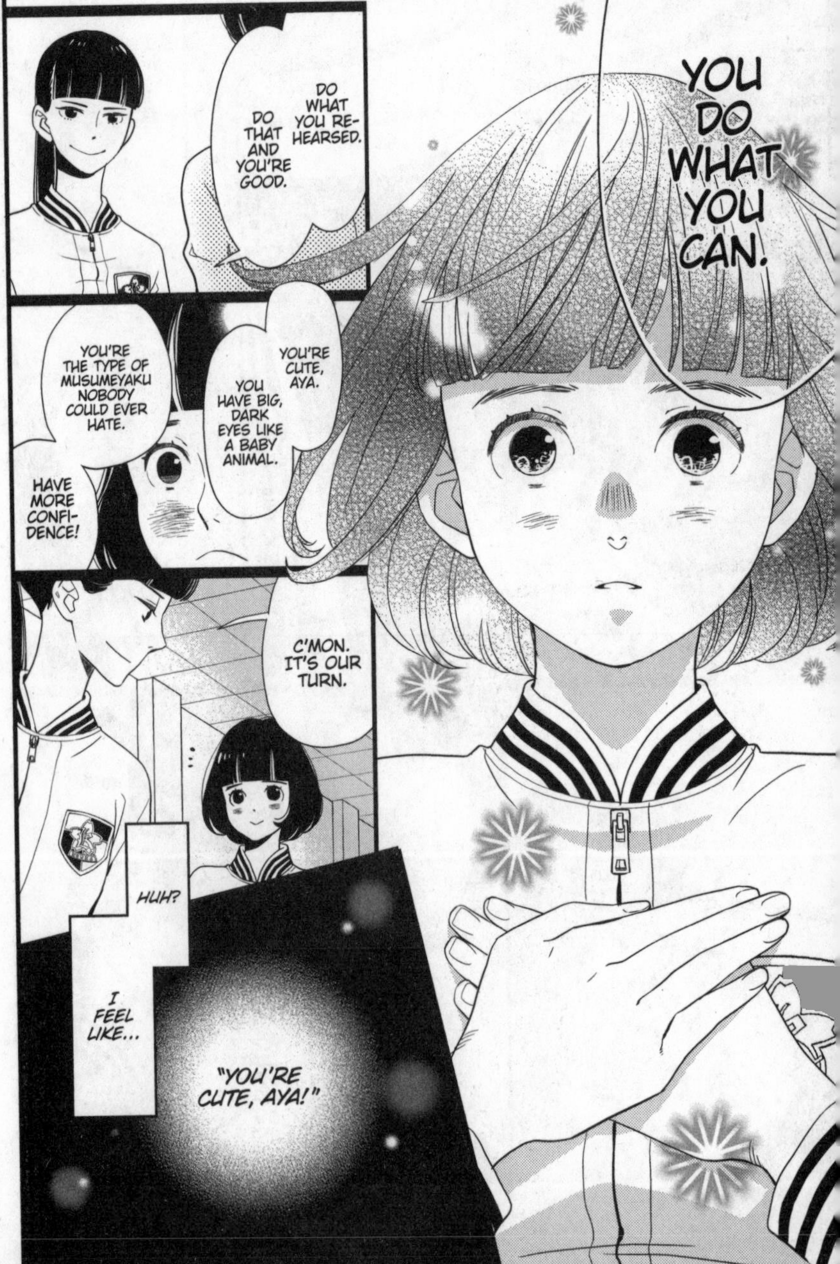
YOU DO WHAT YOU CAN.
DO WHAT YOU RE-HEARSED.
DO THAT AND YOU'RE GOOD.
YOU'RE CUTE, AYA.
YOU HAVE BIG, DARK EYES LIKE A BABY ANIMAL.
YOU'RE THE TYPE OF MUSUMEYAKU NOBODY COULD EVER HATE.
HAVE MORE CONFI-DENCE!
C'MON. IT'S OUR TURN.
...
HUH?
I FEEL LIKE...
"YOU'RE CUTE, AYA!"

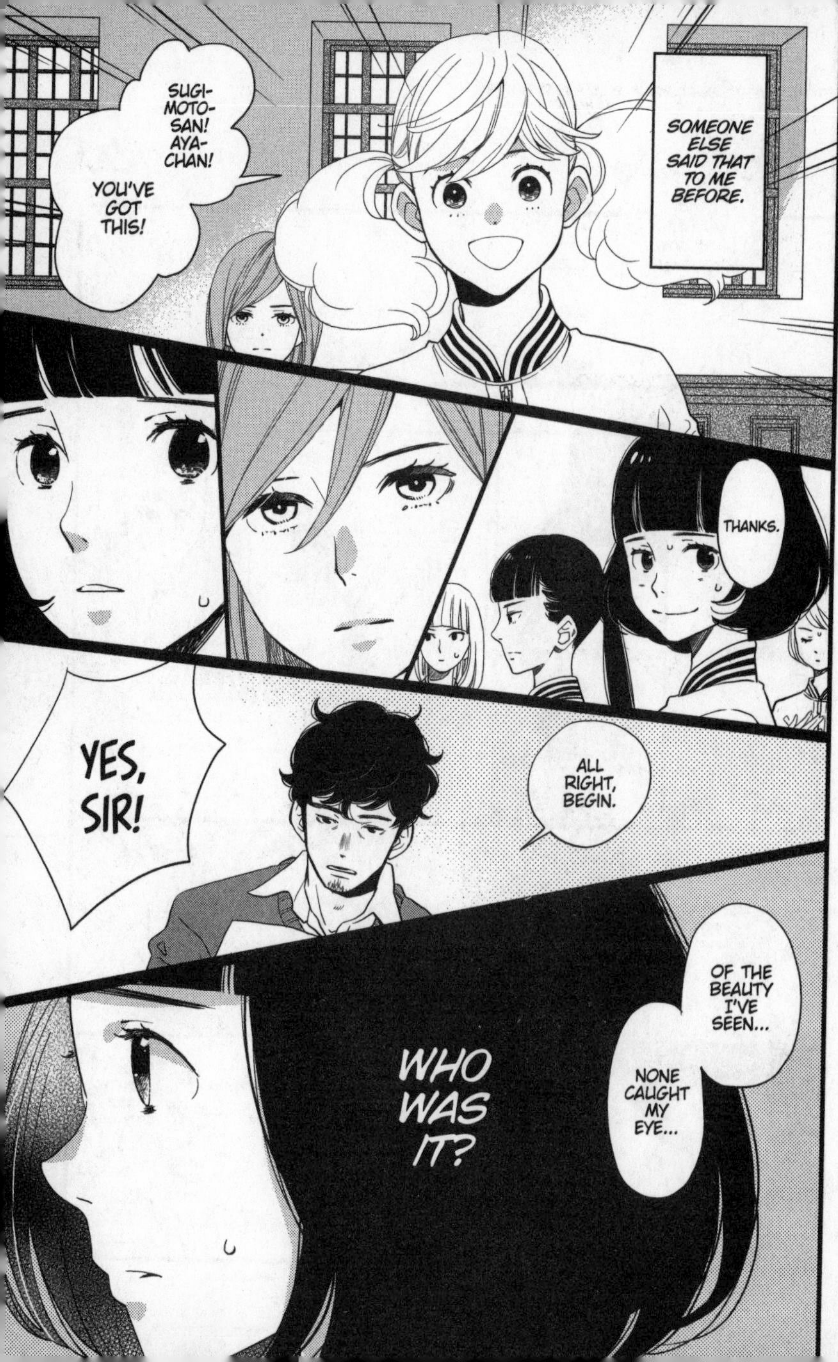
SOMEONE ELSE SAID THAT TO ME BEFORE.
SUGI-MOTO-SAN! AYA-CHAN!
YOU'VE GOT THIS!
THANKS.
ALL RIGHT, BEGIN.
YES, SIR!
OF THE BEAUTY I'VE SEEN...
NONE CAUGHT MY EYE...
WHO WAS IT?

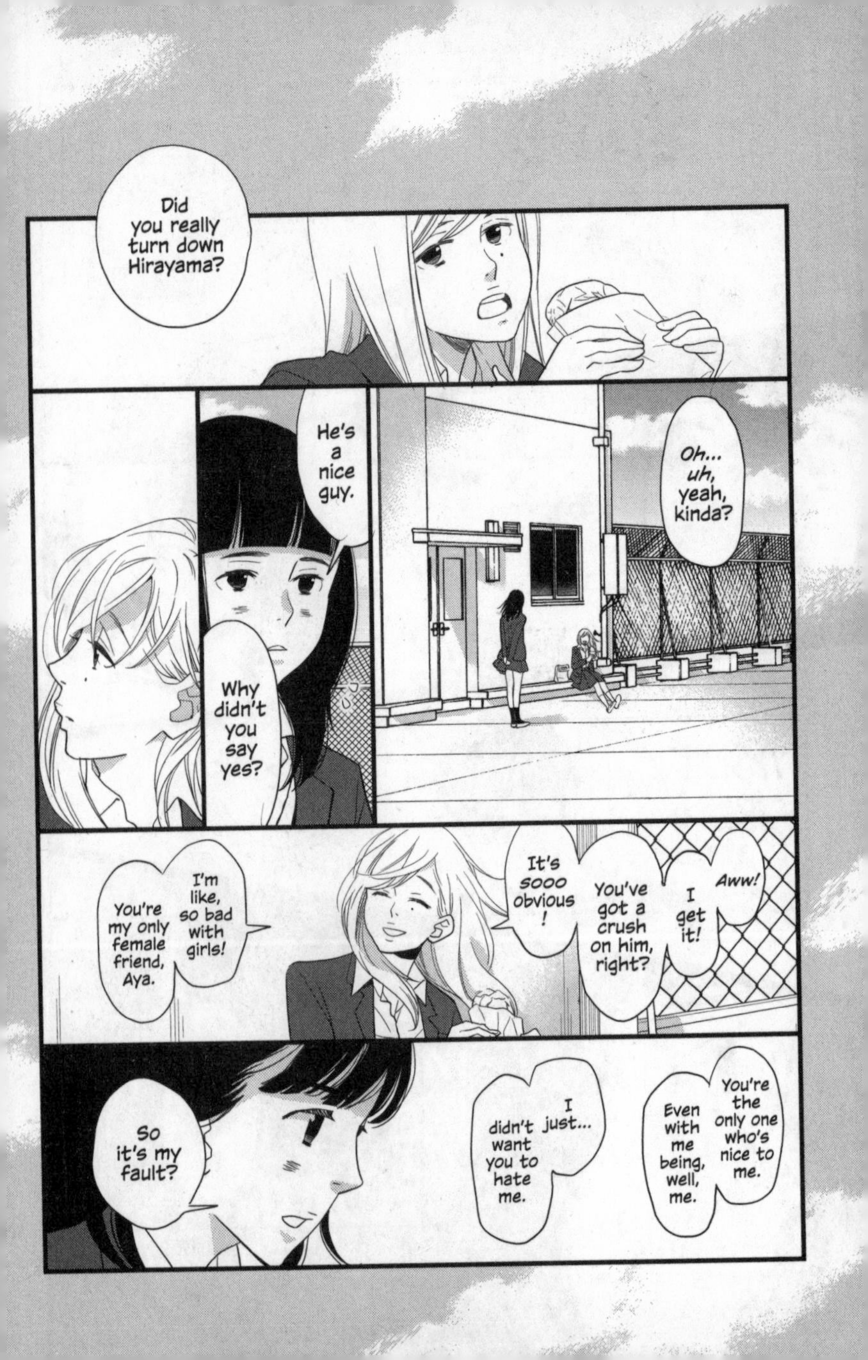
Did you really turn down Hirayama?
Oh... uh, yeah, kinda?
He's a nice guy.
Why didn't you say yes?
Aww!
I get it!
You've got a crush on him, right?
It's sooo obvious!
I'm like, so bad with girls!
You're my only female friend, Aya.
You're the only one who's nice to me.
Even with me being, well, me.
I just...
didn't want you to hate me.
So it's my fault?

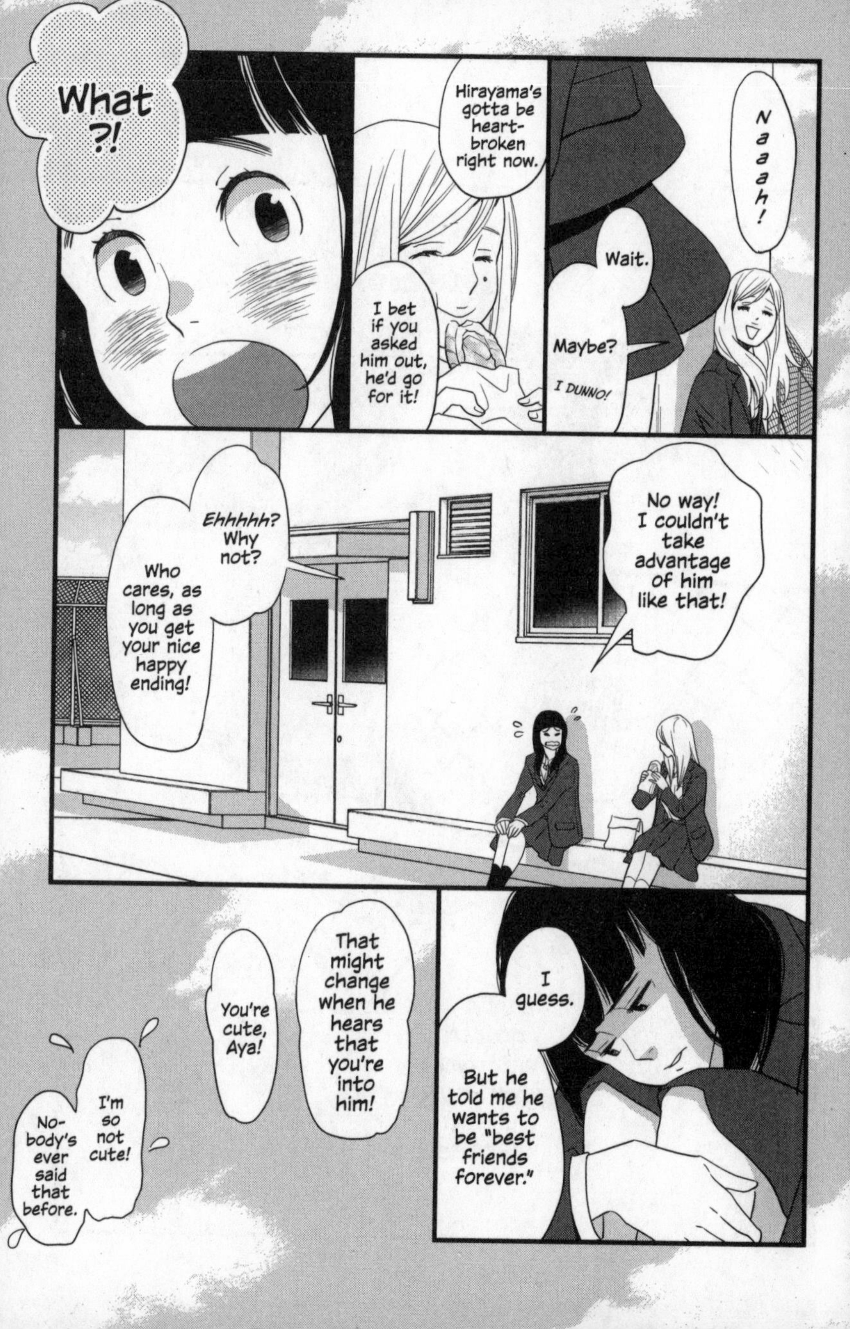
Naaah!
Wait.
Maybe?
I DUNNO!
Hirayama's gotta be heart-broken right now.
I bet if you asked him out, he'd go for it!
What ?!
No way! I couldn't take advantage of him like that!
Ehhhhh? Why not?
Who cares, as long as you get your nice happy ending!
I guess.
But he told me he wants to be "best friends forever."
That might change when he hears that you're into him!
You're cute, Aya!
I'm so not cute!
No-body's ever said that before.

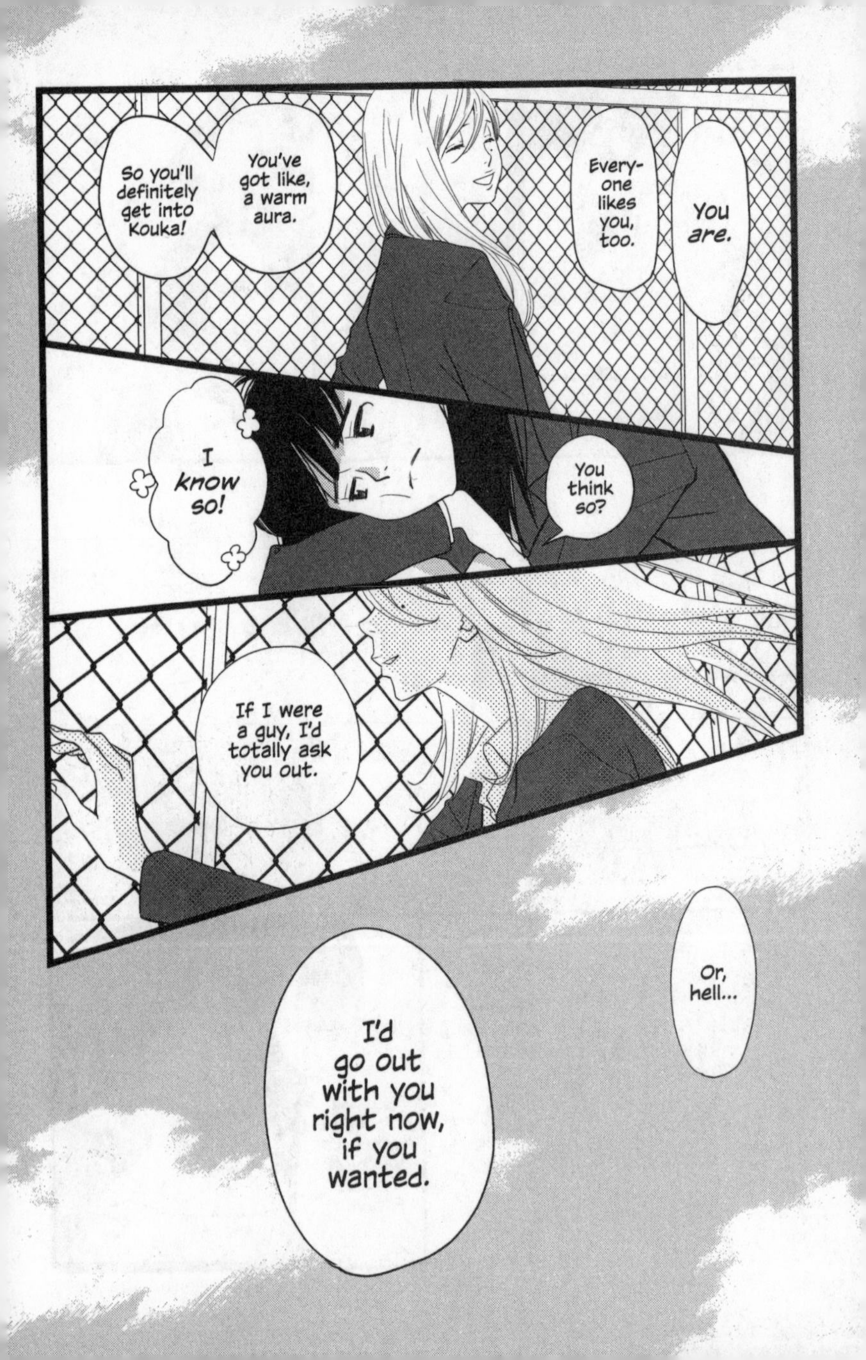
You are.
Every-one likes you, too.
You've got like, a warm aura.
So you'll definitely get into Kouka!
You think so?
I know so!
If I were a guy, I'd totally ask you out.
Or, hell...
I'd go out with you right now, if you wanted.

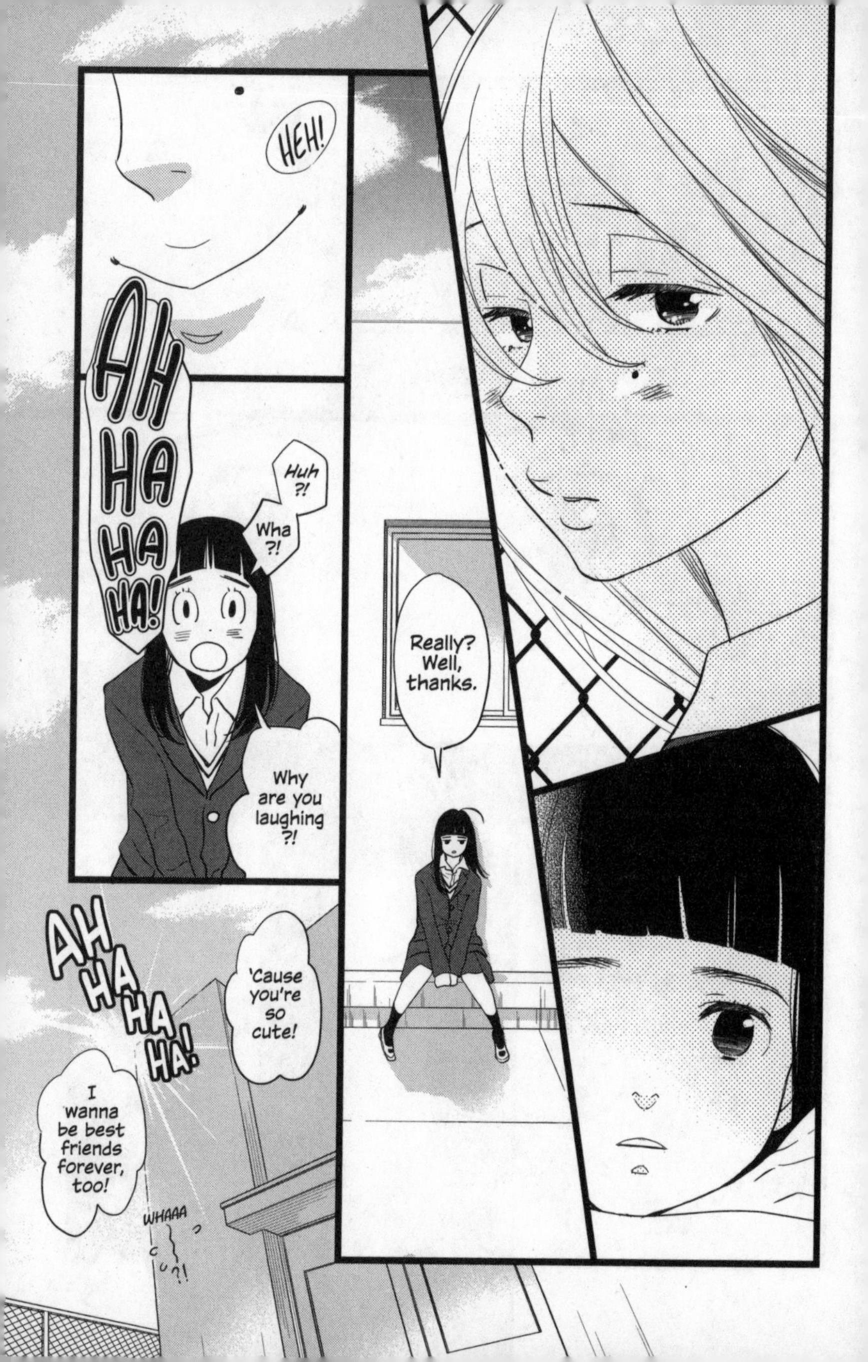
Really? Well, thanks.
HEH!
AHHAHAHAHA!
Huh?!
Wha?!
Why are you laughing?!
'Cause you're so cute!
AHHAHAHAHA!
I wanna be best friends forever, too!
WHAAA?!

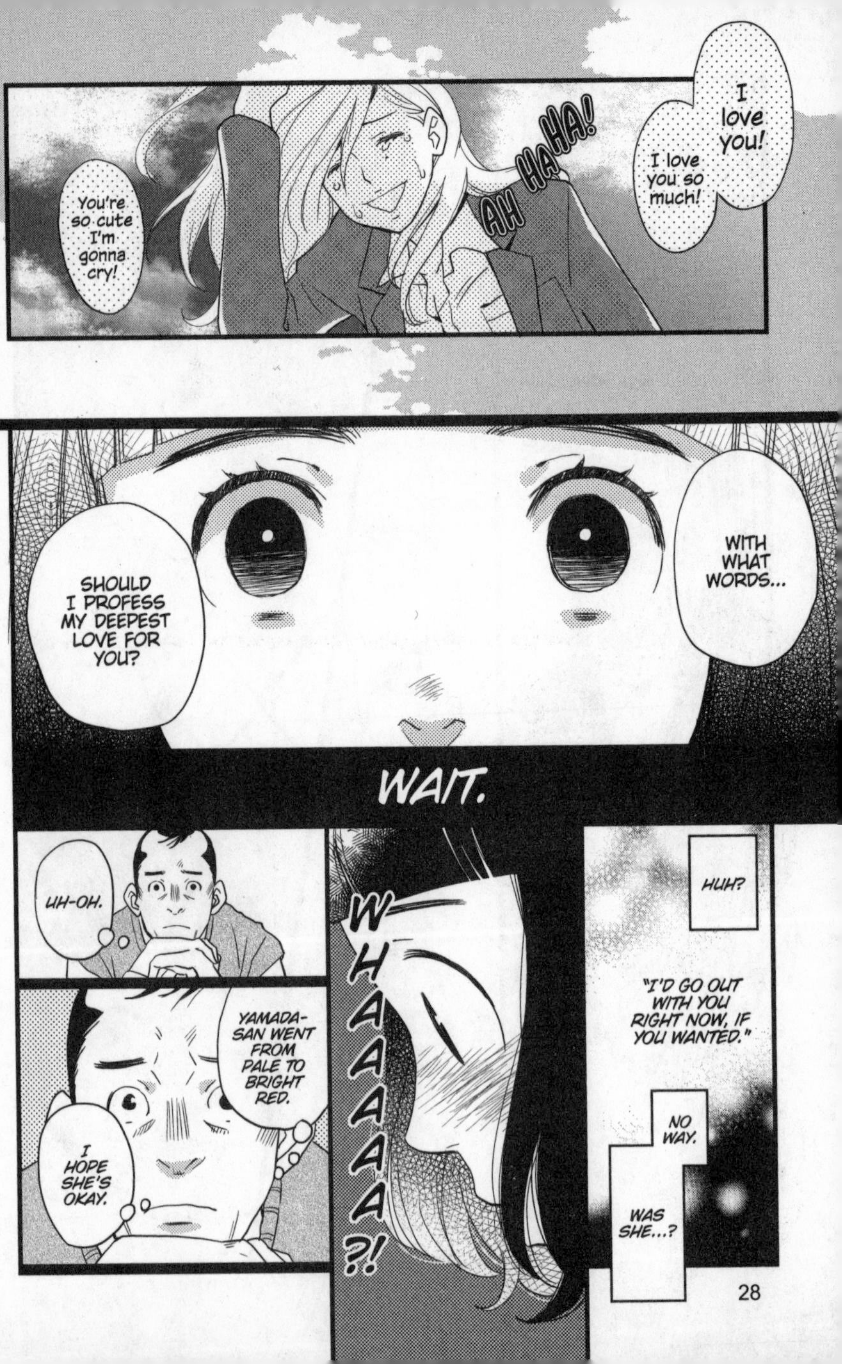
I love you!
I love you so much!
AH HA HA HA!
You're so cute I'm gonna cry!
WITH WHAT WORDS...
SHOULD I PROFESS MY DEEPEST LOVE FOR YOU?
WAIT.
HUH?
"I'D GO OUT WITH YOU RIGHT NOW, IF YOU WANTED."
NO WAY.
WAS SHE...?
WHAAAAAAA?!
UH-OH.
YAMADA-SAN WENT FROM PALE TO BRIGHT RED.
I HOPE SHE'S OKAY.

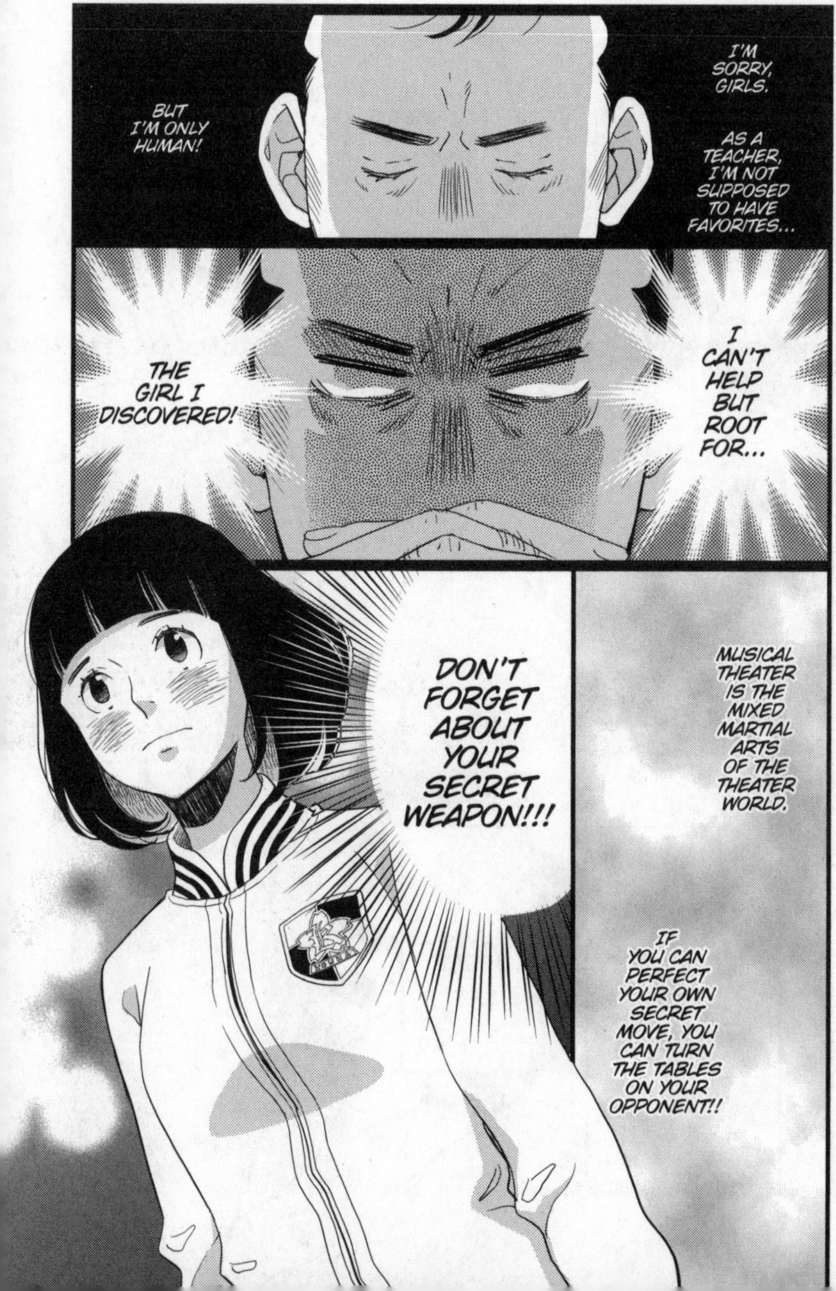
I'M SORRY, GIRLS.
AS A TEACHER, I'M NOT SUPPOSED TO HAVE FAVORITES...
BUT I'M ONLY HUMAN!
I CAN'T HELP BUT ROOT FOR...
THE GIRL I DISCOVERED!
MUSICAL THEATER IS THE MIXED MARTIAL ARTS OF THE THEATER WORLD.
IF YOU CAN PERFECT YOUR OWN SECRET MOVE, YOU CAN TURN THE TABLES ON YOUR OPPONENT!!
DON'T FORGET ABOUT YOUR SECRET WEAPON!!!

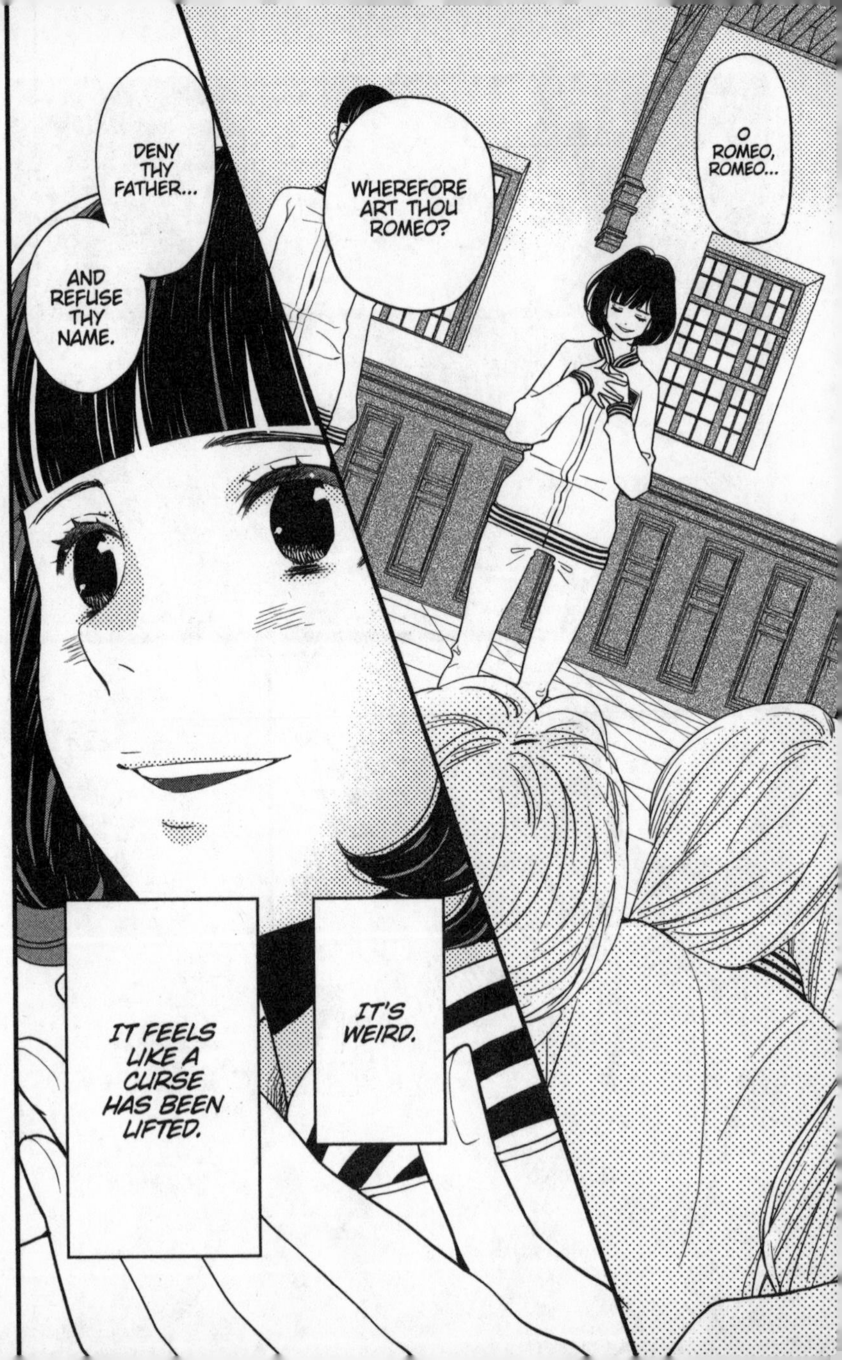
O ROMEO, ROMEO...
WHEREFORE ART THOU ROMEO?
DENY THY FATHER...
AND REFUSE THY NAME.
IT'S WEIRD.
IT FEELS LIKE A CURSE HAS BEEN LIFTED.

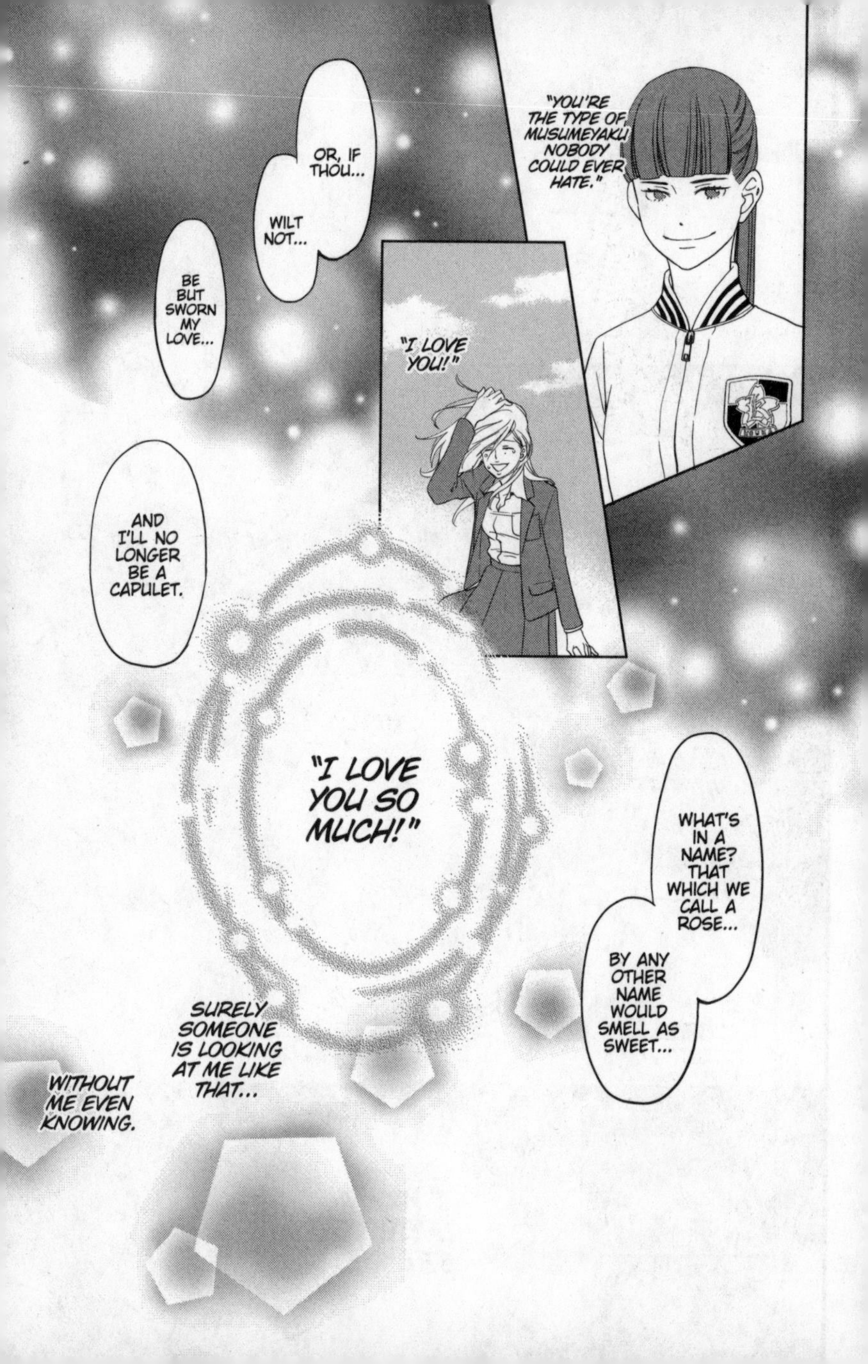
"YOU'RE THE TYPE OF MUSUMEYAKU NOBODY COULD EVER HATE."
"I LOVE YOU!"
OR, IF THOU...
WILT NOT...
BE BUT SWORN MY LOVE...
AND I'LL NO LONGER BE A CAPULET.
"I LOVE YOU SO MUCH!"
WHAT'S IN A NAME? THAT WHICH WE CALL A ROSE...
BY ANY OTHER NAME WOULD SMELL AS SWEET...
SURELY SOMEONE IS LOOKING AT ME LIKE THAT...
WITHOUT ME EVEN KNOWING.

I'LL NEVER BE LIKE NARACCHI, BUT...
YOU CAN DO IT!
WHEN I STAND ON THAT STAGE...
SOMEONE IN THAT AUDIENCE WILL SEE ME.
I WANT THEM TO SEE ME.

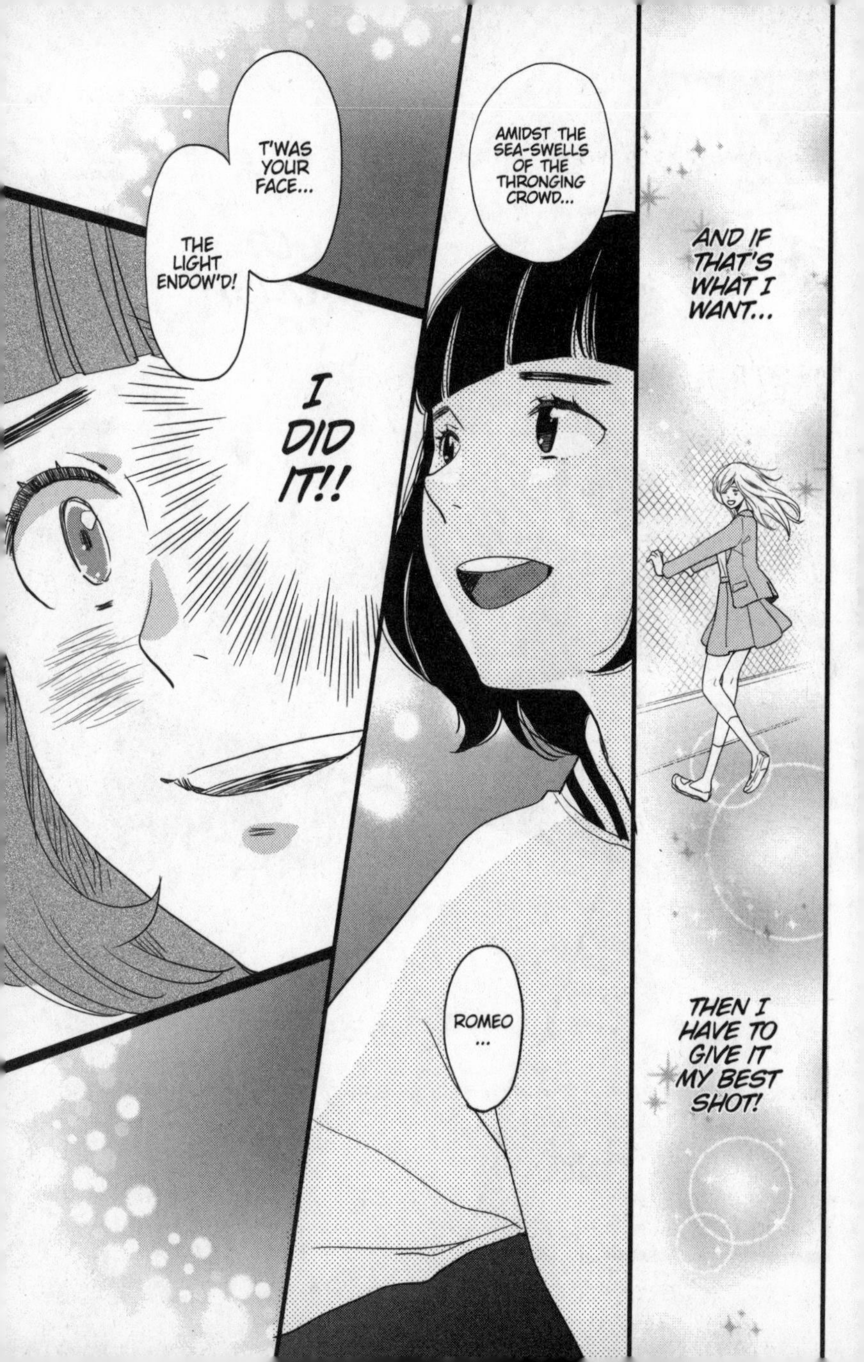
AND IF THAT'S WHAT I WANT...
THEN I HAVE TO GIVE IT MY BEST SHOT!
AMIDST THE SEA-SWELLS OF THE THRONGING CROWD...
T'WAS YOUR FACE... THE LIGHT ENDOW'D!
I DID IT!!
ROMEO ...

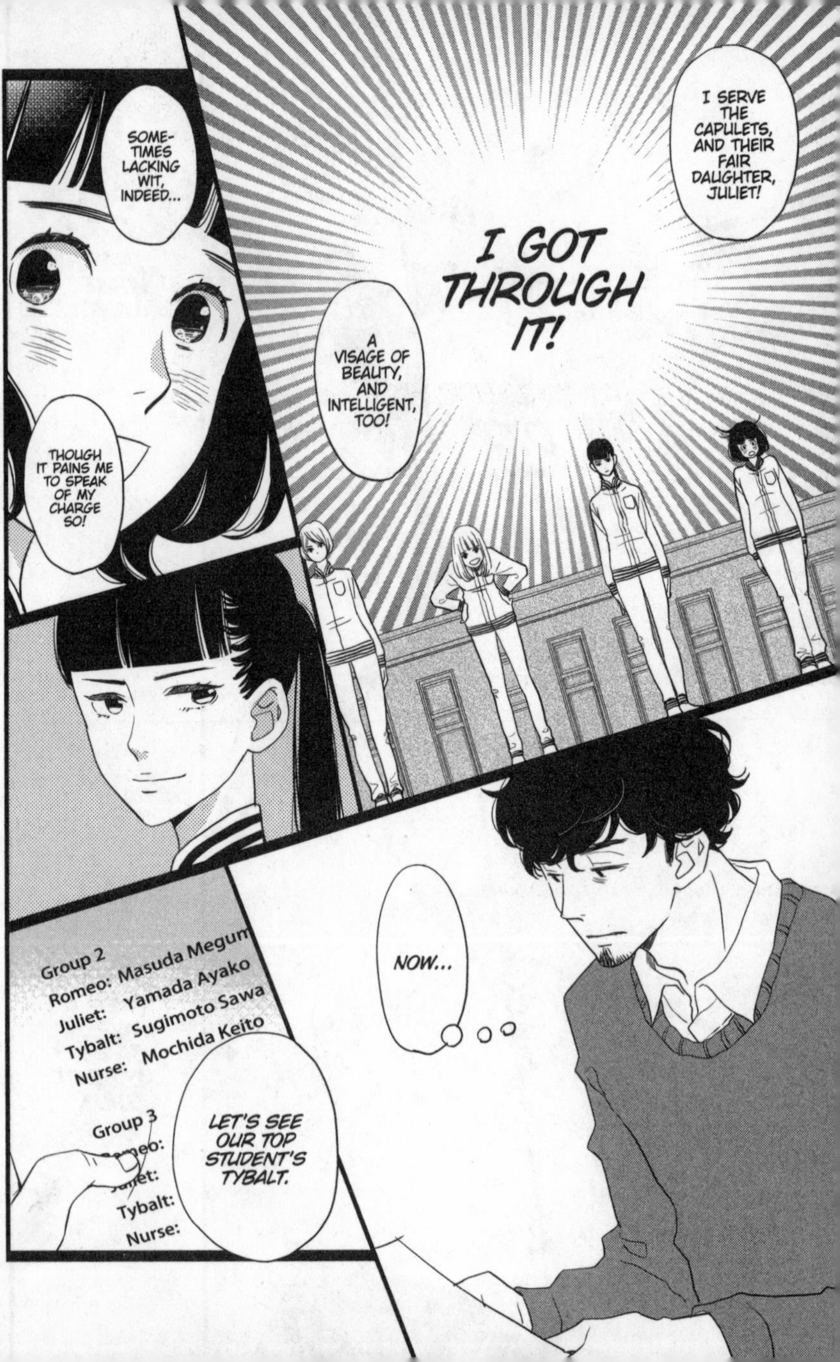
I SERVE THE CAPULETS, AND THEIR FAIR DAUGHTER, JULIET!
I GOT THROUGH IT!
A VISAGE OF BEAUTY, AND INTELLIGENT, TOO!
SOME-TIMES LACKING WIT, INDEED...
THOUGH IT PAINS ME TO SPEAK OF MY CHARGE SO!
NOW...
Group 2
Romeo: Masuda Megum
Juliet: Yamada Ayako
Tybalt: Sugimoto Sawa
Nurse: Mochida Keito
Group 3
Tybalt:
Nurse:
LET'S SEE OUR TOP STUDENT'S TYBALT.

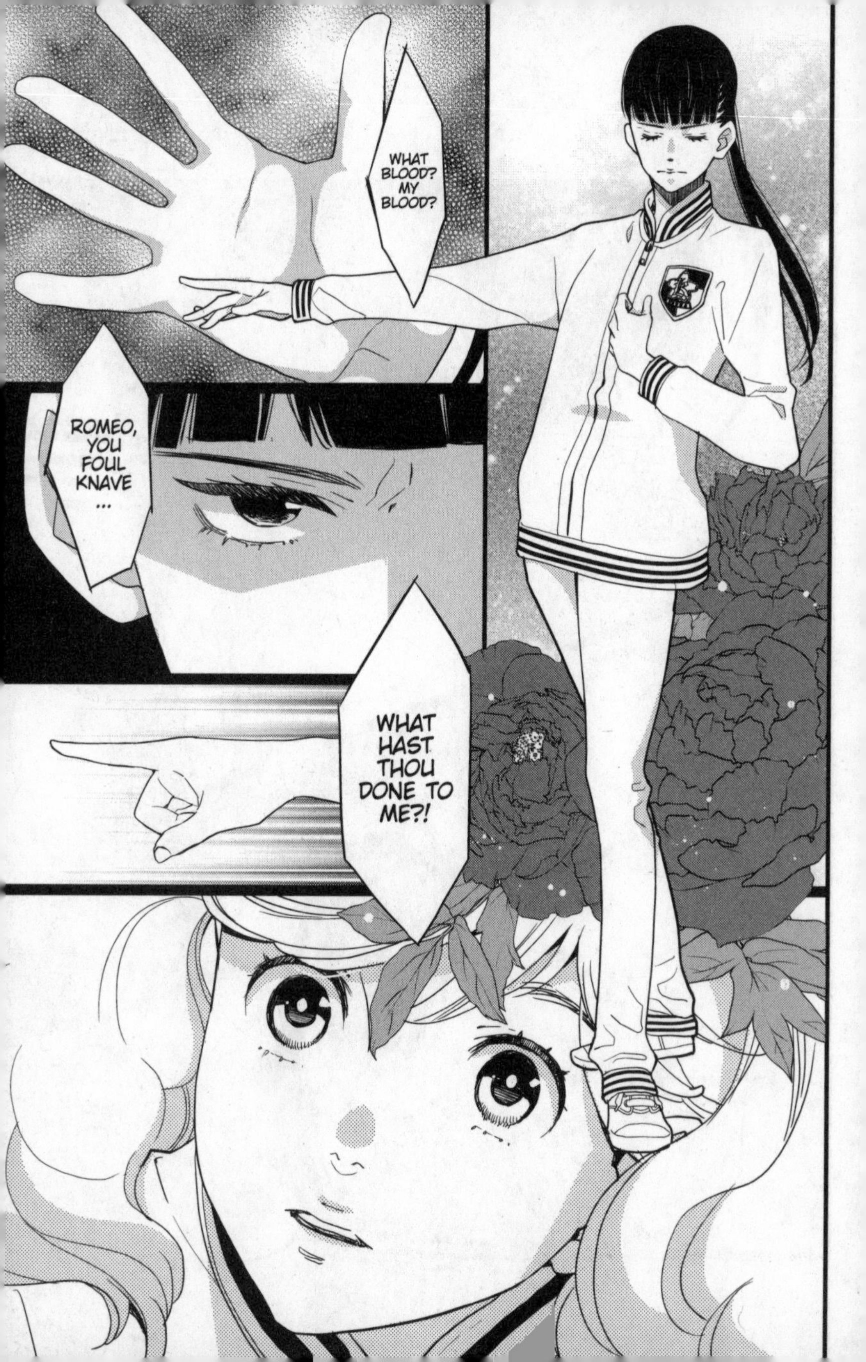
WHAT BLOOD? MY BLOOD?
ROMEO, YOU FOUL KNAVE ...
WHAT HAST THOU DONE TO ME?!

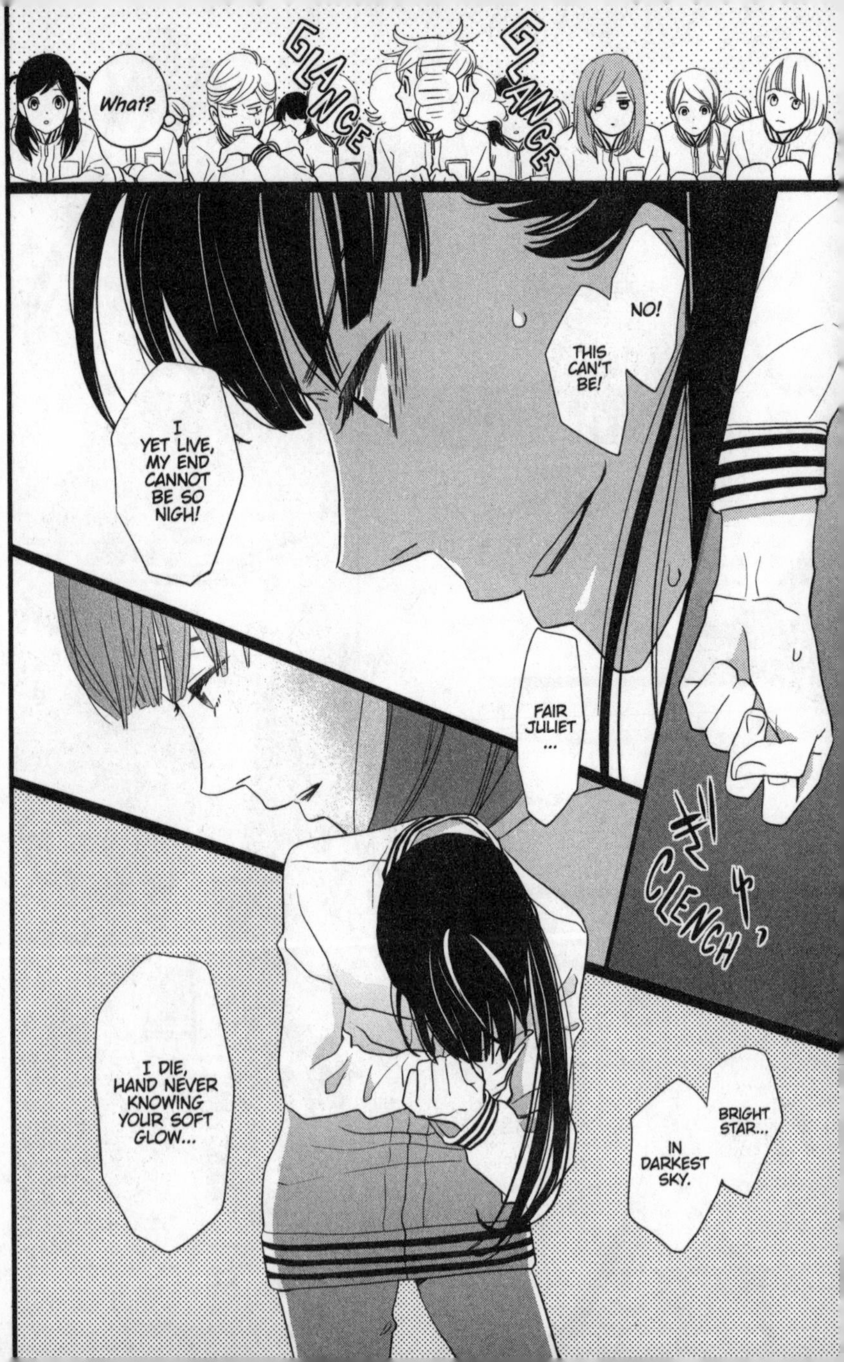
GLANCE
GLANCE
What?
NO!
THIS CAN'T BE!
I YET LIVE, MY END CANNOT BE SO NIGH!
FAIR JULIET ...
CLENCH
BRIGHT STAR...
IN DARKEST SKY.
I DIE, HAND NEVER KNOWING YOUR SOFT GLOW...

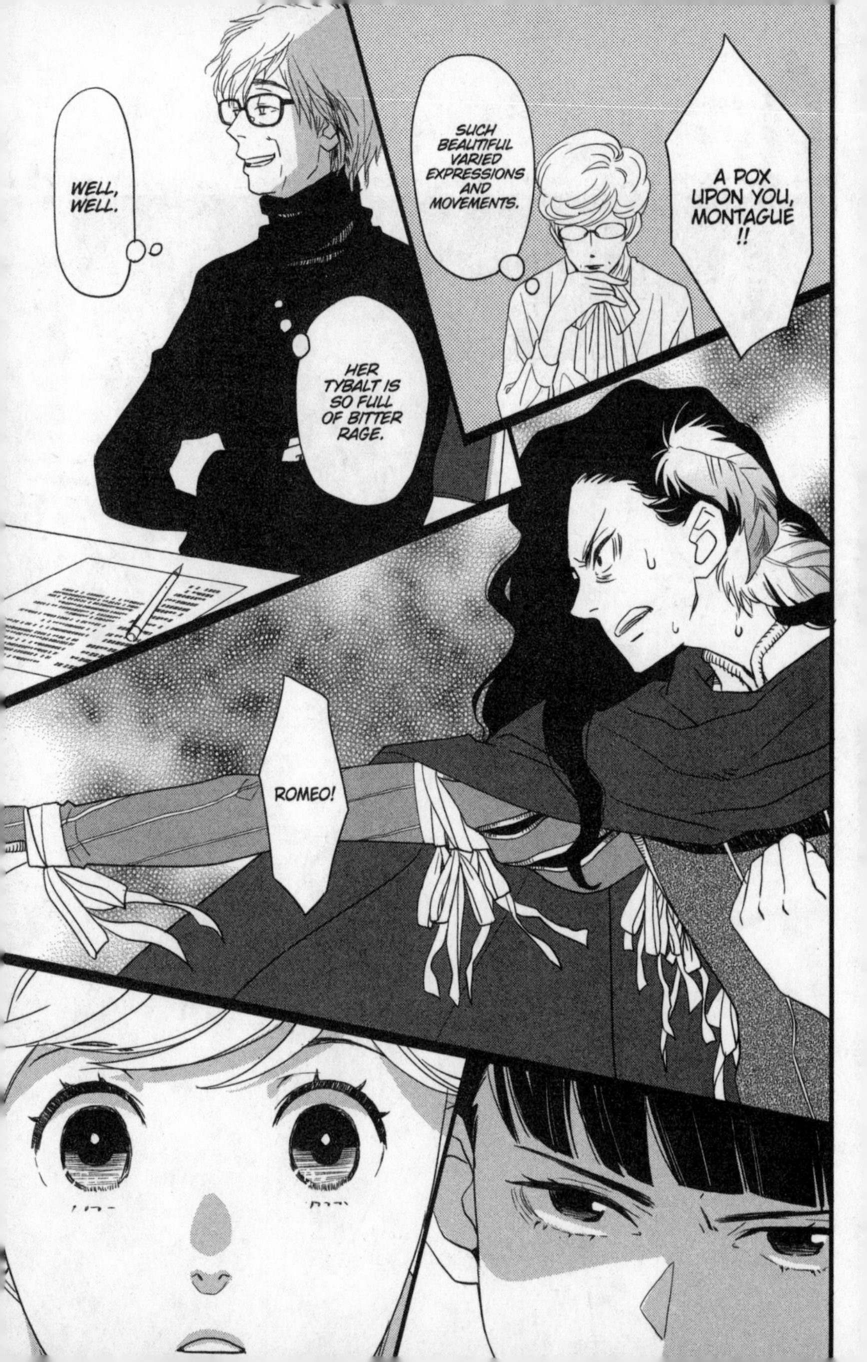
A POX UPON YOU, MONTAGUE!!
SUCH BEAUTIFUL VARIED EXPRESSIONS AND MOVEMENTS.
WELL, WELL.
HER TYBALT IS SO FULL OF BITTER RAGE.
ROMEO!

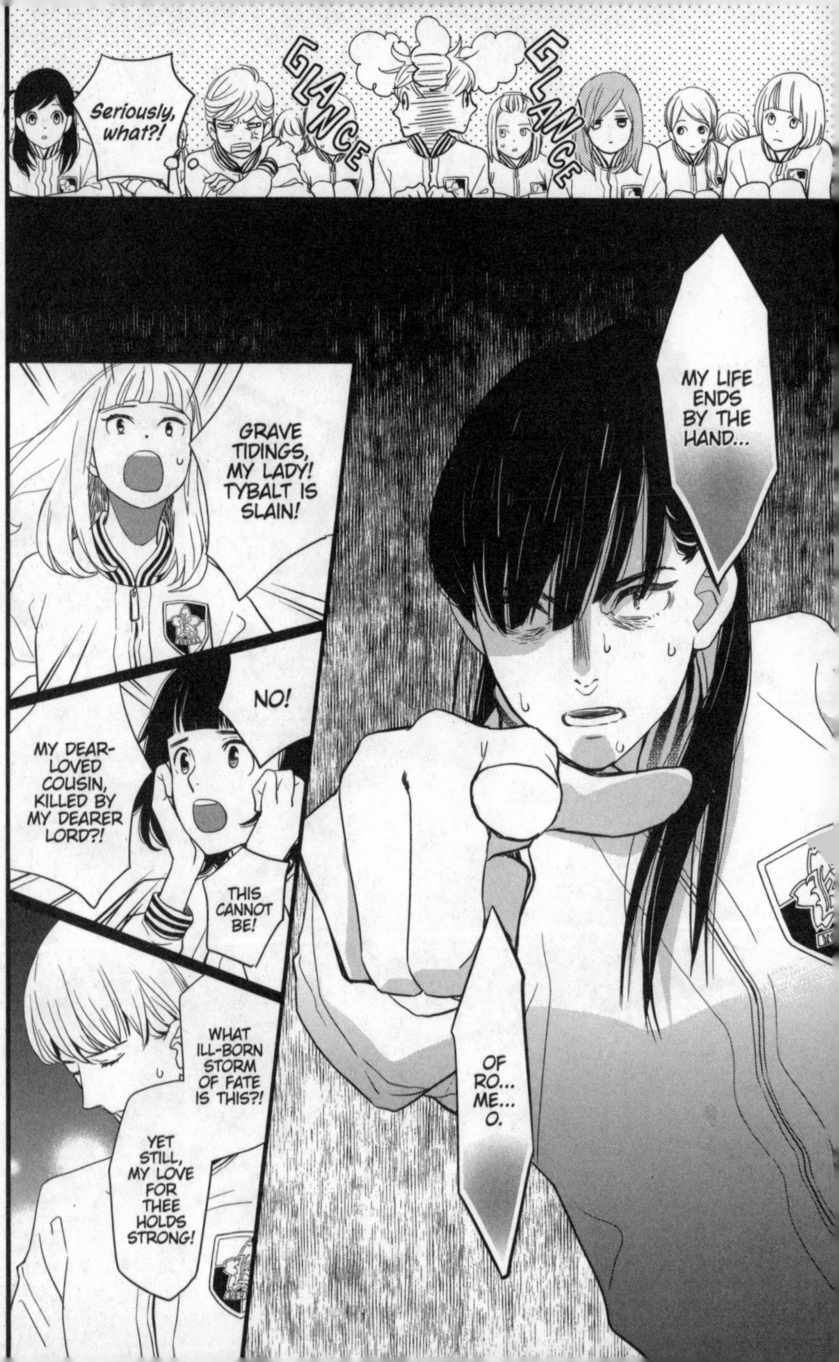
GLANCE
GLANCE
Seriously, what?!
MY LIFE ENDS BY THE HAND...
OF RO... ME... O.
GRAVE TIDINGS, MY LADY! TYBALT IS SLAIN!
NO!
MY DEAR-LOVED COUSIN, KILLED BY MY DEARER LORD?!
THIS CANNOT BE!
WHAT ILL-BORN STORM OF FATE IS THIS?!
YET STILL, MY LOVE FOR THEE HOLDS STRONG!

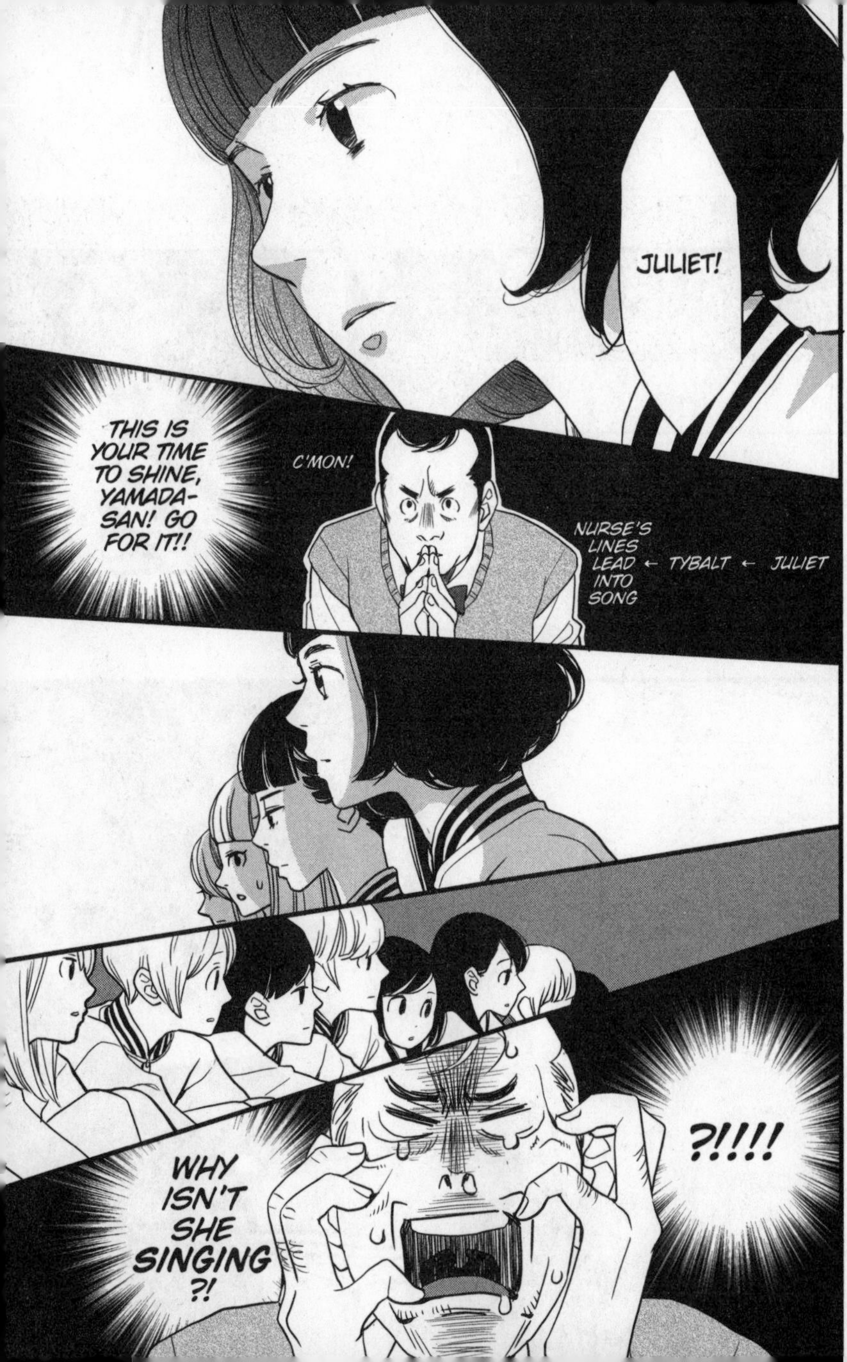
JULIET!
NURSE'S LINES LEAD INTO SONG ← TYBALT ← JULIET
C'MON!
THIS IS YOUR TIME TO SHINE, YAMADA-SAN! GO FOR IT!!
?!!!!
WHY ISN'T SHE SINGING?!

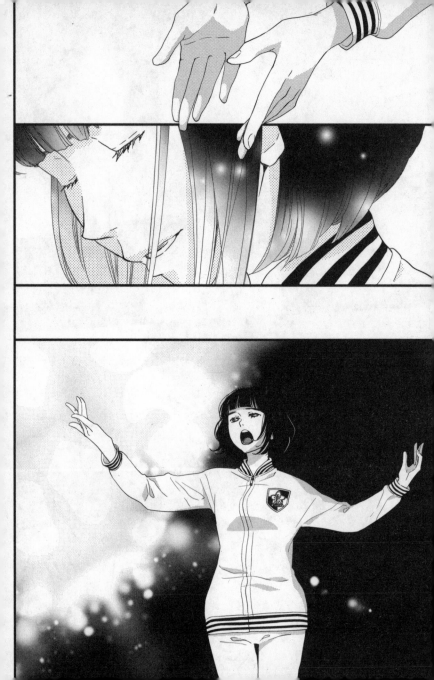

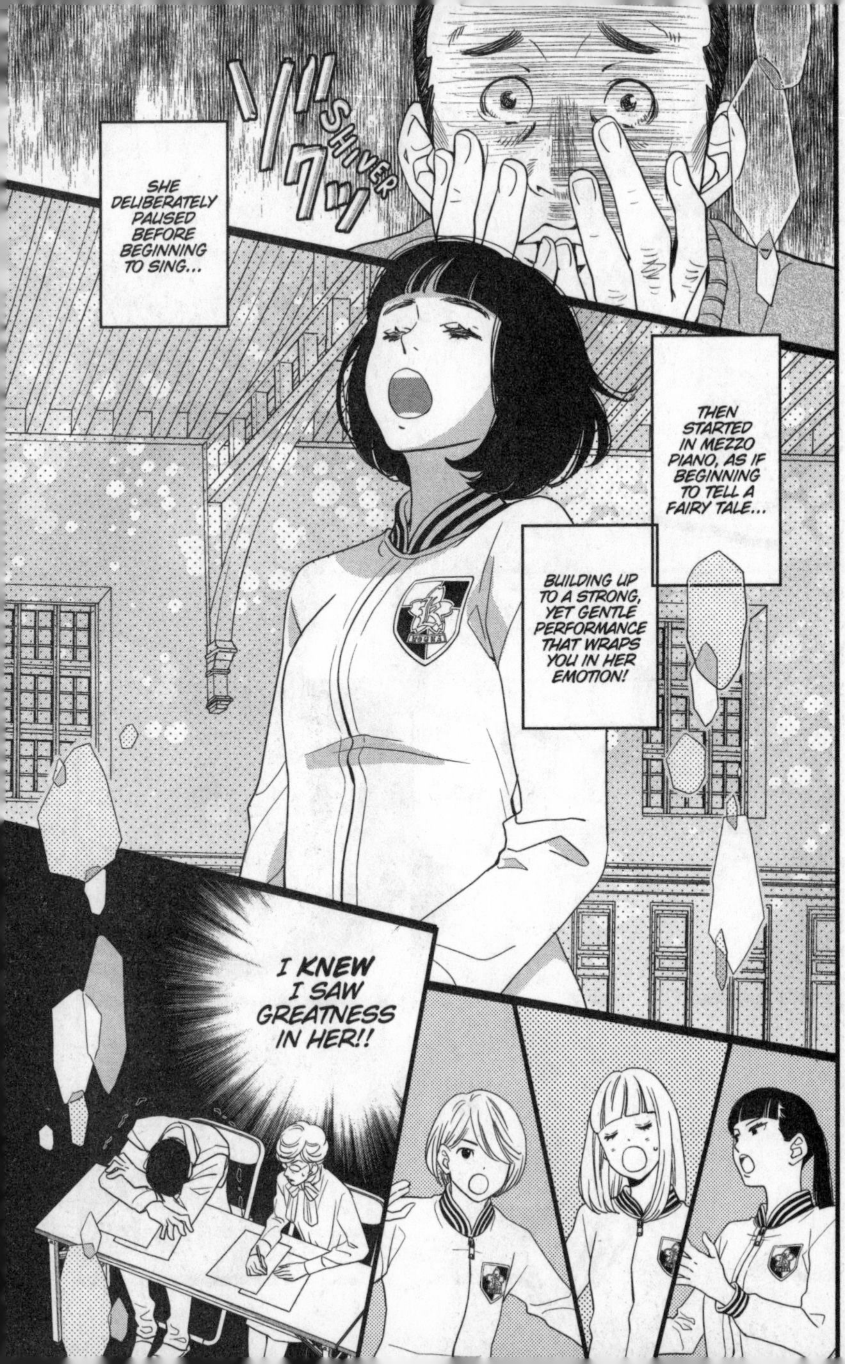
SHIVER
SHE DELIBERATELY PAUSED BEFORE BEGINNING TO SING...
THEN STARTED IN MEZZO PIANO, AS IF BEGINNING TO TELL A FAIRY TALE...
BUILDING UP TO A STRONG, YET GENTLE PERFORMANCE THAT WRAPS YOU IN HER EMOTION!
I KNEW I SAW GREATNESS IN HER!!

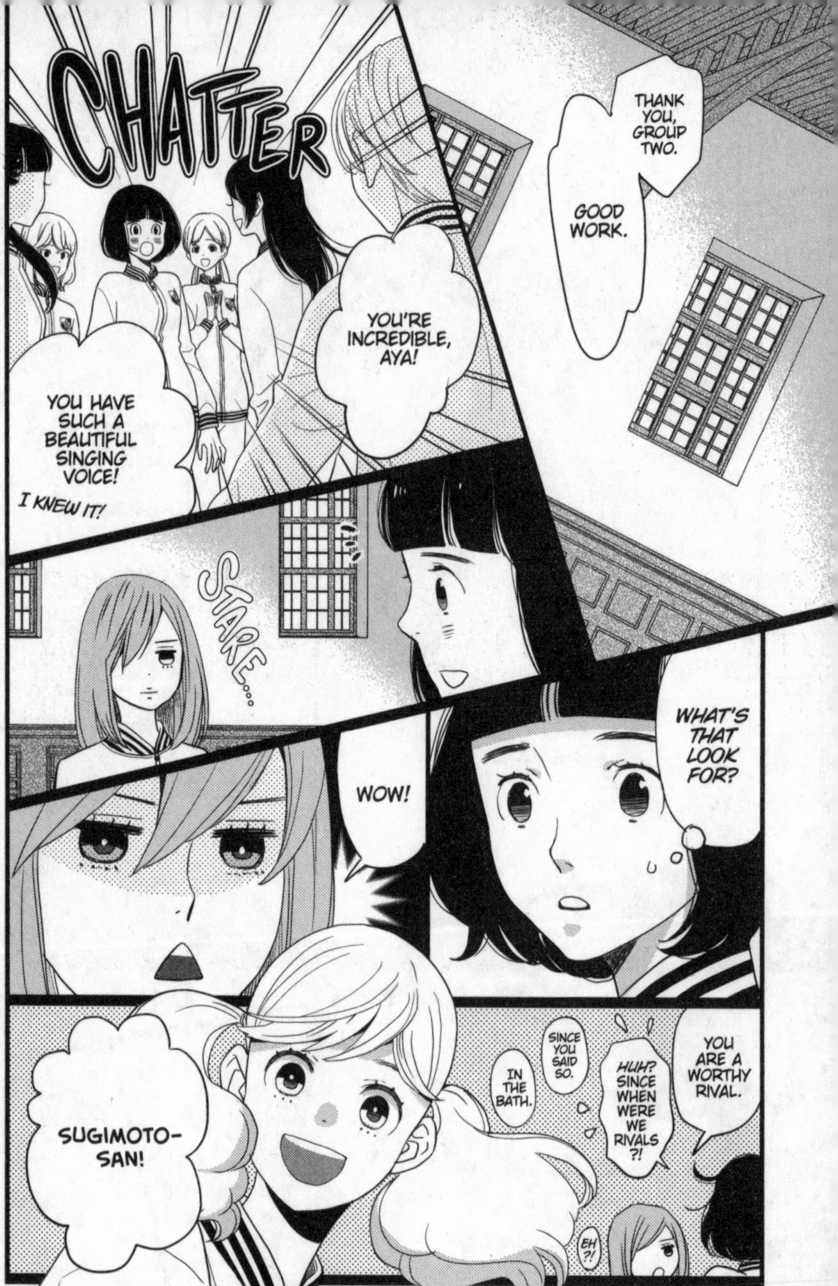
THANK YOU, GROUP TWO.
GOOD WORK.
CHATTER
YOU'RE INCREDIBLE, AYA!
YOU HAVE SUCH A BEAUTIFUL SINGING VOICE!
I KNEW IT!
!!
STARE...
WHAT'S THAT LOOK FOR?
WOW!
YOU ARE A WORTHY RIVAL.
HUH? SINCE WHEN WERE WE RIVALS?!
SINCE YOU SAID SO.
IN THE BATH.
EH?!
SUGIMOTO-SAN!

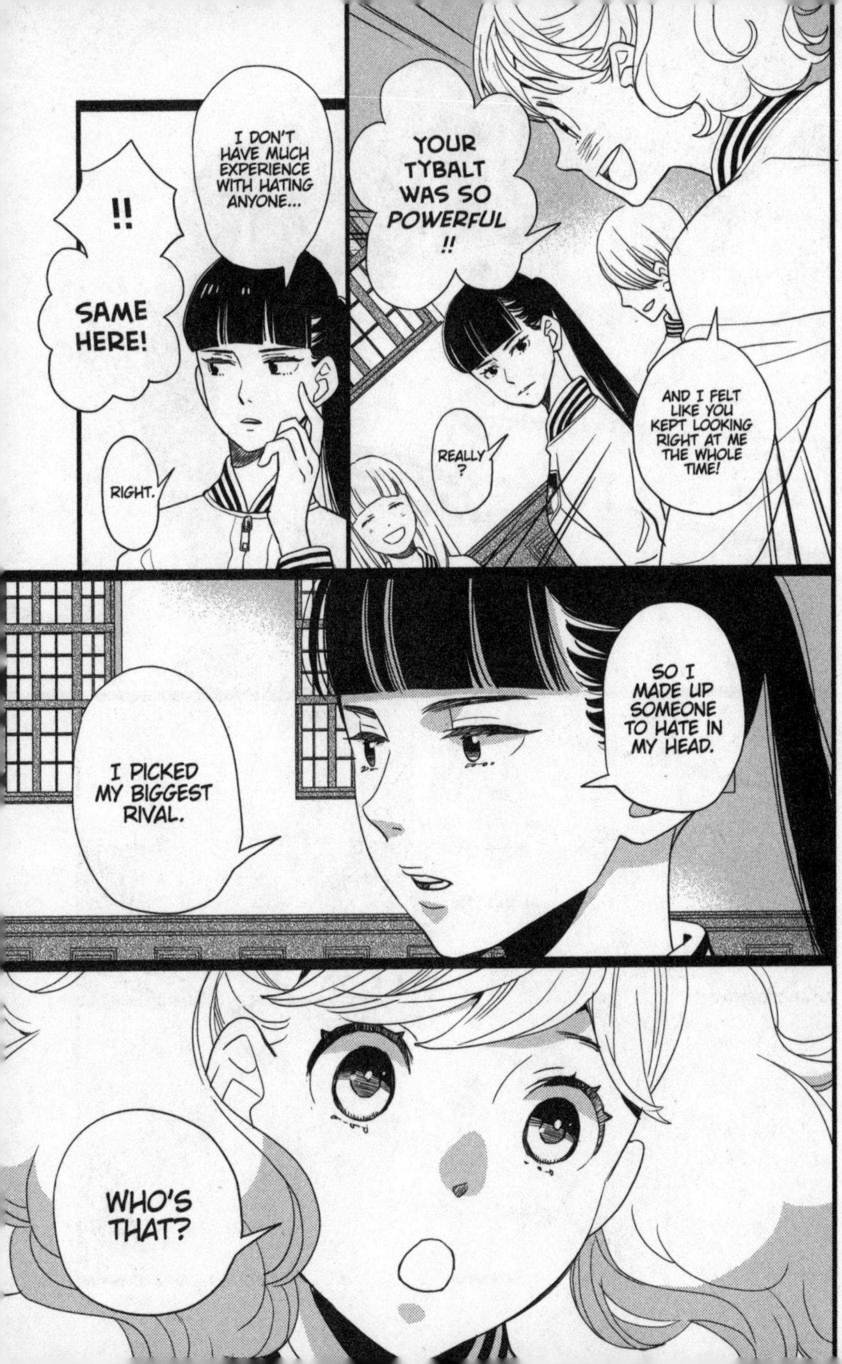
YOUR TYBALT WAS SO POWERFUL!!
AND I FELT LIKE YOU KEPT LOOKING RIGHT AT ME THE WHOLE TIME!
REALLY?
I DON'T HAVE MUCH EXPERIENCE WITH HATING ANYONE...
!!
SAME HERE!
RIGHT.
SO I MADE UP SOMEONE TO HATE IN MY HEAD.
I PICKED MY BIGGEST RIVAL.
WHO'S THAT?

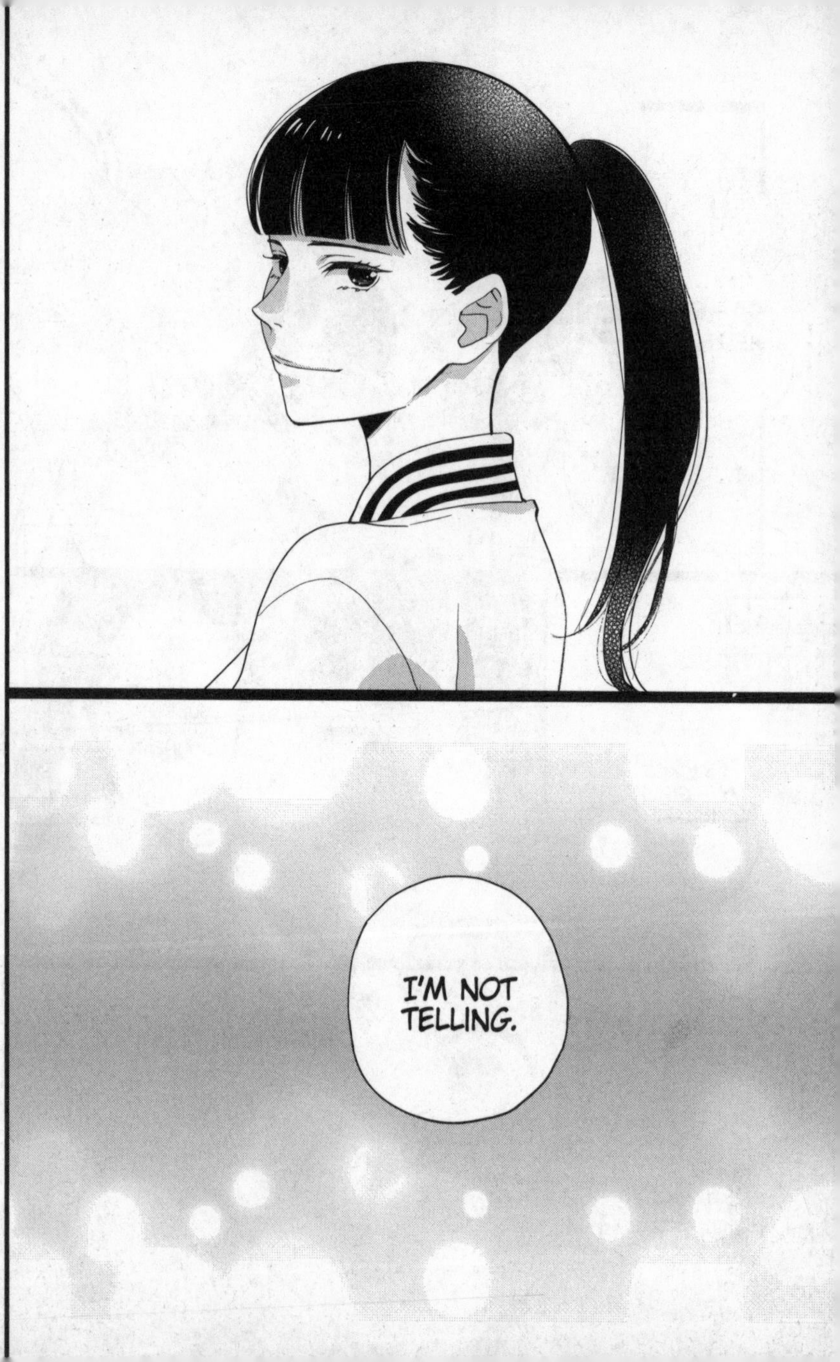
I'M NOT TELLING.

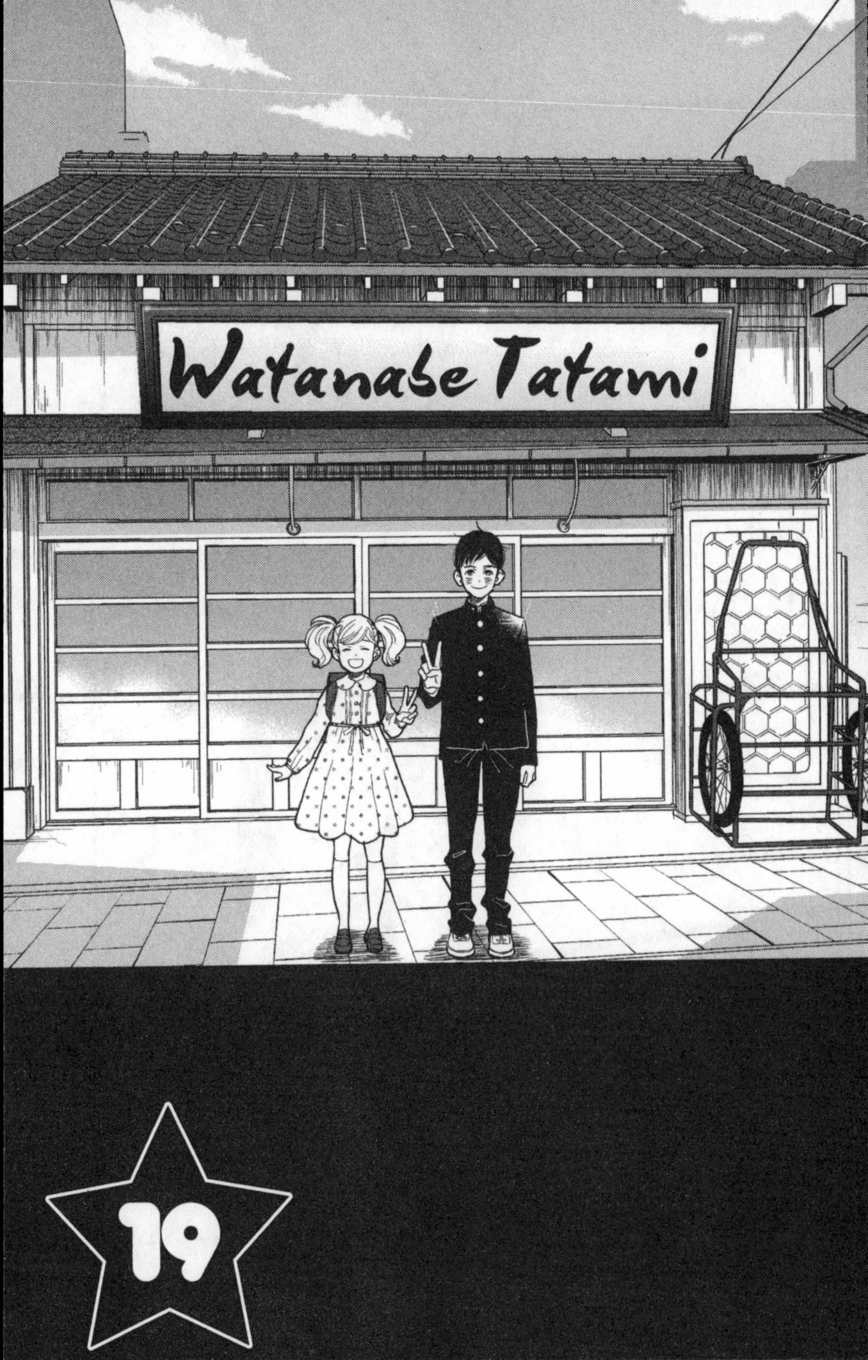
Watanabe Tatami
19

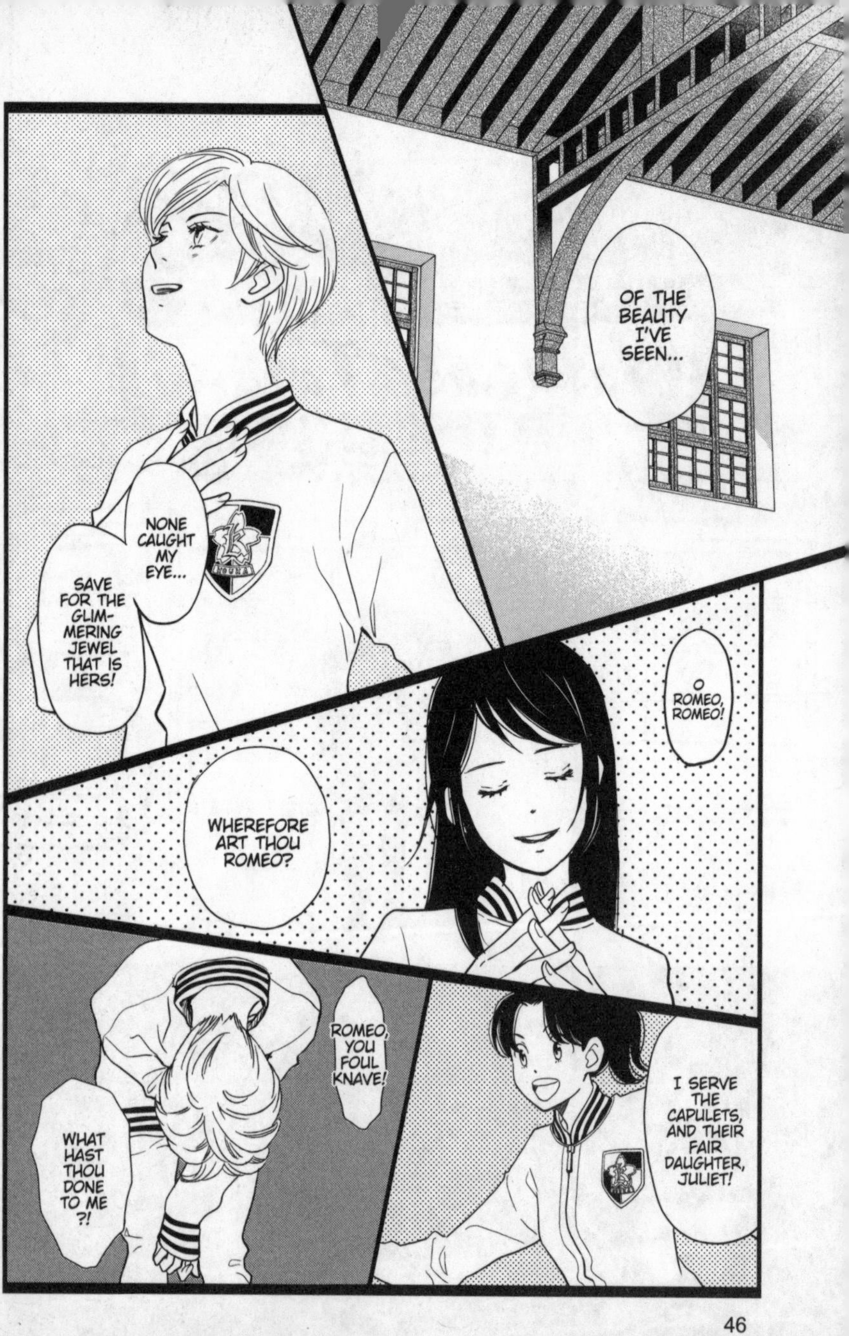
OF THE BEAUTY I'VE SEEN...
NONE CAUGHT MY EYE...
SAVE FOR THE GLIM-MERING JEWEL THAT IS HERS!
O ROMEO, ROMEO!
WHEREFORE ART THOU ROMEO?
I SERVE THE CAPULETS, AND THEIR FAIR DAUGHTER, JULIET!
ROMEO, YOU FOUL KNAVE!
WHAT HAST THOU DONE TO ME ?!

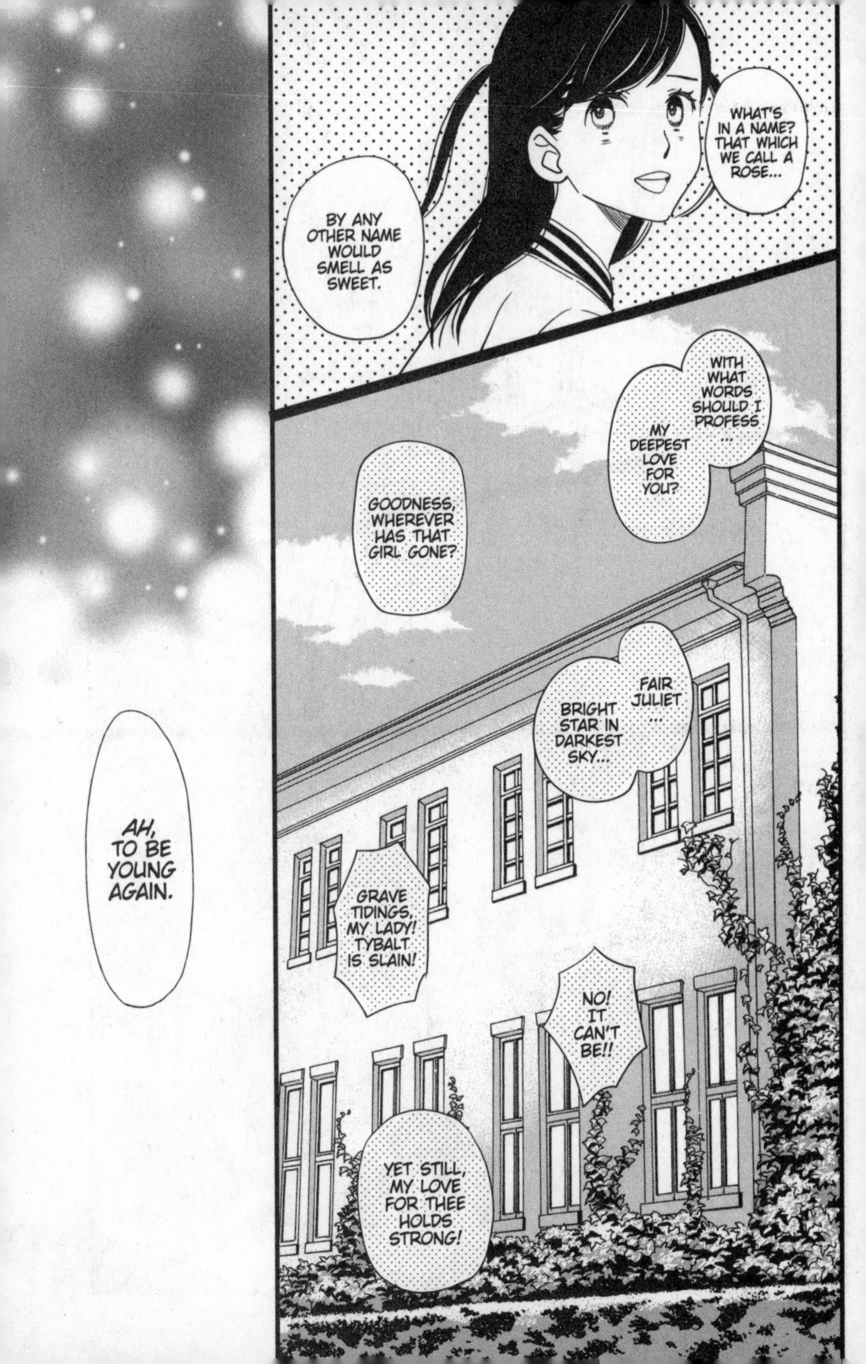
WHAT'S IN A NAME? THAT WHICH WE CALL A ROSE...
BY ANY OTHER NAME WOULD SMELL AS SWEET.
WITH WHAT WORDS SHOULD I PROFESS...
MY DEEPEST LOVE FOR YOU?
GOODNESS, WHEREVER HAS THAT GIRL GONE?
FAIR JULIET...
BRIGHT STAR IN DARKEST SKY...
GRAVE TIDINGS, MY LADY! TYBALT IS SLAIN!
NO! IT CAN'T BE!!
YET STILL, MY LOVE FOR THEE HOLDS STRONG!
AH, TO BE YOUNG AGAIN.

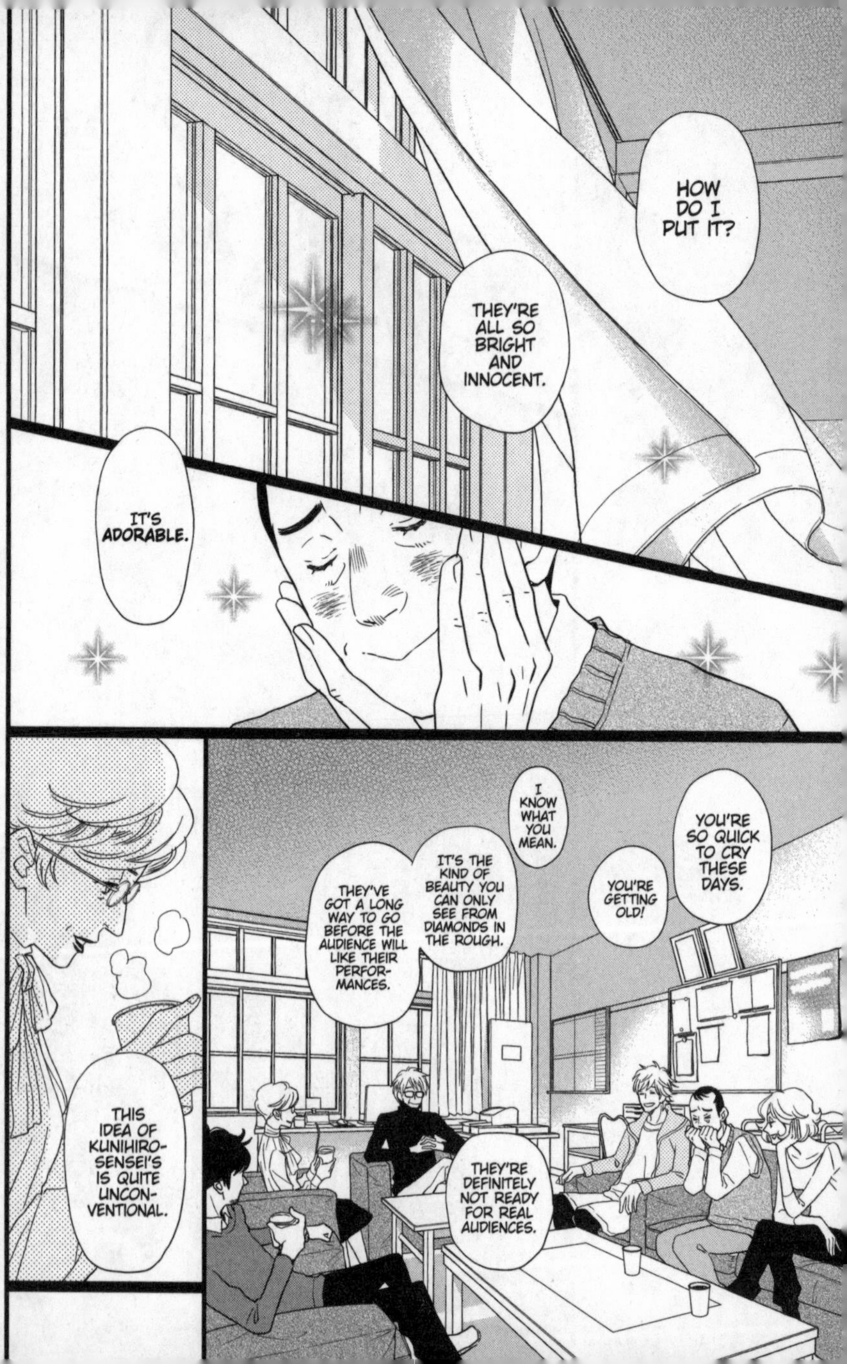
HOW DO I PUT IT?
THEY'RE ALL SO BRIGHT AND INNOCENT.
IT'S ADORABLE.
YOU'RE SO QUICK TO CRY THESE DAYS.
YOU'RE GETTING OLD!
I KNOW WHAT YOU MEAN.
IT'S THE KIND OF BEAUTY YOU CAN ONLY SEE FROM DIAMONDS IN THE ROUGH.
THEY'VE GOT A LONG WAY TO GO BEFORE THE AUDIENCE WILL LIKE THEIR PERFOR-MANCES.
THEY'RE DEFINITELY NOT READY FOR REAL AUDIENCES.
THIS IDEA OF KUNIHIRO-SENSEI'S IS QUITE UNCON-VENTIONAL.

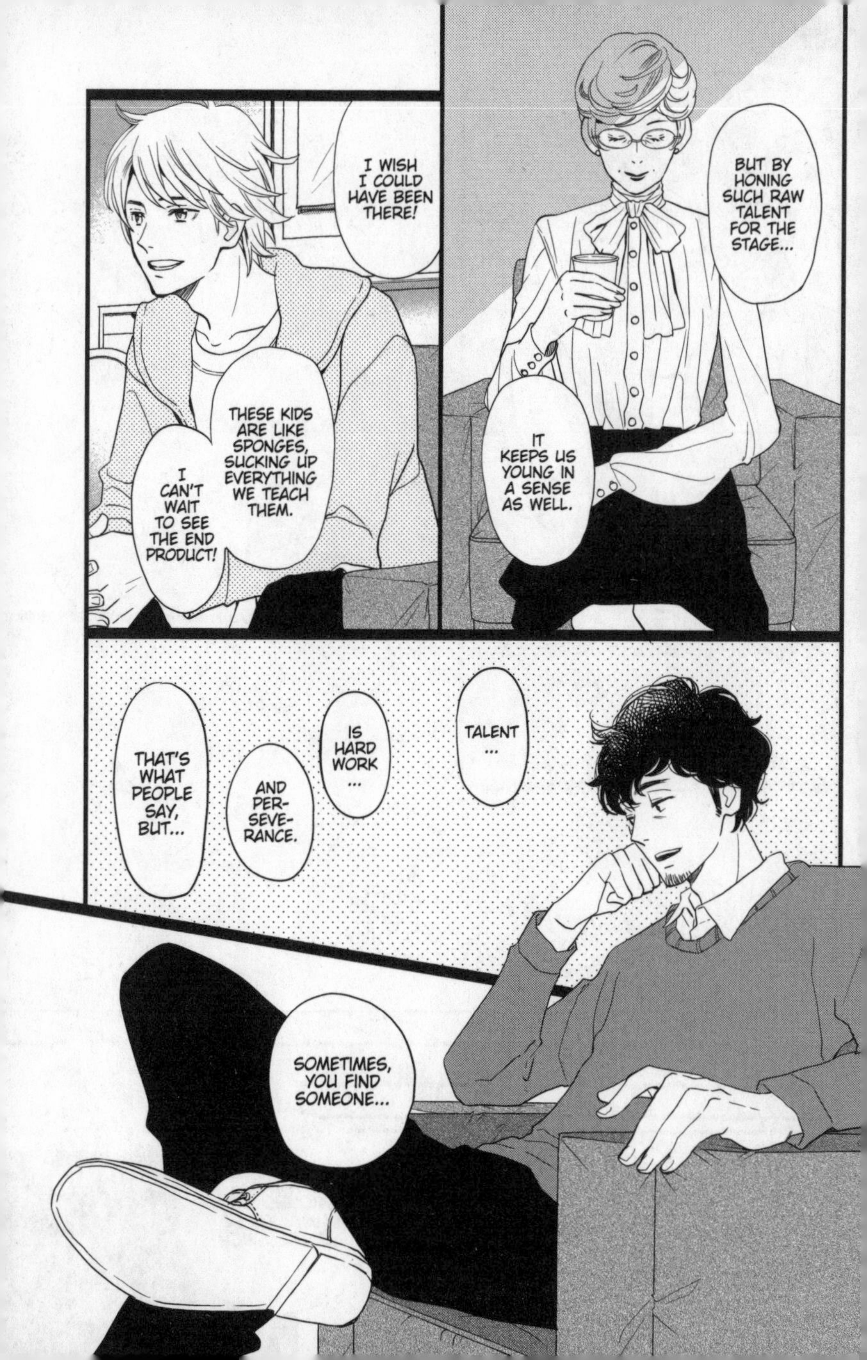
BUT BY HONING SUCH RAW TALENT FOR THE STAGE...
IT KEEPS US YOUNG IN A SENSE AS WELL.
I WISH I COULD HAVE BEEN THERE!
THESE KIDS ARE LIKE SPONGES, SUCKING UP EVERYTHING WE TEACH THEM.
I CAN'T WAIT TO SEE THE END PRODUCT!
TALENT...
IS HARD WORK...
AND PER-SEVE-RANCE.
THAT'S WHAT PEOPLE SAY, BUT...
SOMETIMES, YOU FIND SOMEONE...

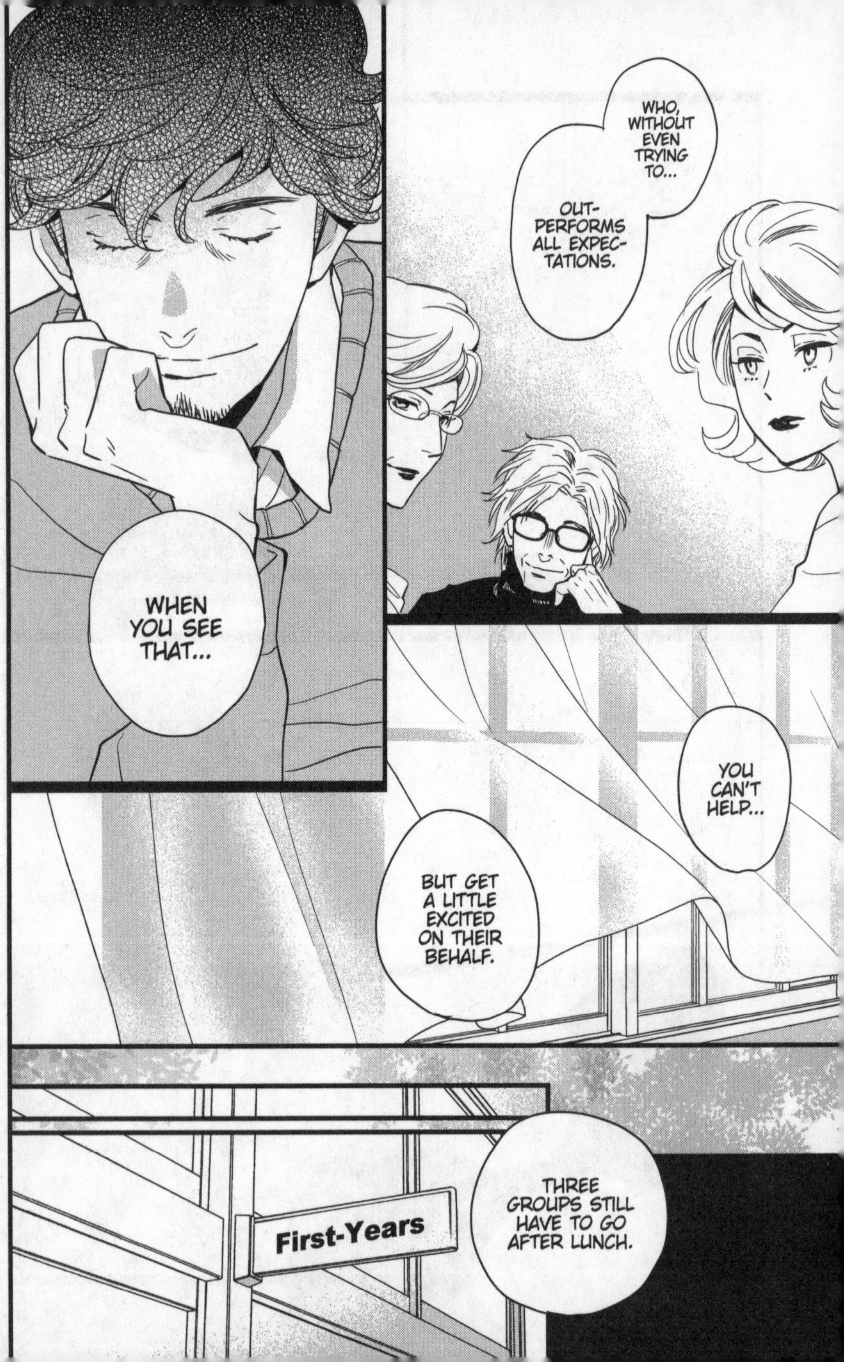
WHO, WITHOUT EVEN TRYING TO...
OUT-PERFORMS ALL EXPECTATIONS.
WHEN YOU SEE THAT...
YOU CAN'T HELP...
BUT GET A LITTLE EXCITED ON THEIR BEHALF.
First-Years
THREE GROUPS STILL HAVE TO GO AFTER LUNCH.

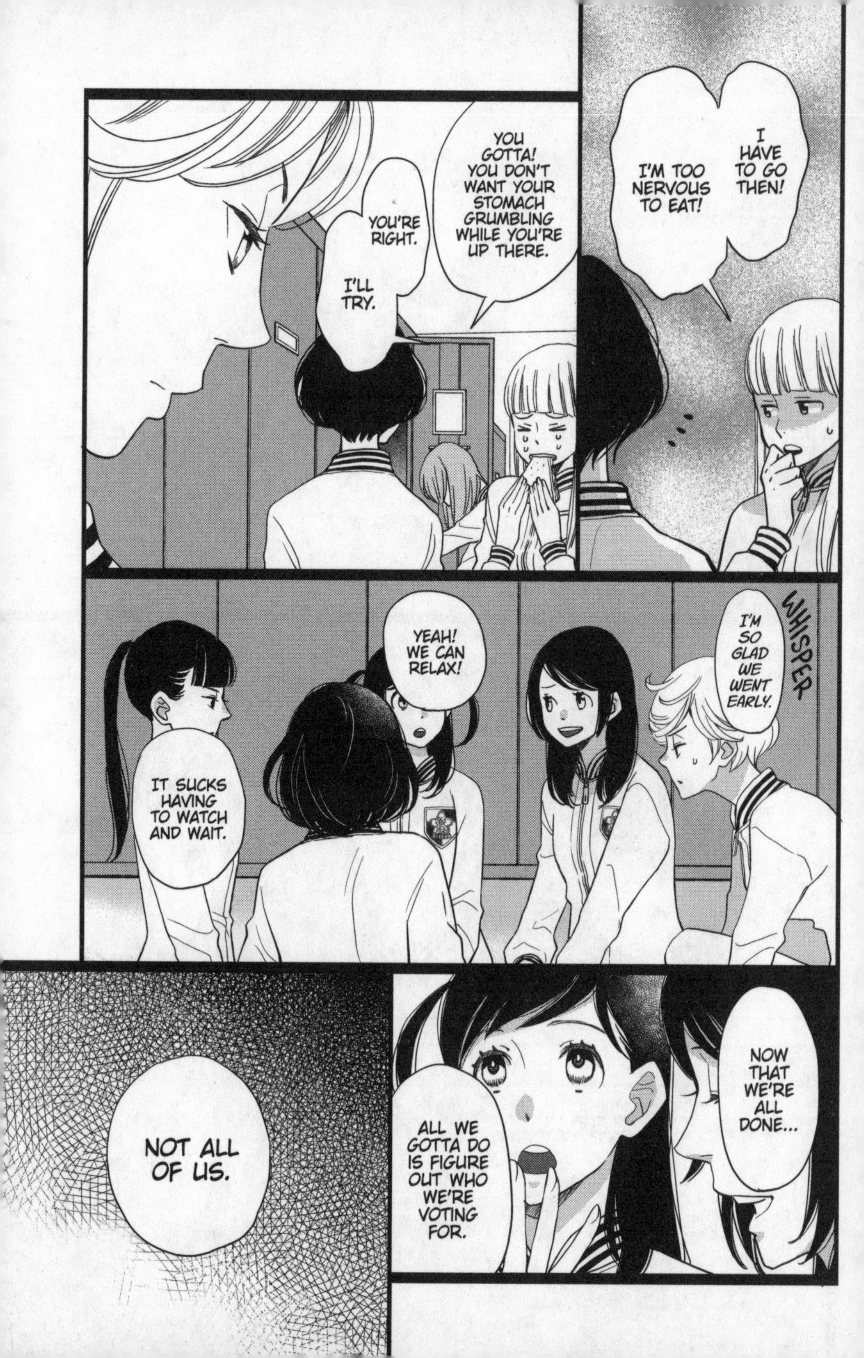
I HAVE TO GO THEN!
I'M TOO NERVOUS TO EAT!
YOU GOTTA! YOU DON'T WANT YOUR STOMACH GRUMBLING WHILE YOU'RE UP THERE.
YOU'RE RIGHT.
I'LL TRY.
WHISPER
I'M SO GLAD WE WENT EARLY.
YEAH! WE CAN RELAX!
IT SUCKS HAVING TO WATCH AND WAIT.
NOW THAT WE'RE ALL DONE...
ALL WE GOTTA DO IS FIGURE OUT WHO WE'RE VOTING FOR.
NOT ALL OF US.

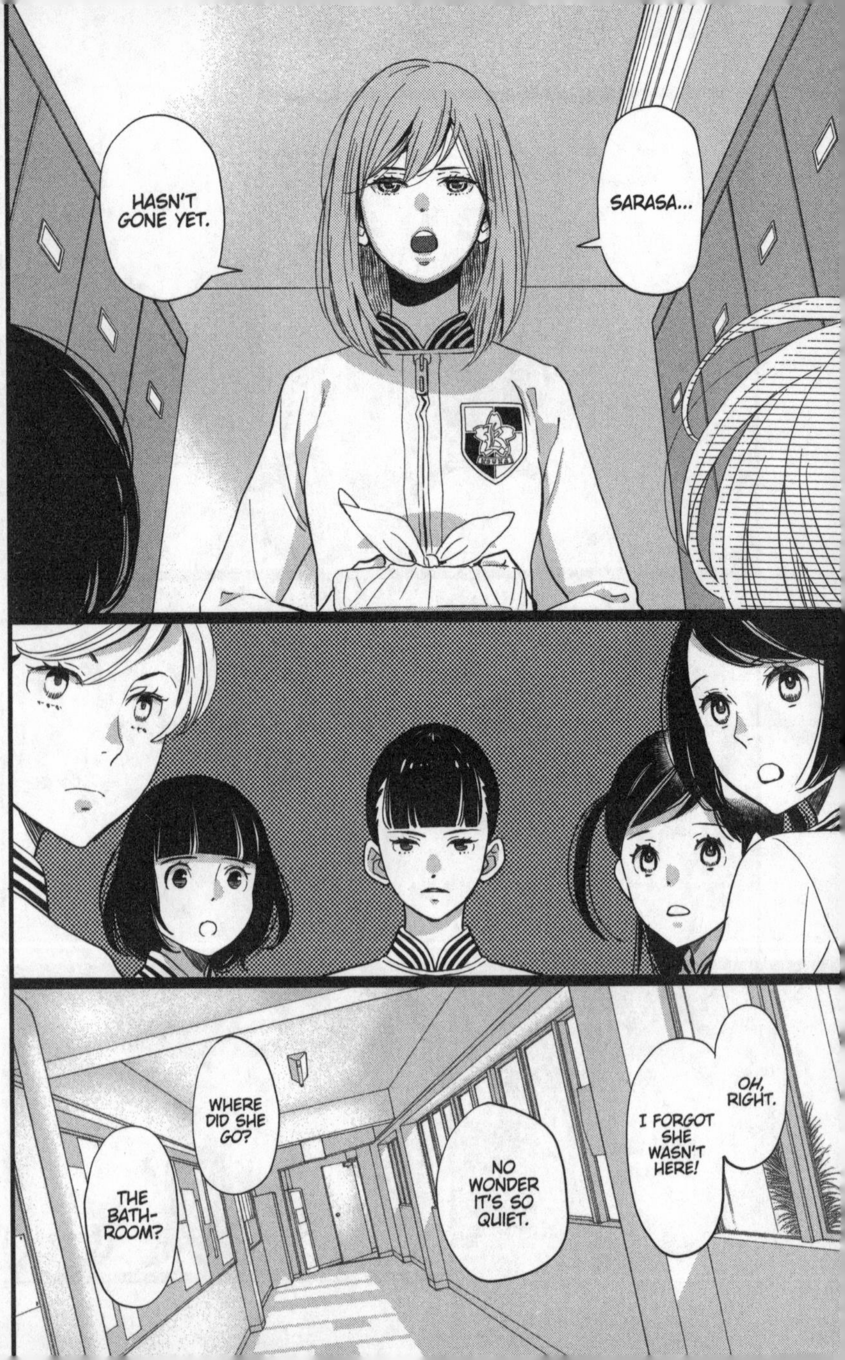
SARASA...
HASN'T GONE YET.
OH, RIGHT.
I FORGOT SHE WASN'T HERE!
NO WONDER IT'S SO QUIET.
WHERE DID SHE GO?
THE BATH-ROOM?

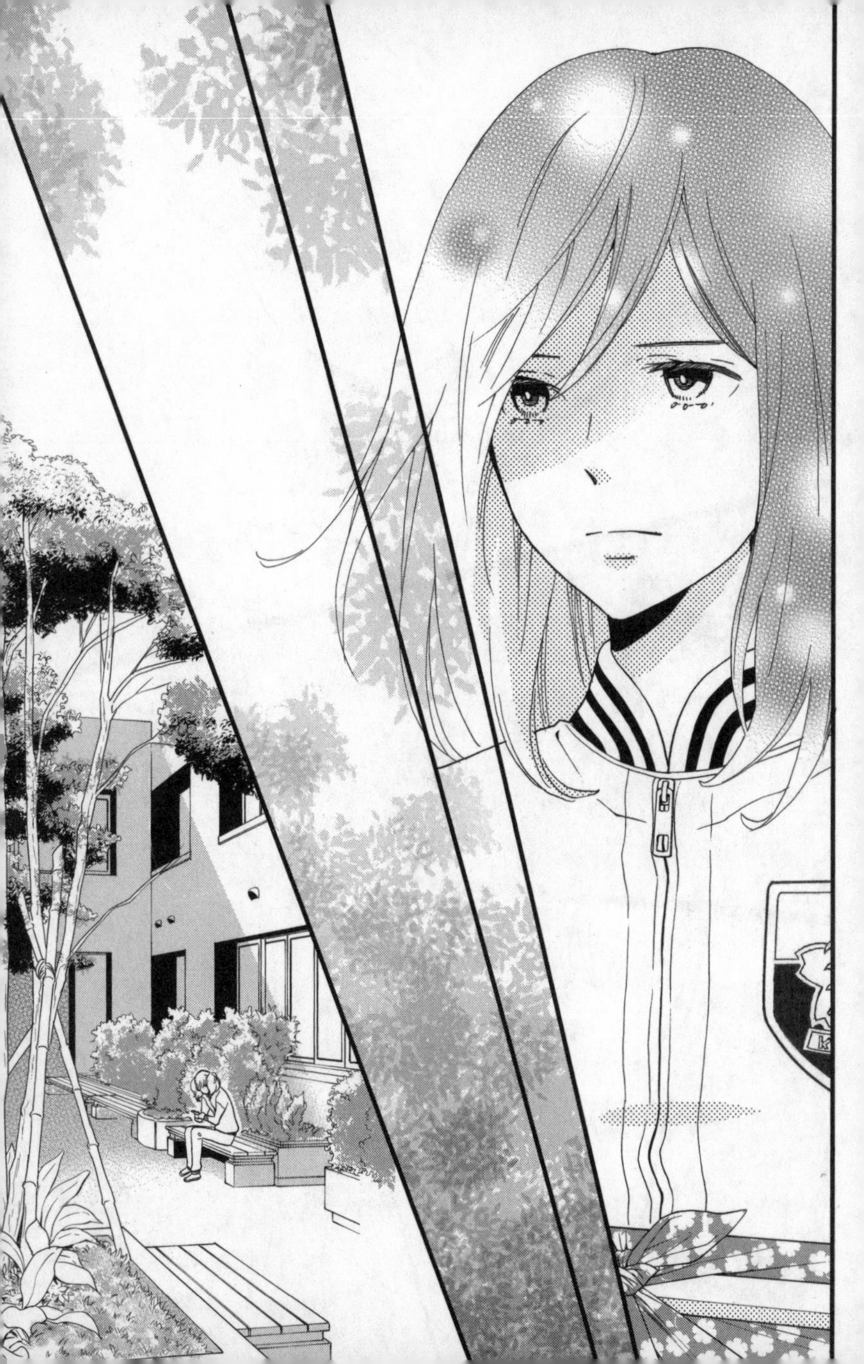

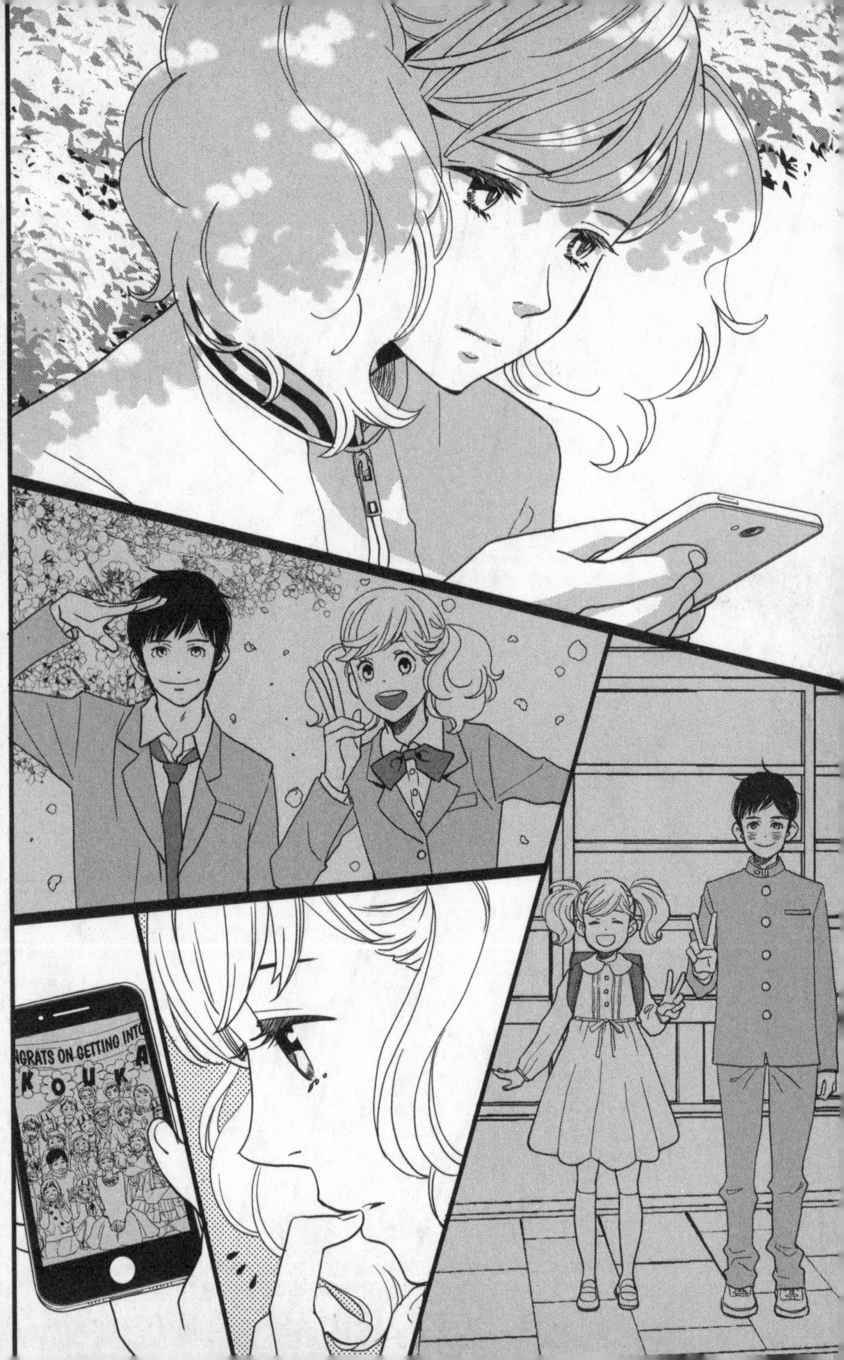
NGRATS ON GETTING INTO
KOUKA

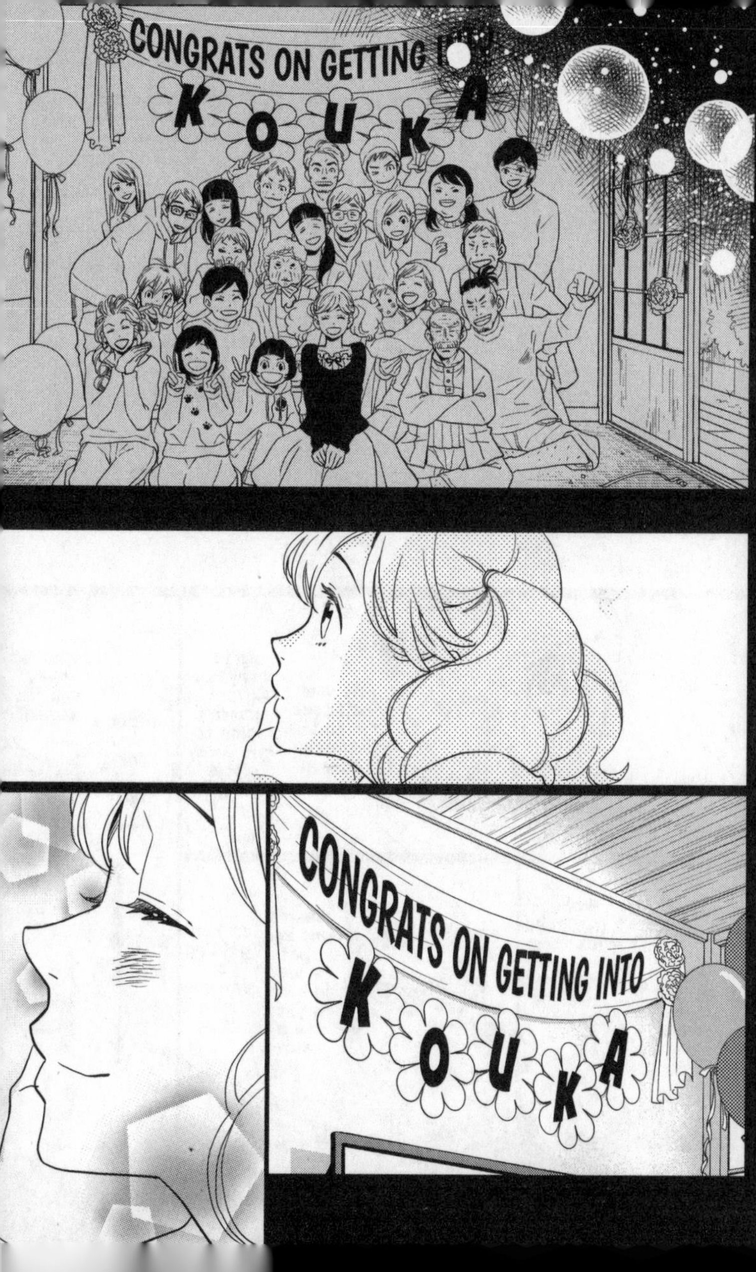
CONGRATS ON GETTING
KOUKA
CONGRATS ON GETTING INTO
KOUKA

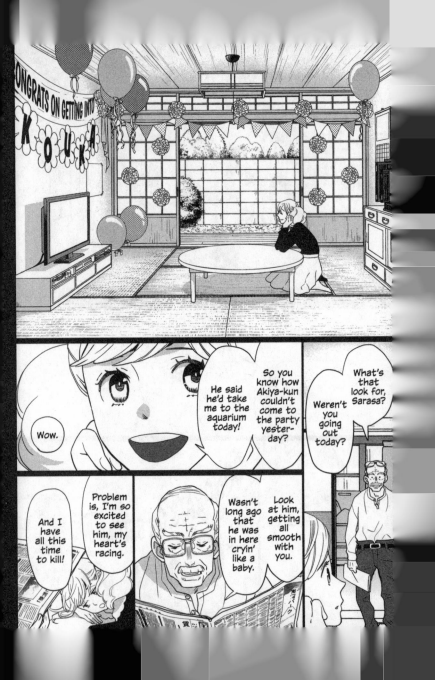

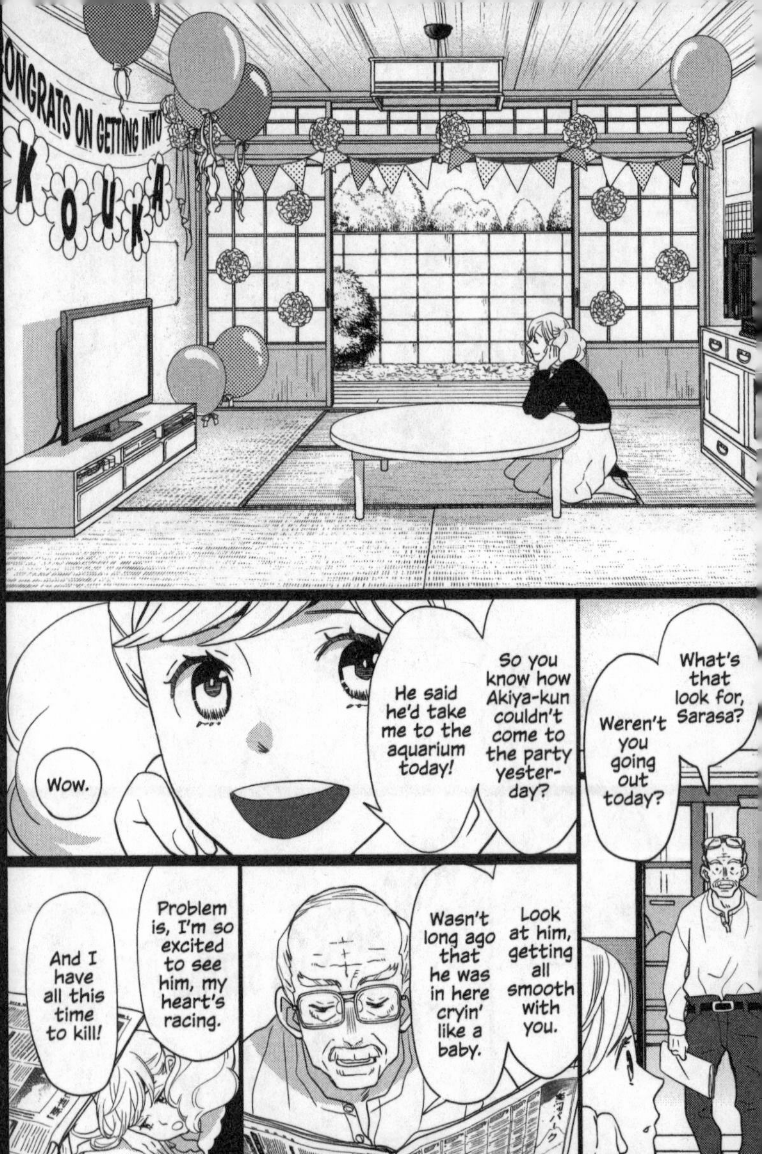
CONGRATS ON GETTING INTO
KOUKA
What's that look for, Sarasa?
Weren't you going out today?
So you know how Akiya-kun couldn't come to the party yester-day?
He said he'd take me to the aquarium today!
Wow.
Look at him, getting all smooth with you.
Wasn't long ago that he was in here cryin' like a baby.
Problem is, I'm so excited to see him, my heart's racing.
And I have all this time to kill!

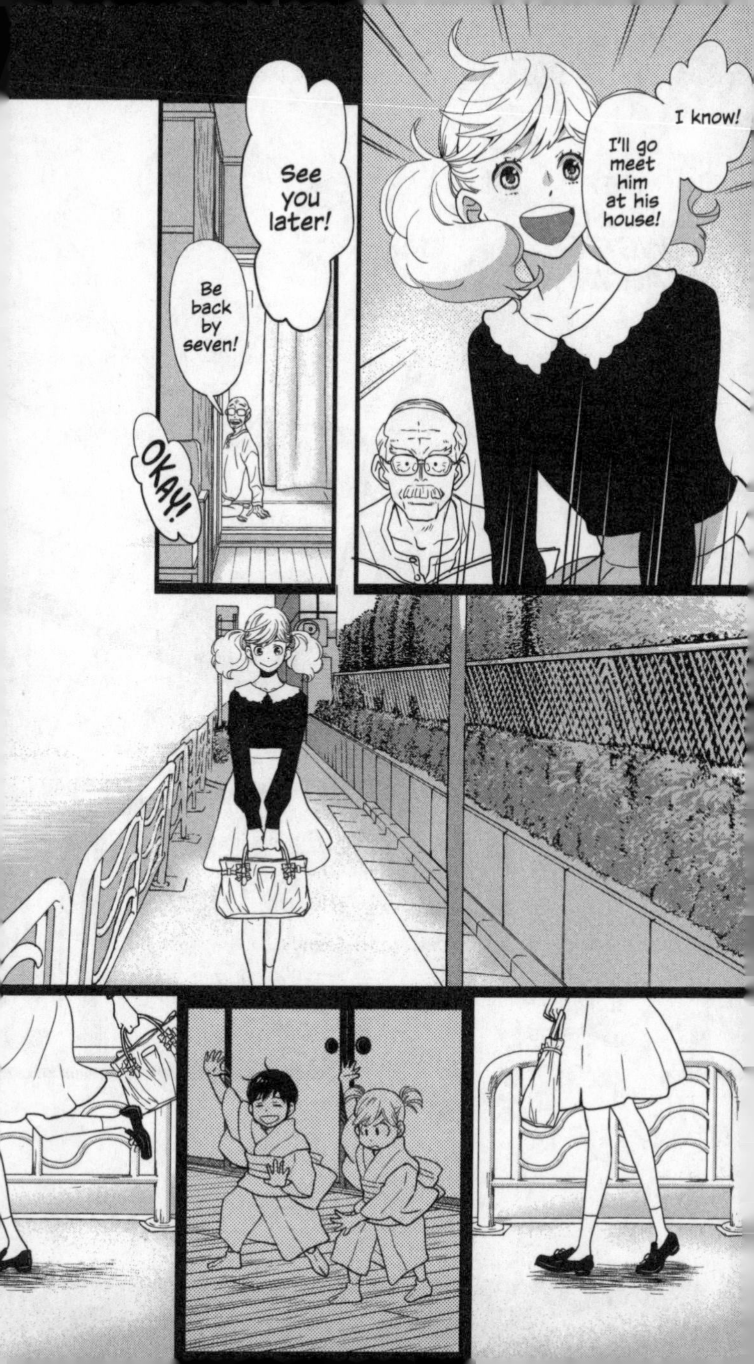
I know!
I'll go meet him at his house!
See you later!
Be back by seven!
OKAY!

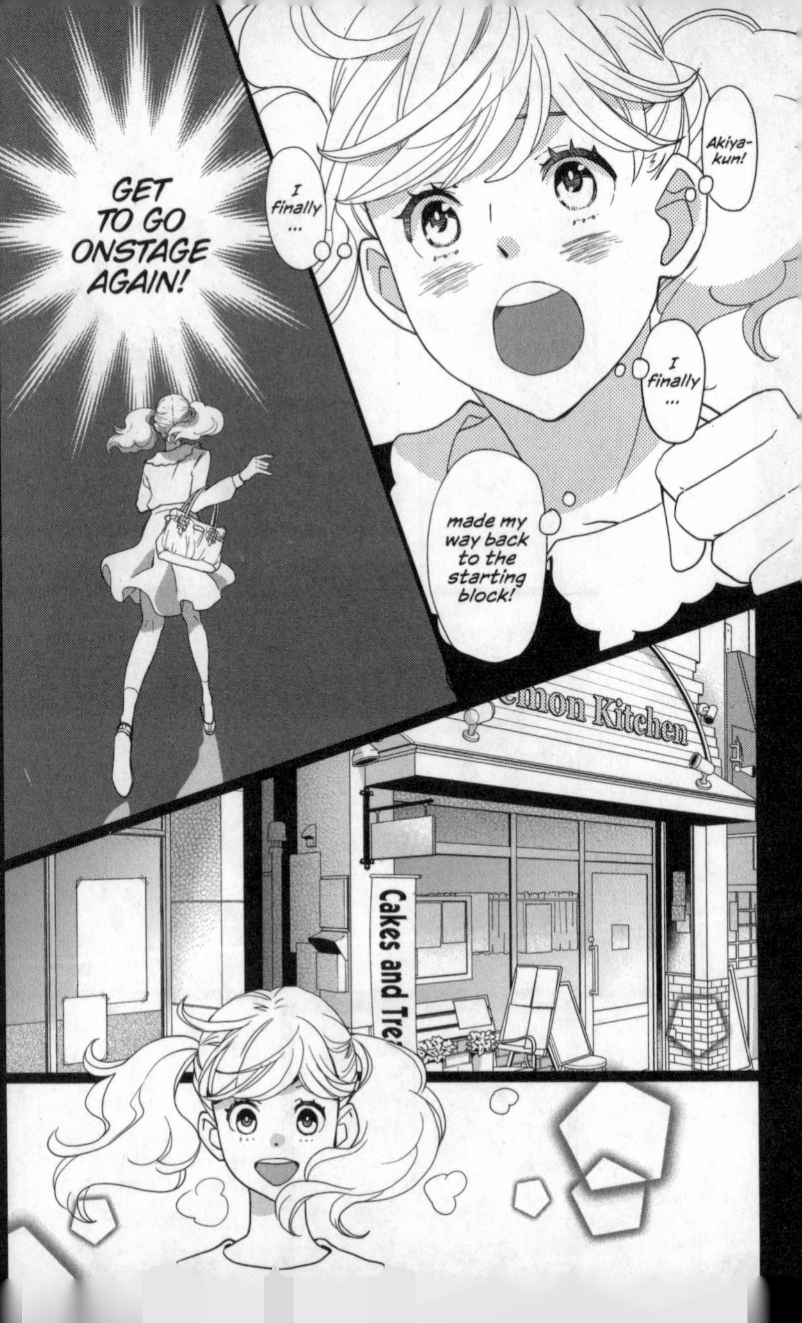
Akiya-kun!
I finally ...
I finally ...
made my way back to the starting block!
GET TO GO ONSTAGE AGAIN!
Kitchen
Cakes and

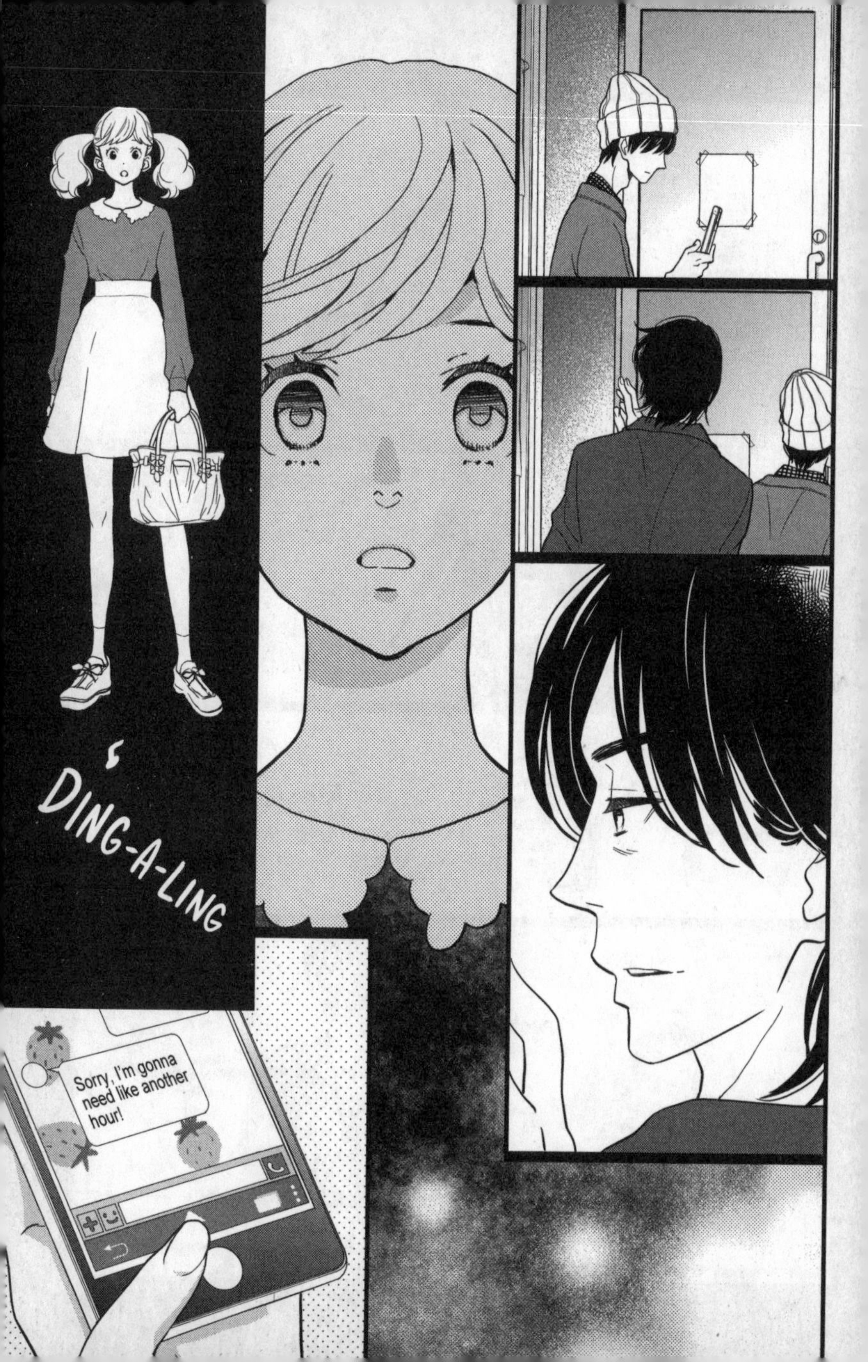
DING-A-LING
Sorry, I'm gonna need like another hour!

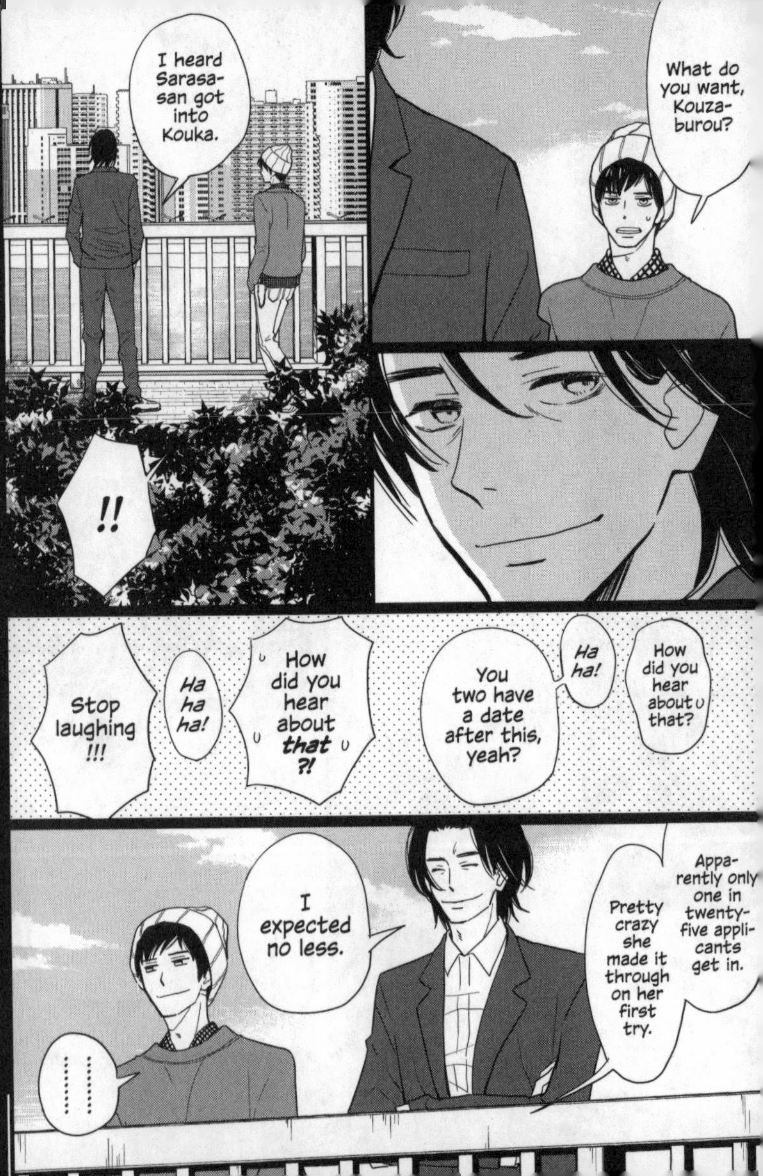
What do you want, Kouzaburou?
I heard Sarasa-san got into Kouka.
!!
How did you hear about that?
Ha ha!
You two have a date after this, yeah?
How did you hear about *that*?!
Ha ha ha!
Stop laughing!!!
Apparently only one in twenty-five applicants get in.
Pretty crazy she made it through on her first try.
I expected no less.
......

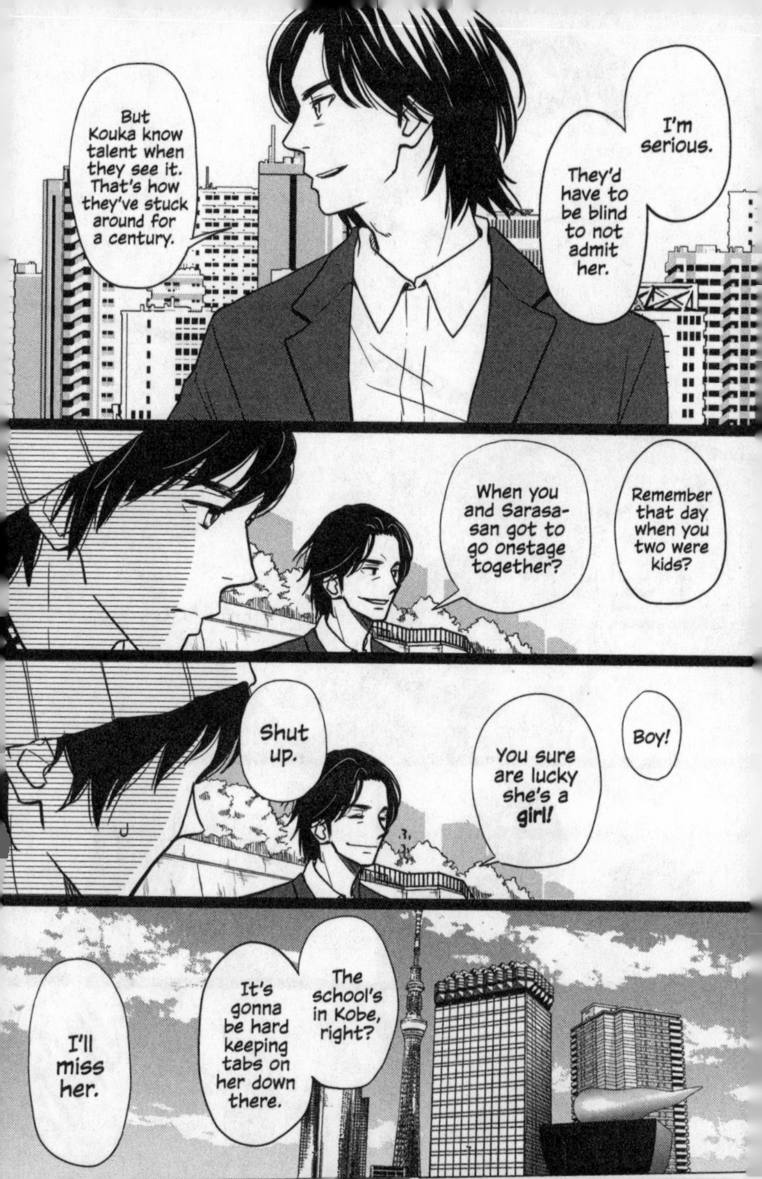
I'm serious.
They'd have to be blind to not admit her.
But Kouka know talent when they see it. That's how they've stuck around for a century.
Remember that day when you two were kids?
When you and Sarasa-san got to go onstage together?
Boy!
You sure are lucky she's a girl!
Shut up.
The school's in Kobe, right?
It's gonna be hard keeping tabs on her down there.
I'll miss her.

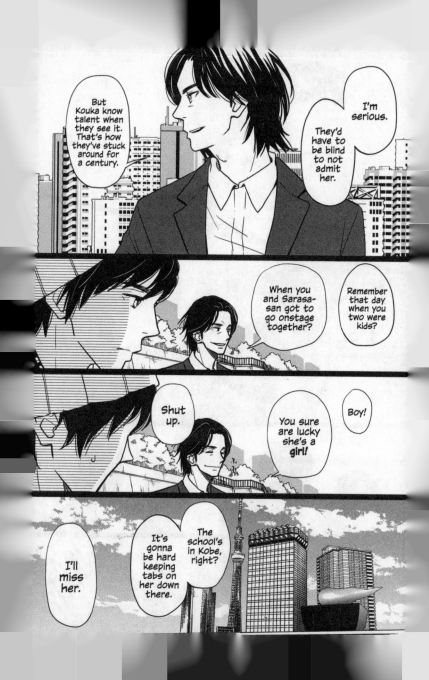

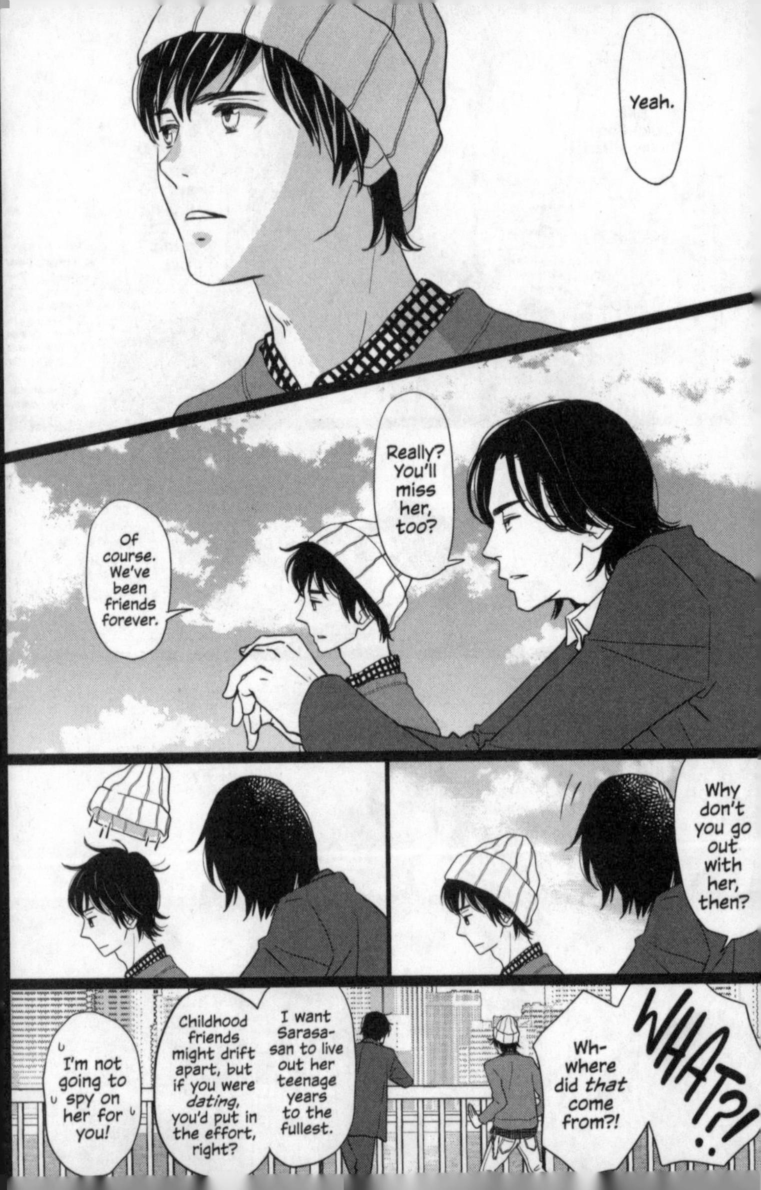
Yeah.
Really? You'll miss her, too?
Of course. We've been friends forever.
Why don't you go out with her, then?
WHAT?!
Wh- where did *that* come from?!
I want Sarasa-san to live out her teenage years to the fullest.
Childhood friends might drift apart, but if you were *dating*, you'd put in the effort, right?
I'm not going to spy on her for you!

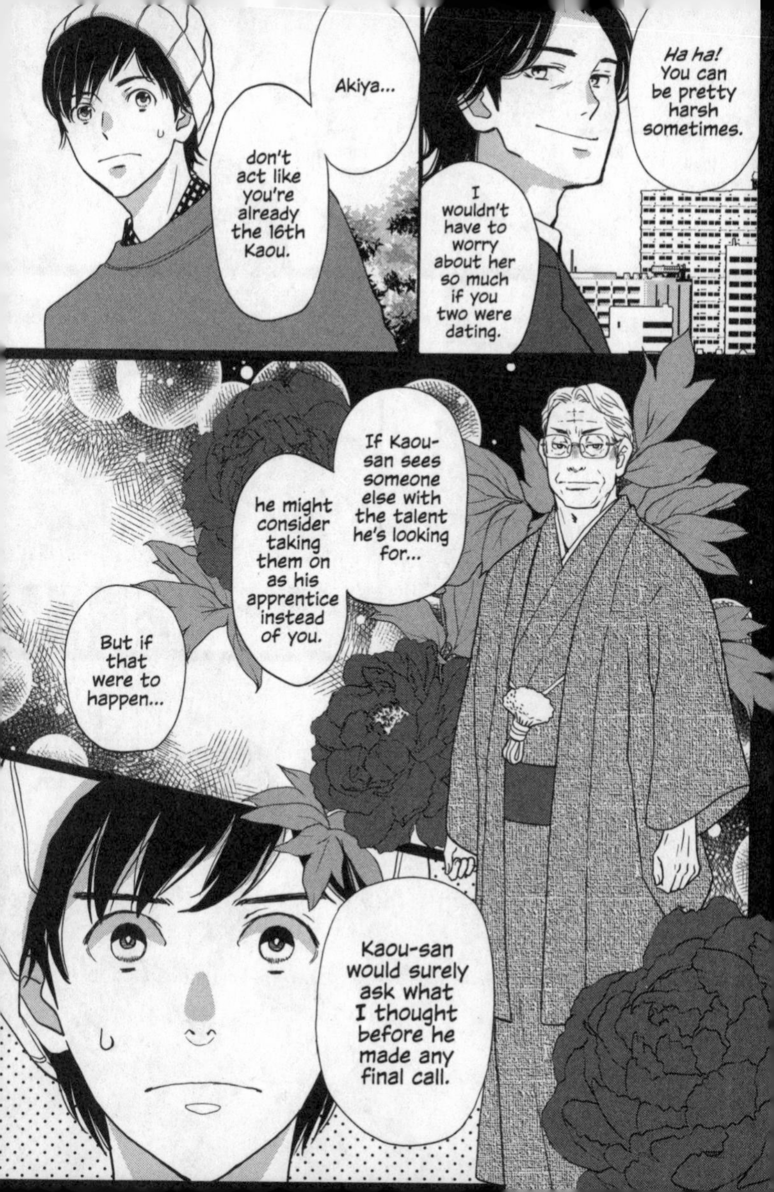

Ha ha! You can be pretty harsh sometimes.
I wouldn't have to worry about her so much if you two were dating.
Akiya...
don't act like you're already the 16th Kaou.
If Kaou-san sees someone else with the talent he's looking for...
he might consider taking them on as his apprentice instead of you.
But if that were to happen...
Kaou-san would surely ask what I thought before he made any final call.

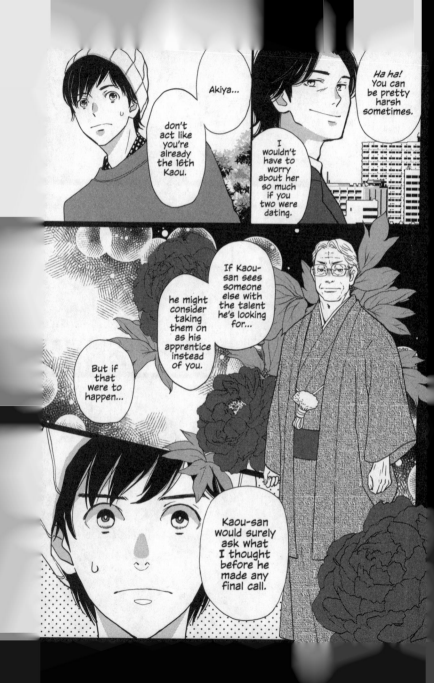

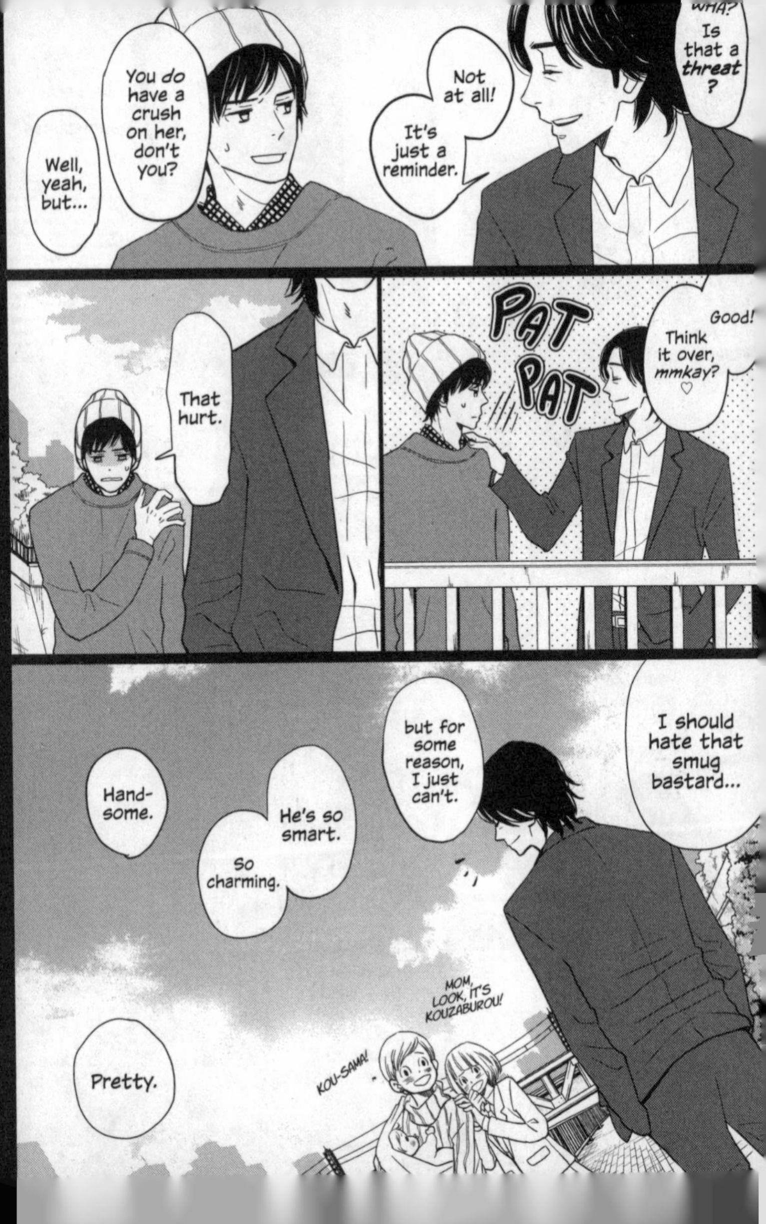
WHA? Is that a threat?
Not at all!
It's just a reminder.
You do have a crush on her, don't you?
Well, yeah, but...
PAT PAT
Good!
Think it over, mmkay? ♡
That hurt.
I should hate that smug bastard...
but for some reason, I just can't.
He's so smart.
So charming.
Hand-some.
MOM, LOOK, IT'S KOUZABUROU!
KOU-SAMA!
Pretty.

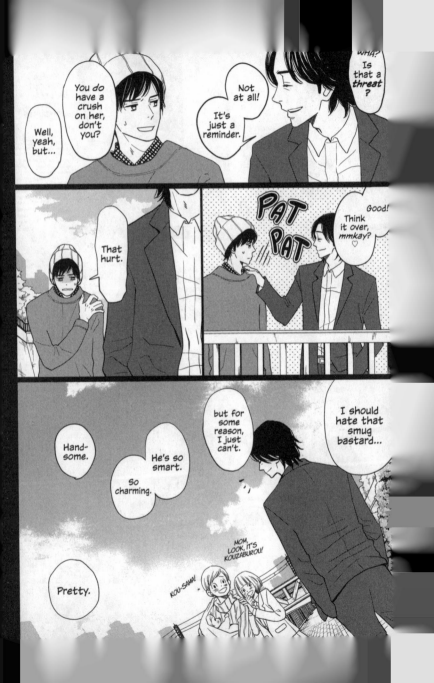

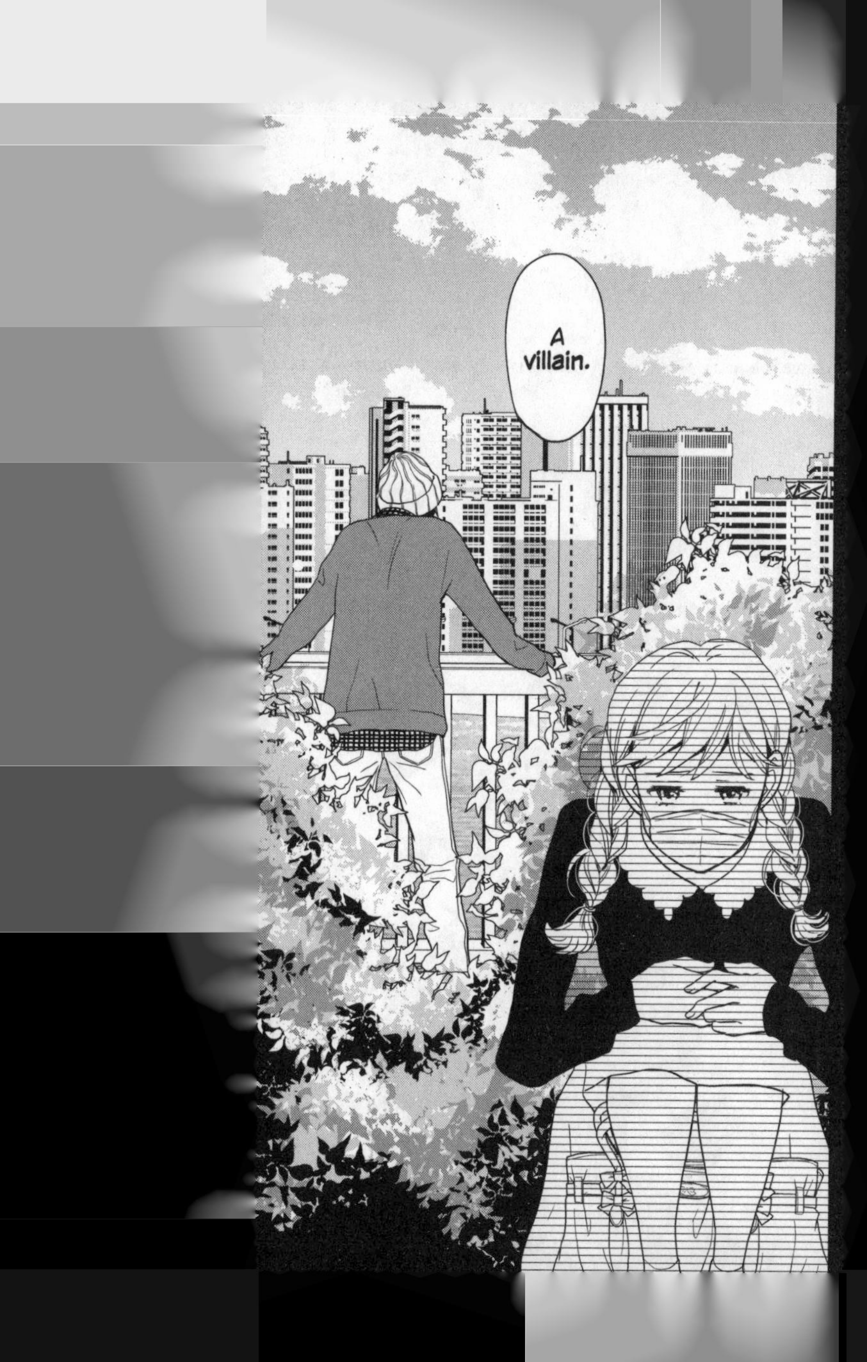
A villain.

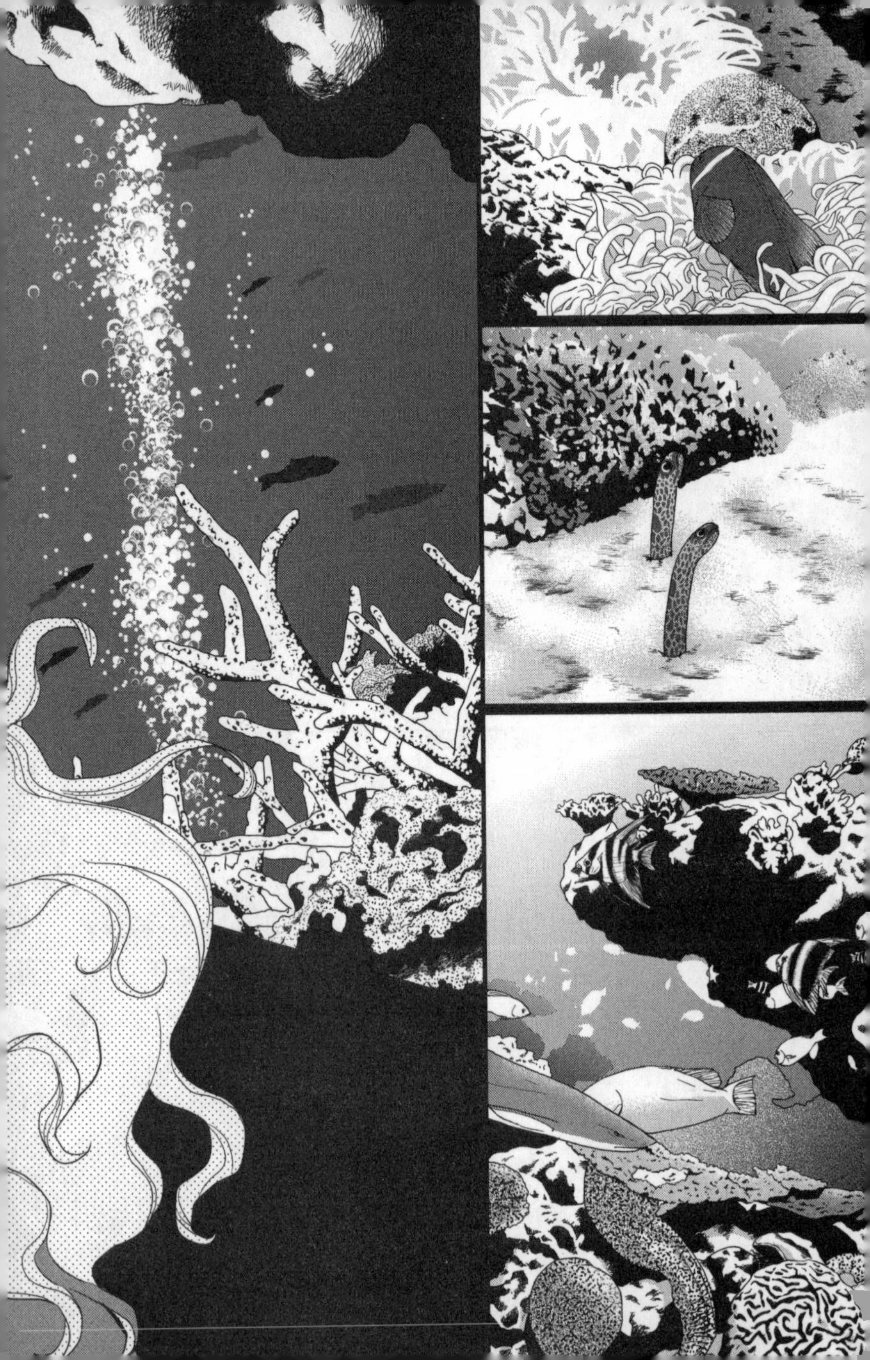

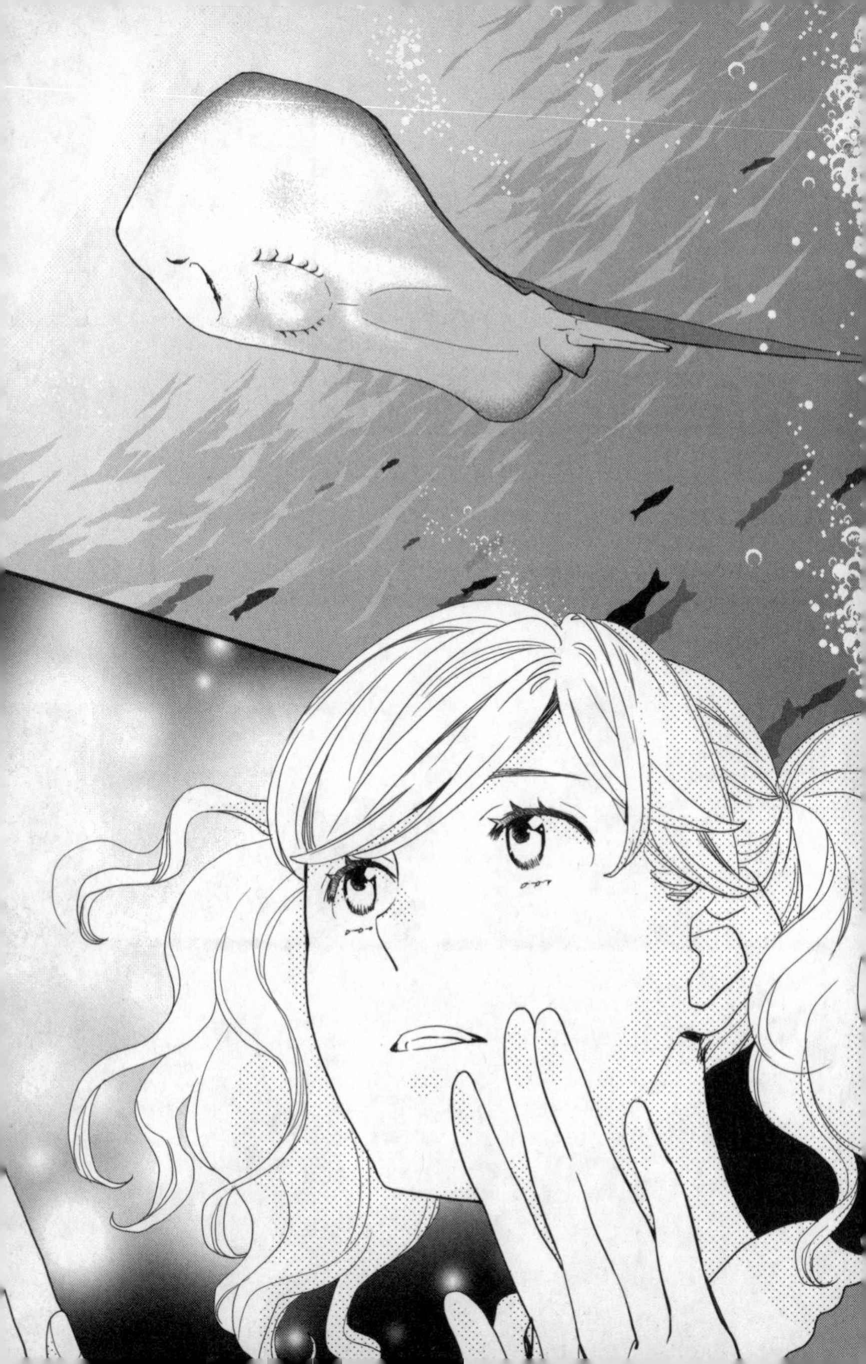

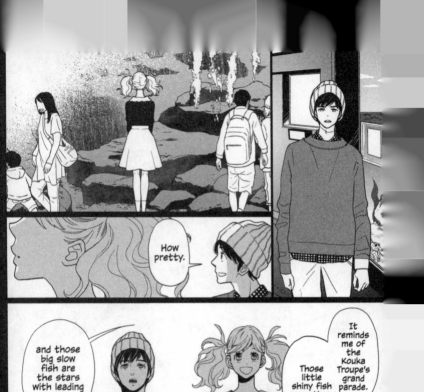

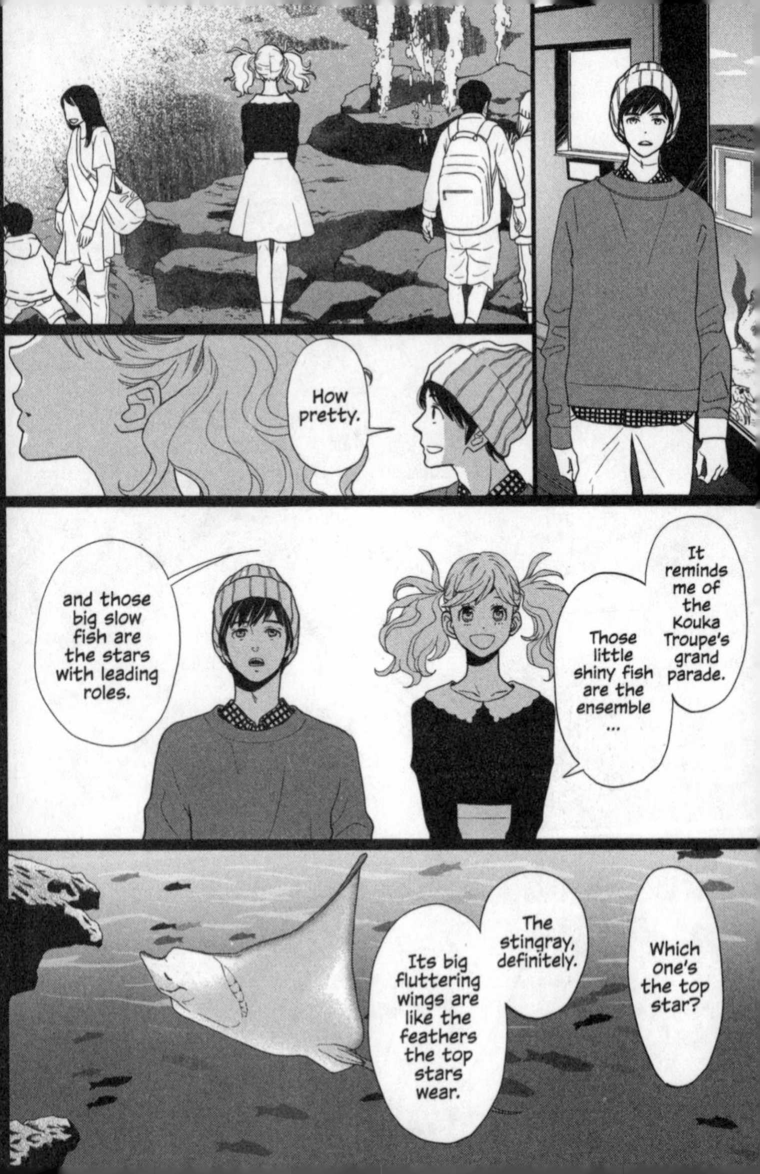
How pretty.
It reminds me of the Kouka Troupe's grand parade.
Those little shiny fish are the ensemble ...
and those big slow fish are the stars with leading roles.
Which one's the top star?
The stingray, definitely.
Its big fluttering wings are like the feathers the top stars wear.

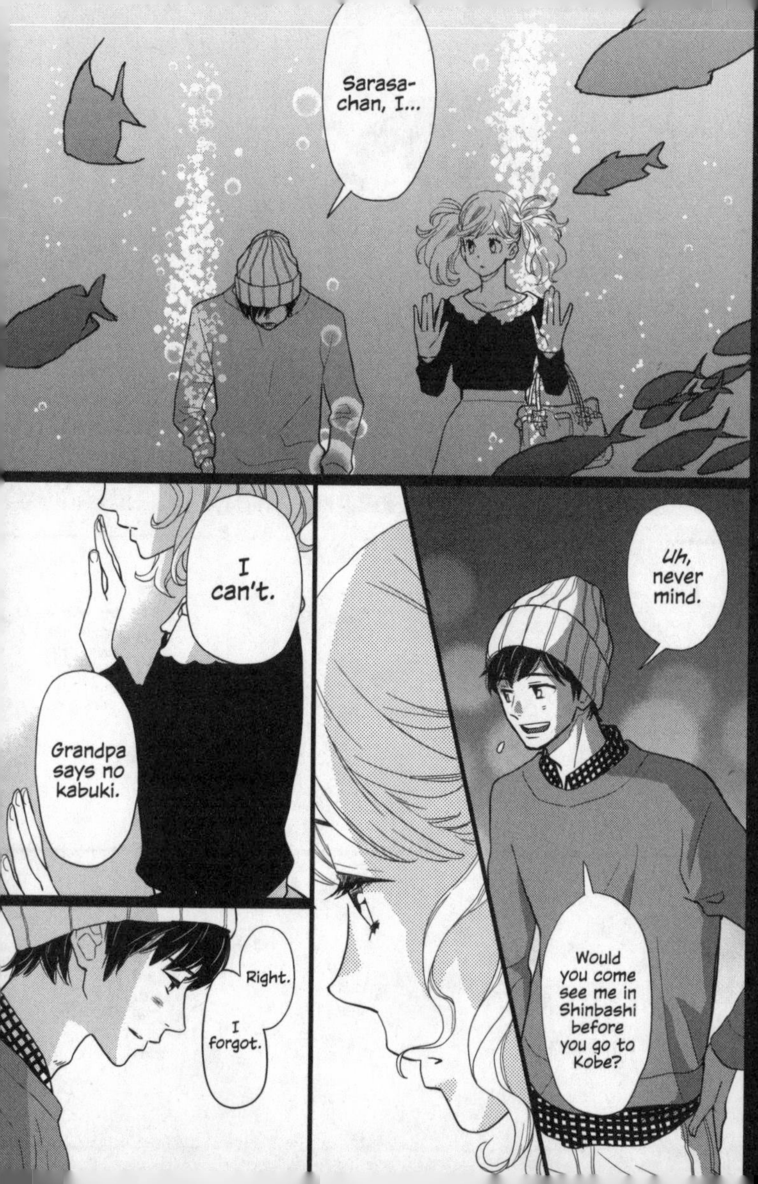
Sarasa-chan, I...
Uh, never mind.
Would you come see me in Shinbashi before you go to Kobe?
I can't.
Grandpa says no kabuki.
Right.
I forgot.

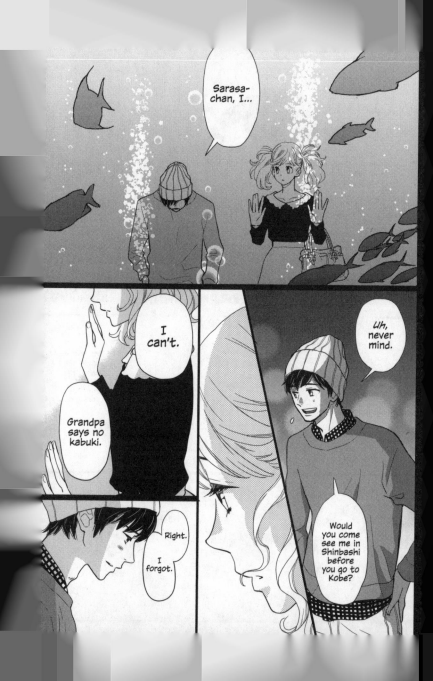

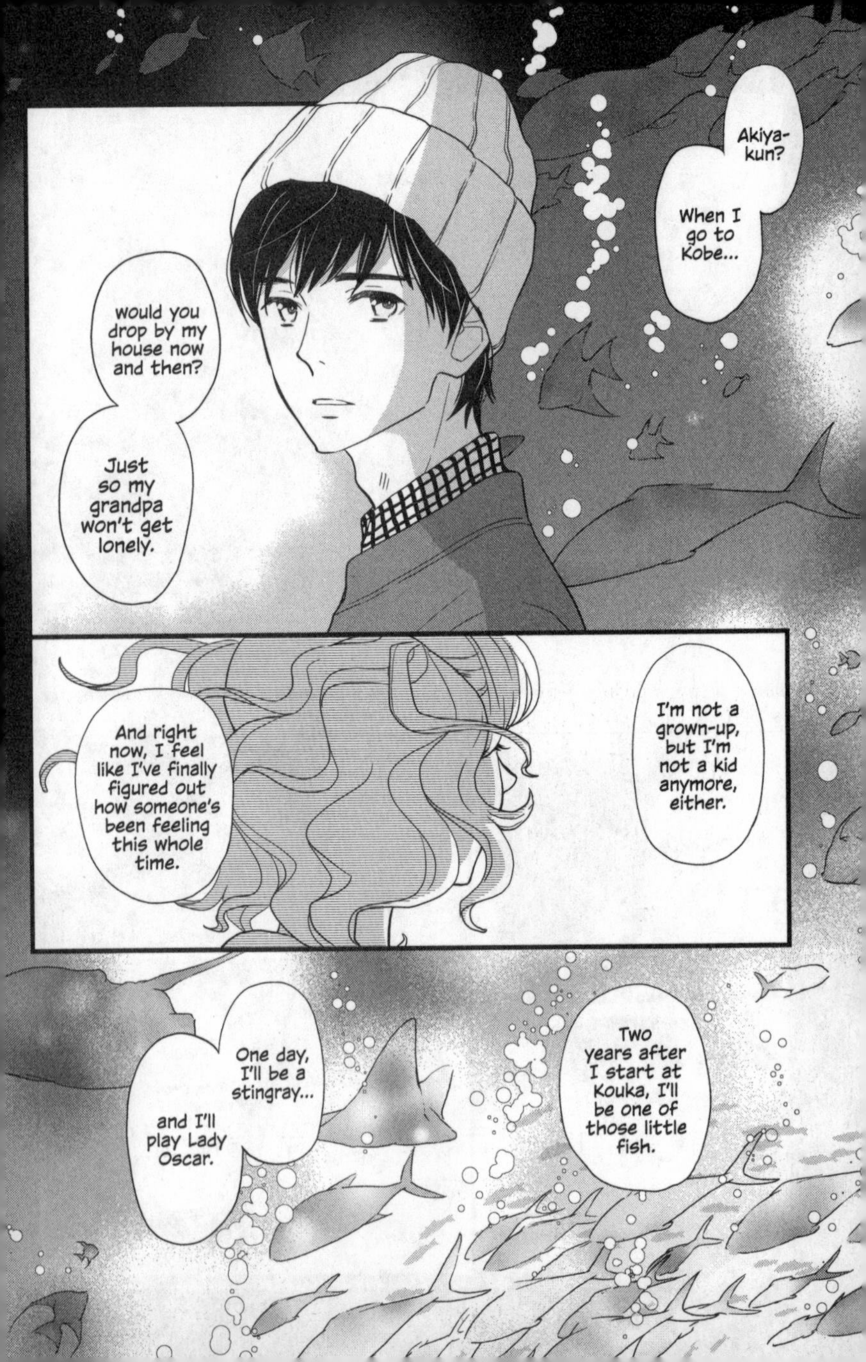
Akiya-kun?
When I go to Kobe...
would you drop by my house now and then?
Just so my grandpa won't get lonely.
I'm not a grown-up, but I'm not a kid anymore, either.
And right now, I feel like I've finally figured out how someone's been feeling this whole time.
Two years after I start at Kouka, I'll be one of those little fish.
One day, I'll be a stingray...
and I'll play Lady Oscar.

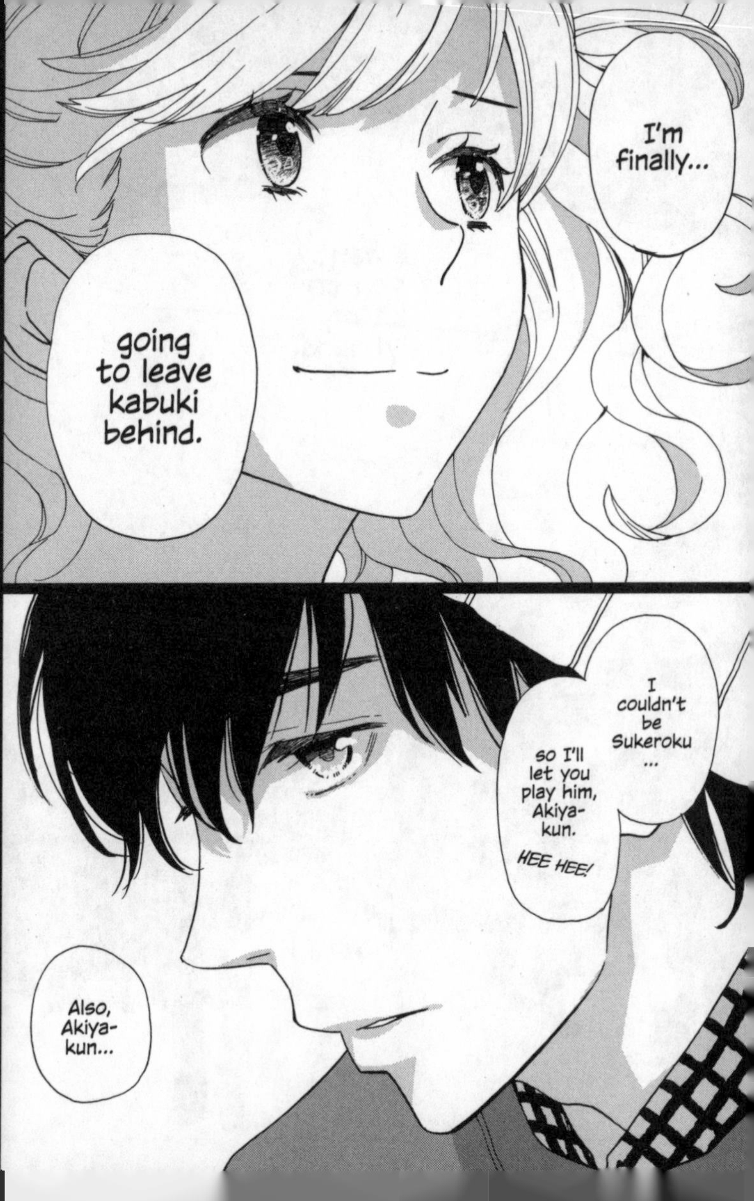
I'm finally...
going to leave kabuki behind.
I couldn't be Sukeroku ...
so I'll let you play him, Akiya-kun.
HEE HEE!
Also, Akiya-kun...

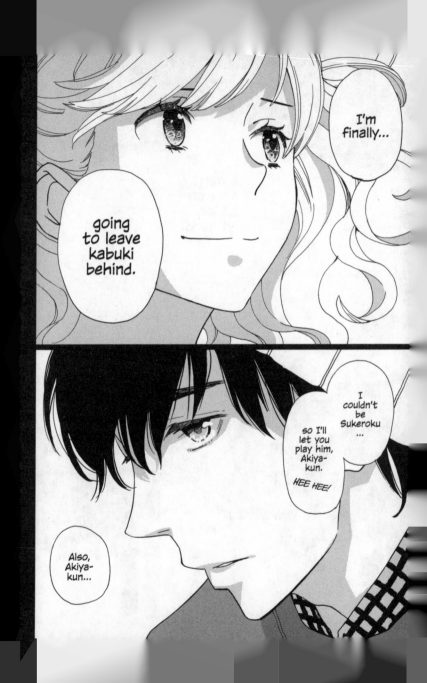

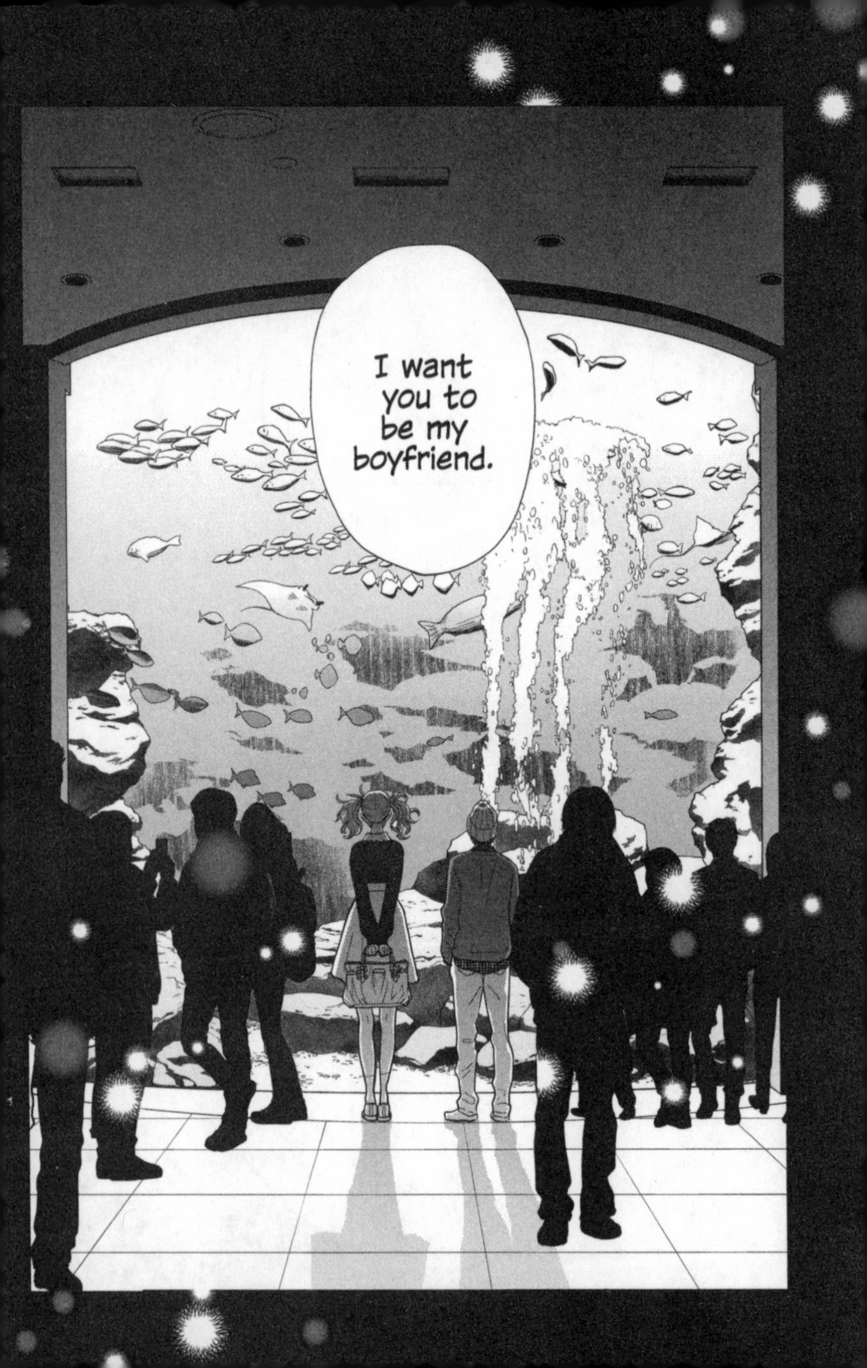
I want you to be my boyfriend.

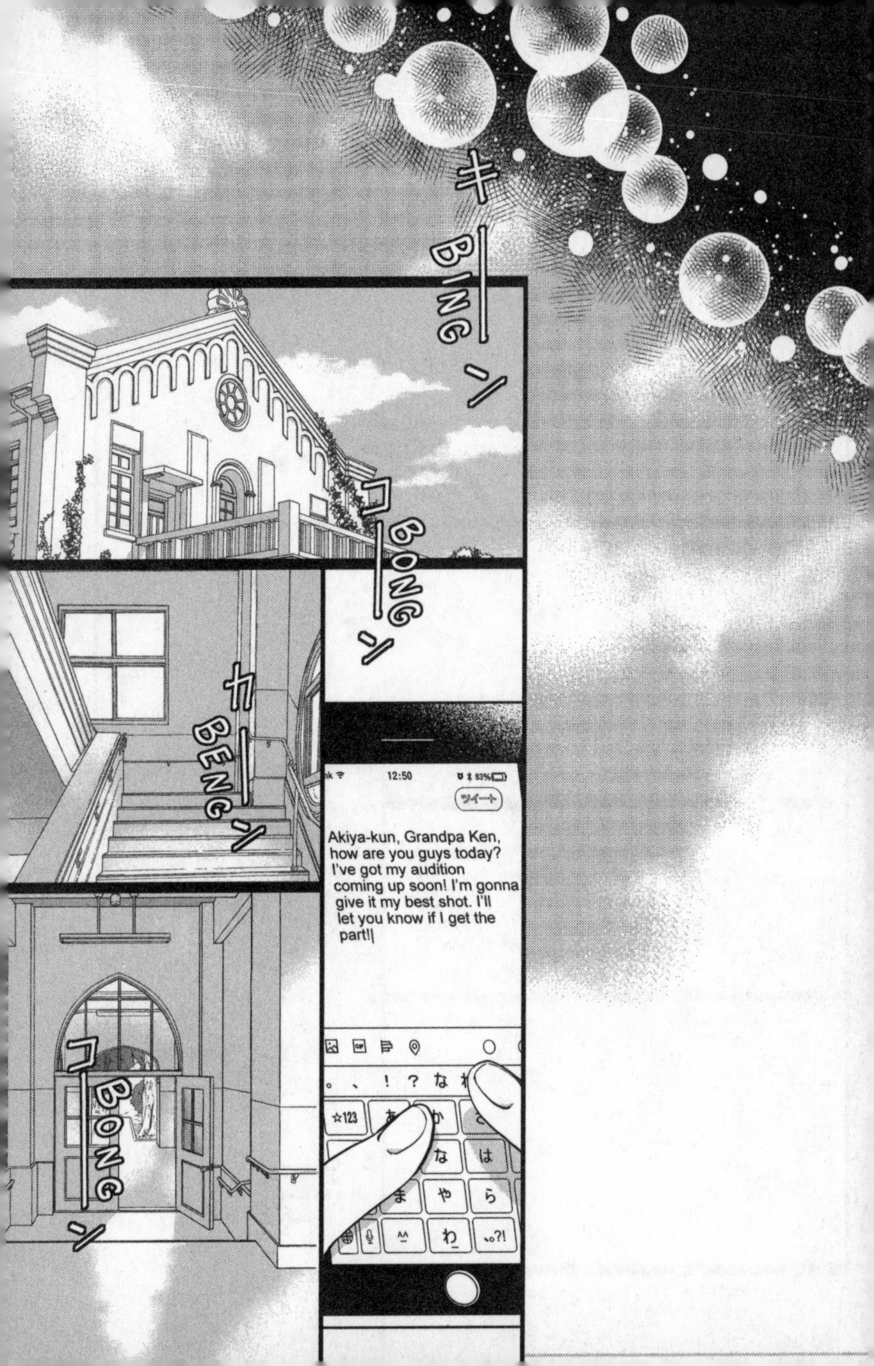

キーン
BING
コーン
BONG
カーン
BENG
12:50
ツイート
Akiya-kun, Grandpa Ken, how are you guys today? I've got my audition coming up soon! I'm gonna give it my best shot. I'll let you know if I get the part!!
コーン
BONG

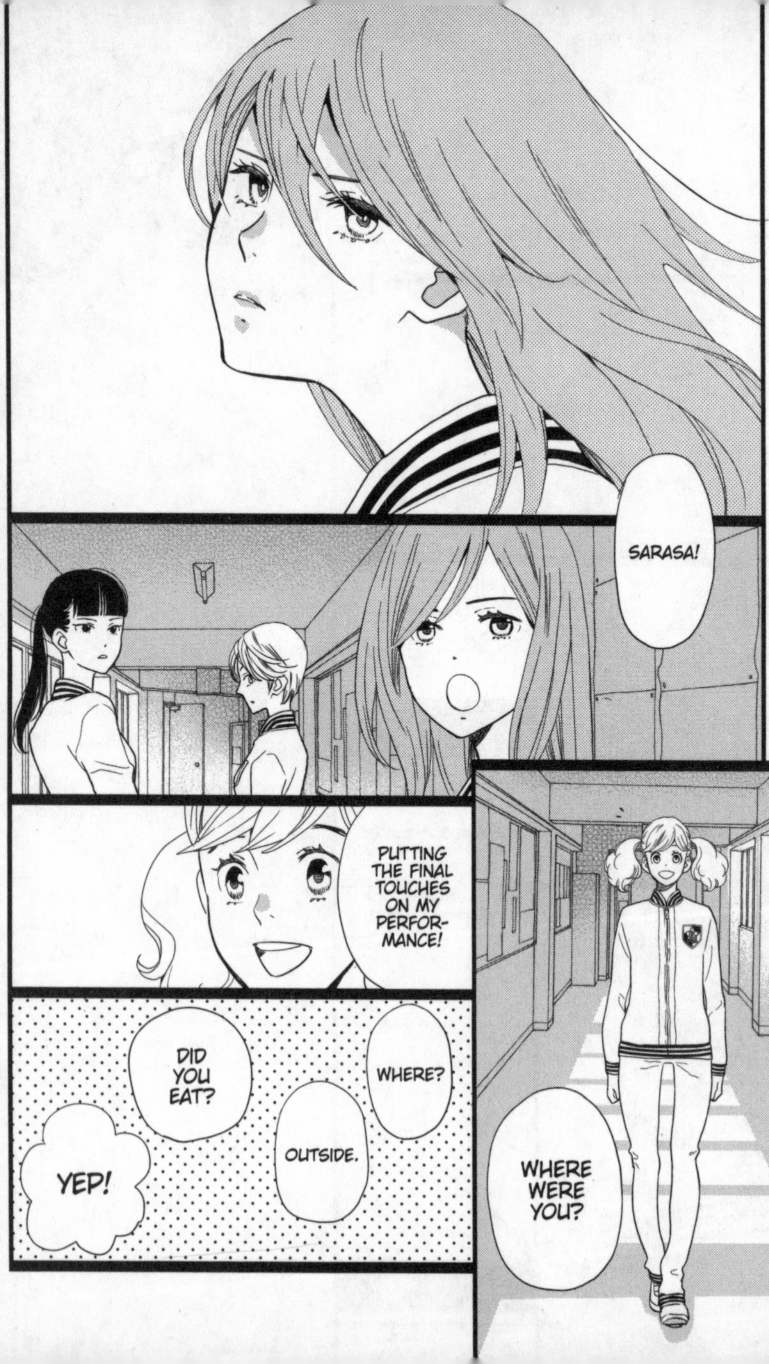
SARASA!
WHERE WERE YOU?
PUTTING THE FINAL TOUCHES ON MY PERFORMANCE!
WHERE?
OUTSIDE.
DID YOU EAT?
YEP!

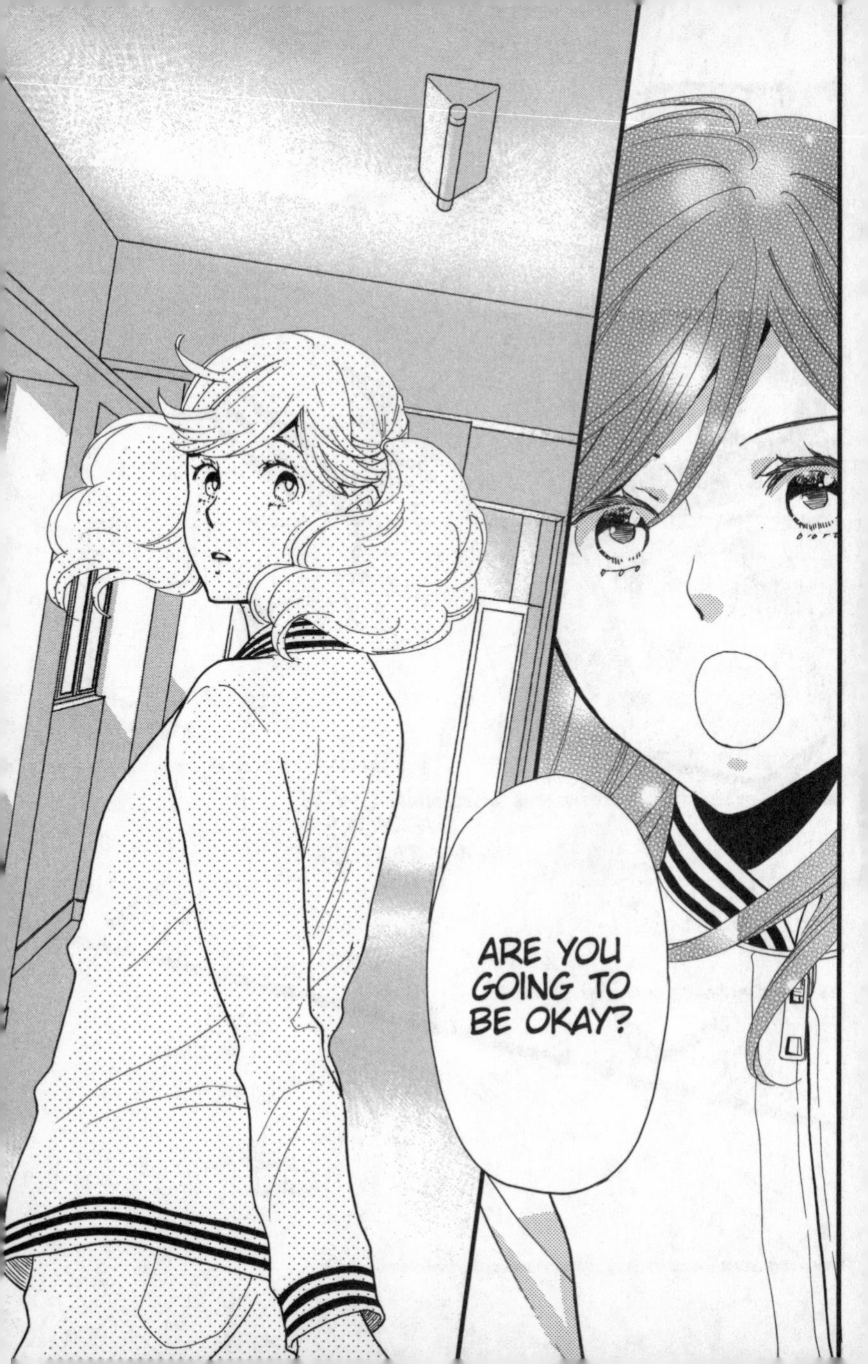
ARE YOU GOING TO BE OKAY?

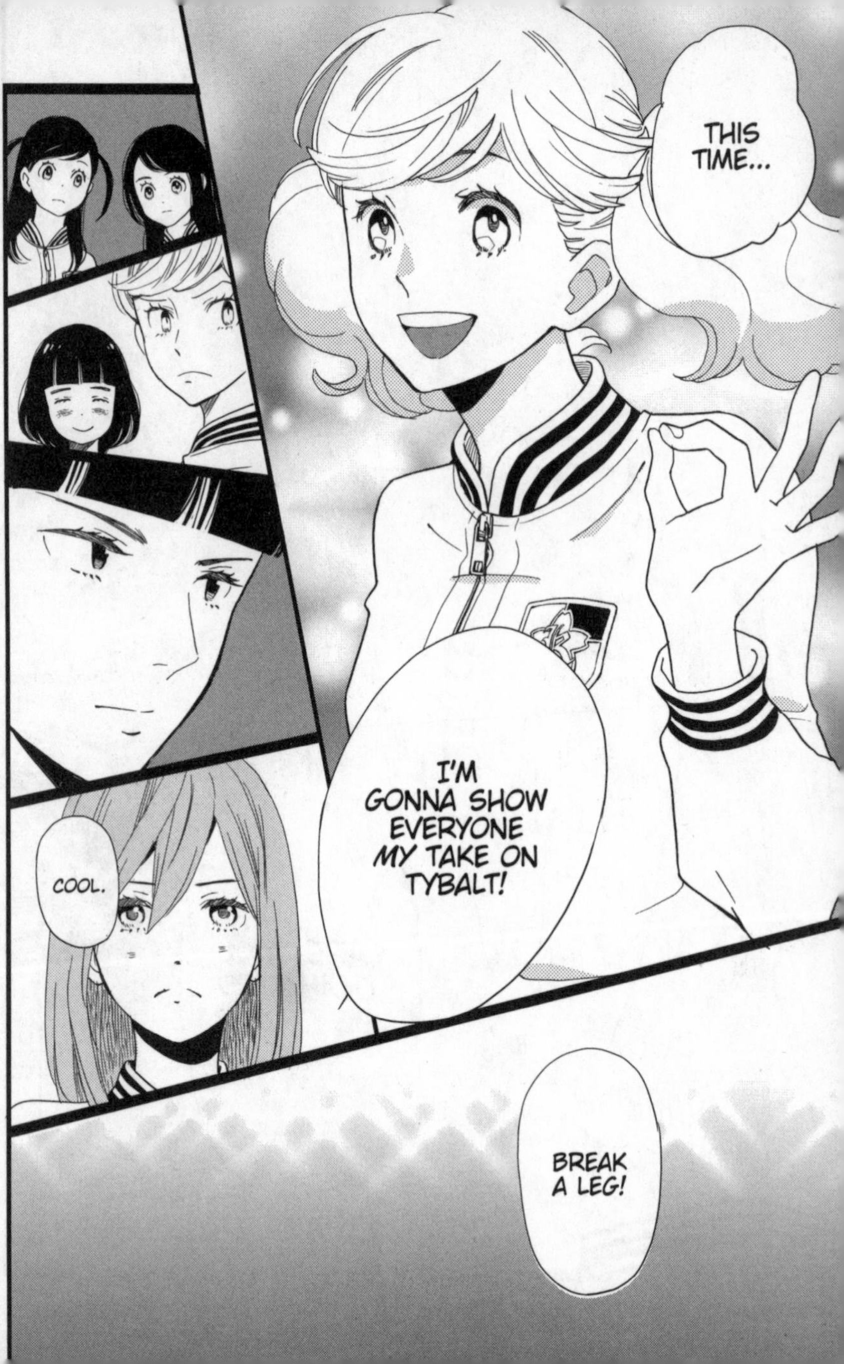
THIS TIME...
I'M GONNA SHOW EVERYONE MY TAKE ON TYBALT!
COOL.
BREAK A LEG!

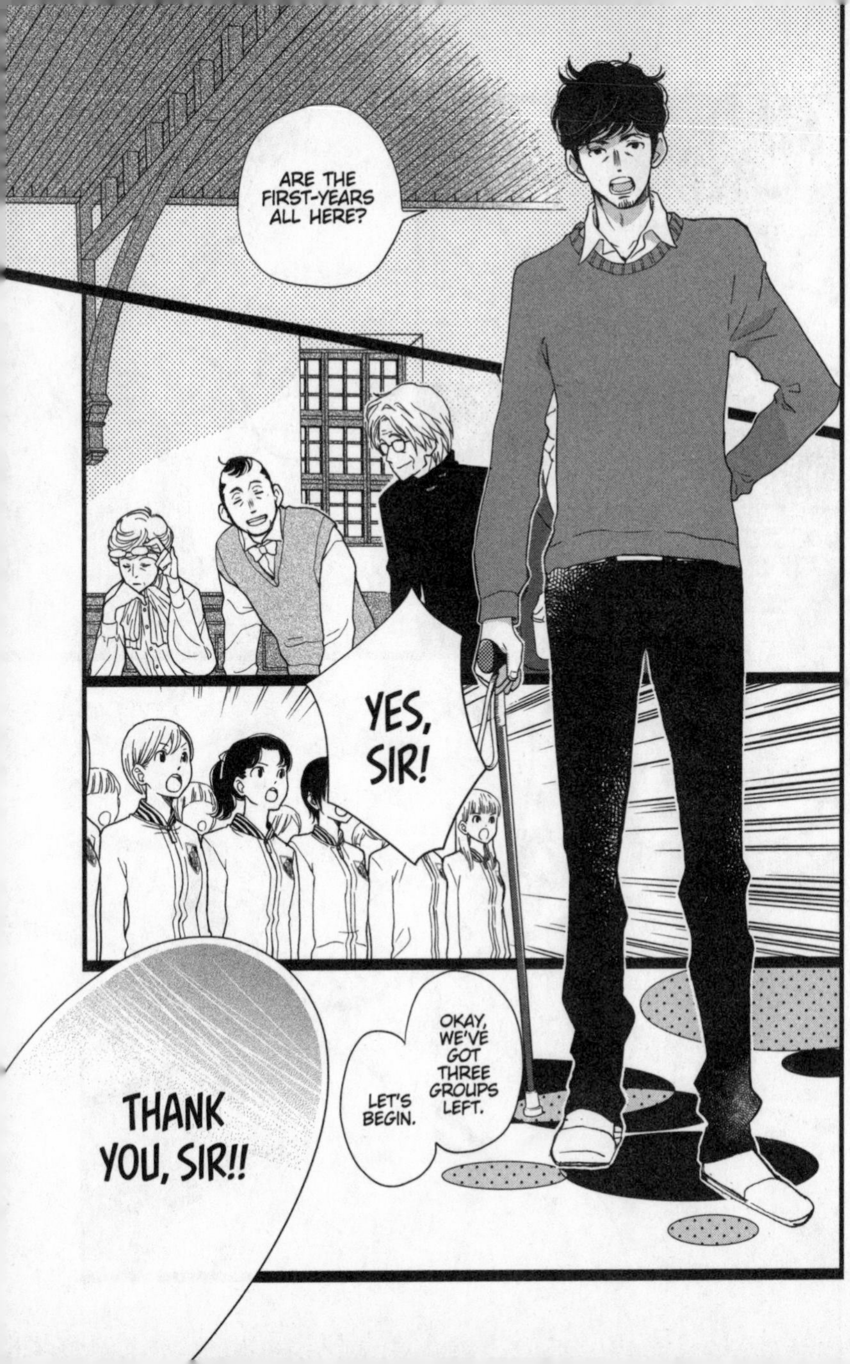
ARE THE FIRST-YEARS ALL HERE?
YES, SIR!
OKAY, WE'VE GOT THREE GROUPS LEFT.
LET'S BEGIN.
THANK YOU, SIR!!

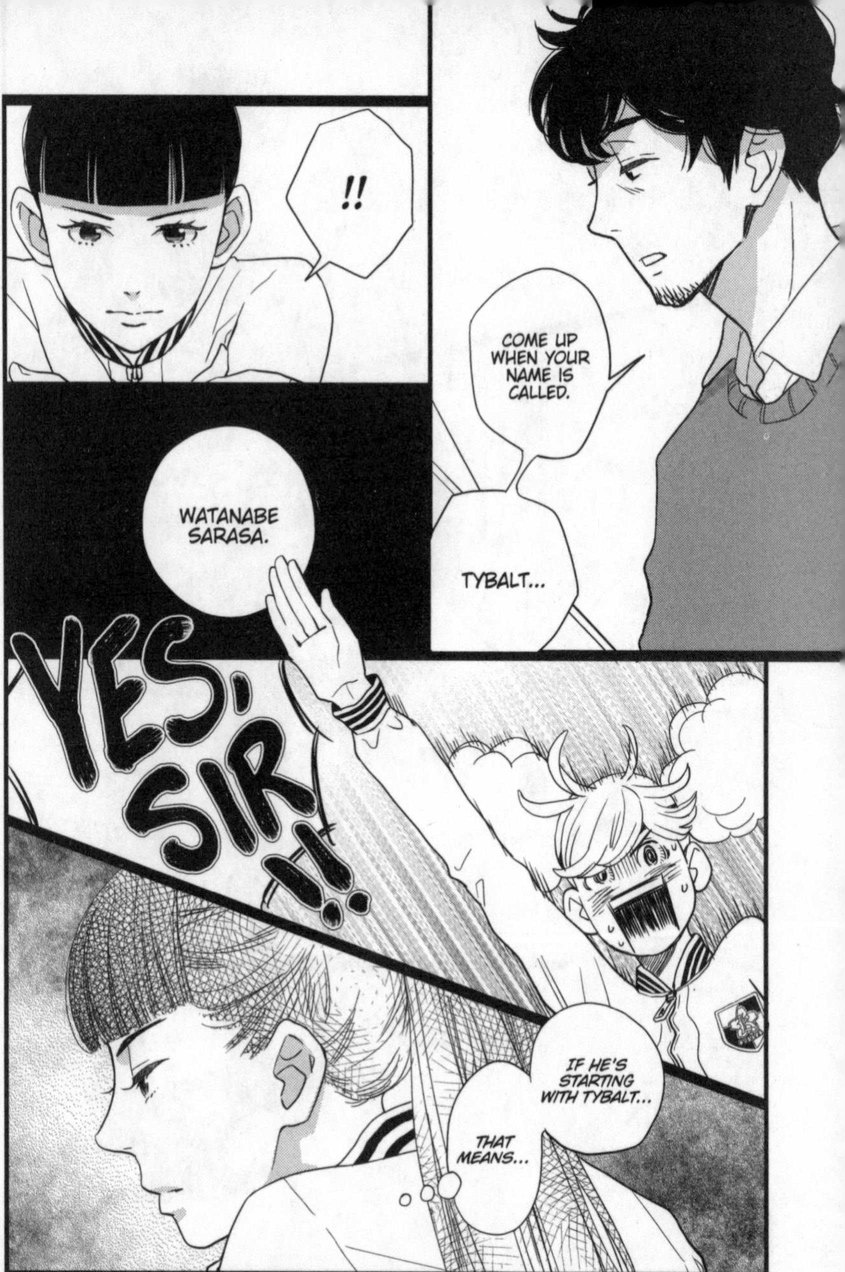
COME UP WHEN YOUR NAME IS CALLED.
TYBALT...
!!
WATANABE SARASA.
YES, SIR!!
IF HE'S STARTING WITH TYBALT...
THAT MEANS...

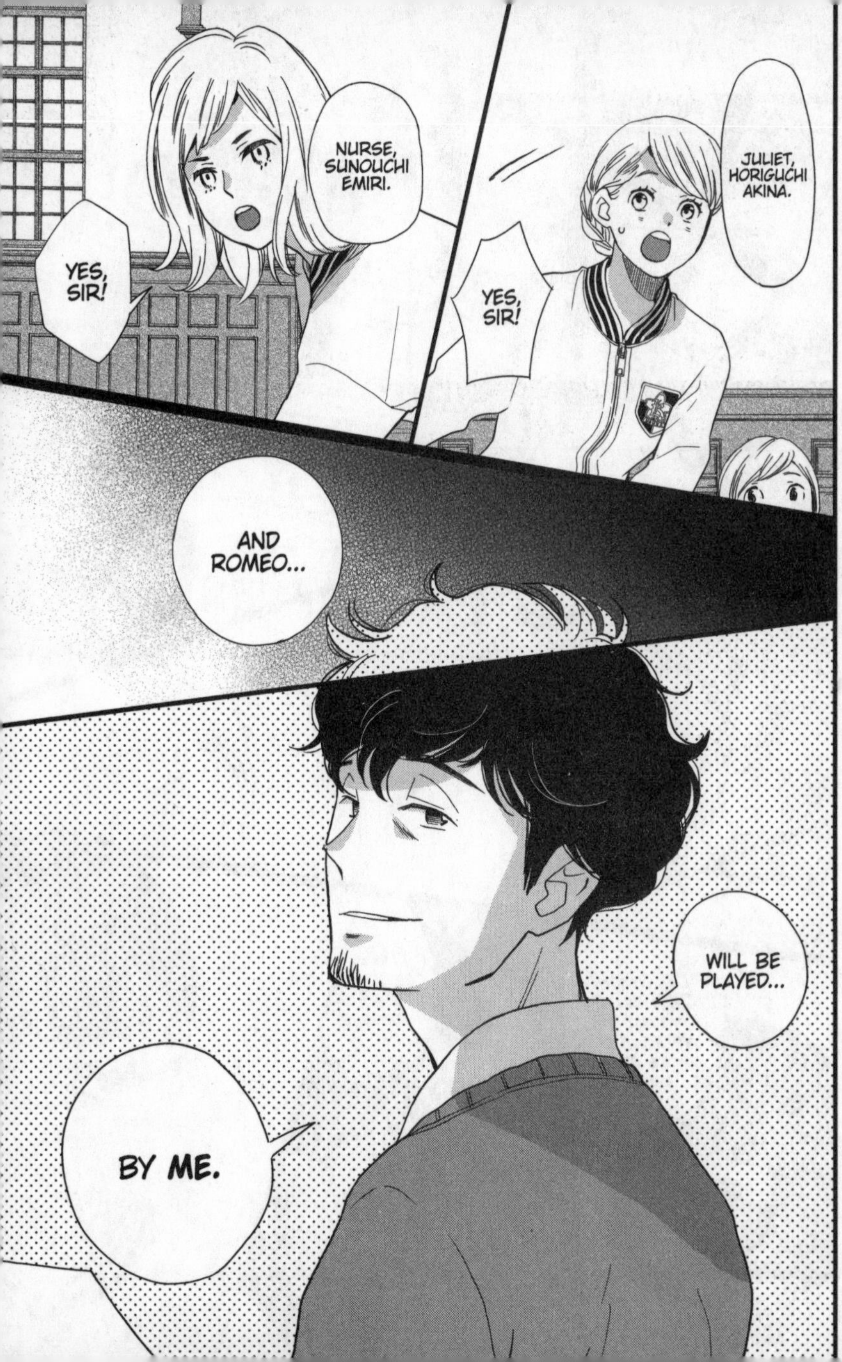
JULIET, HORIGUCHI AKINA.
YES, SIR!
NURSE, SUNOUCHI EMIRI.
YES, SIR!
AND ROMEO...
WILL BE PLAYED...
BY ME.

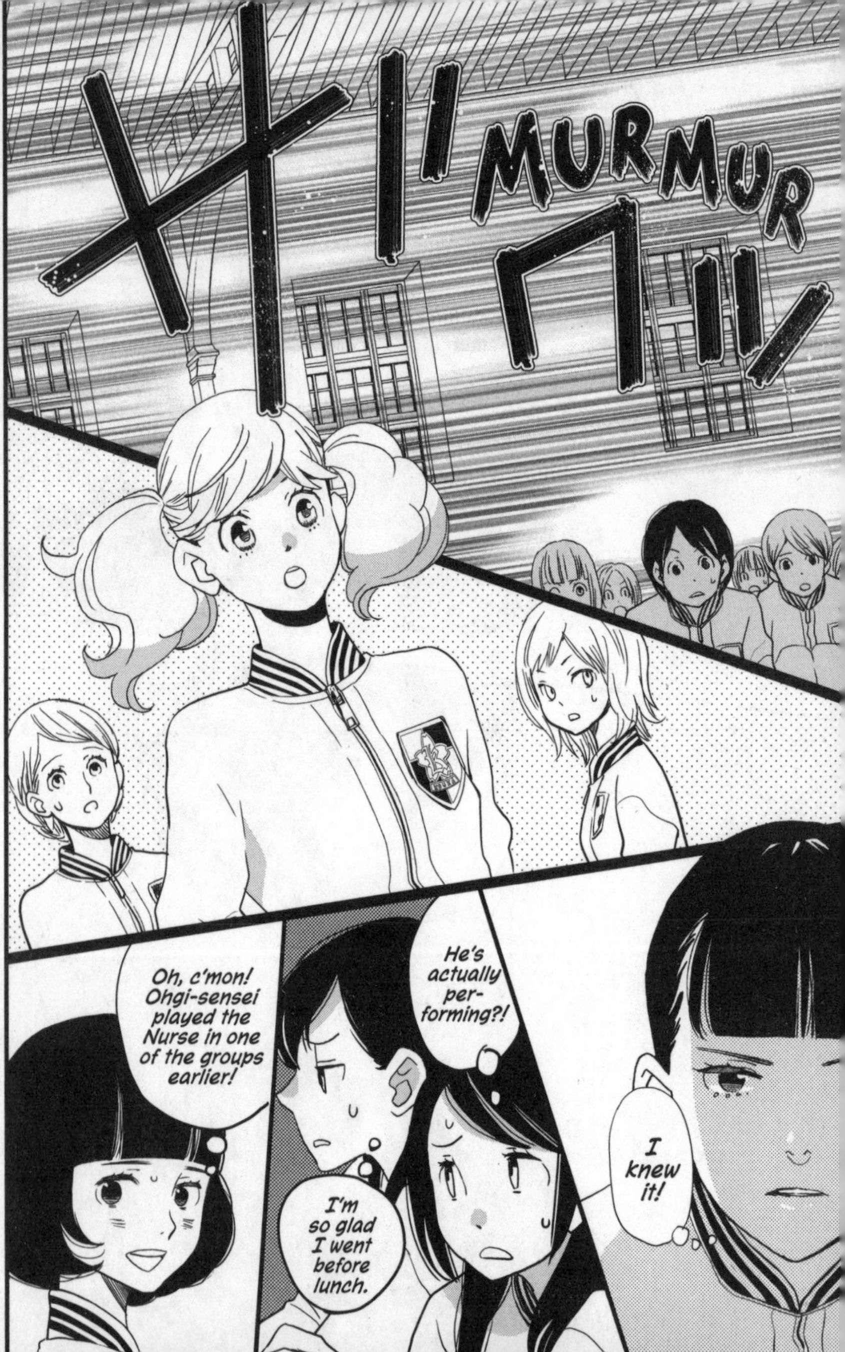
MURMUR
I knew it!
He's actually per-forming?!
I'm so glad I went before lunch.
Oh, c'mon! Ohgi-sensei played the Nurse in one of the groups earlier!

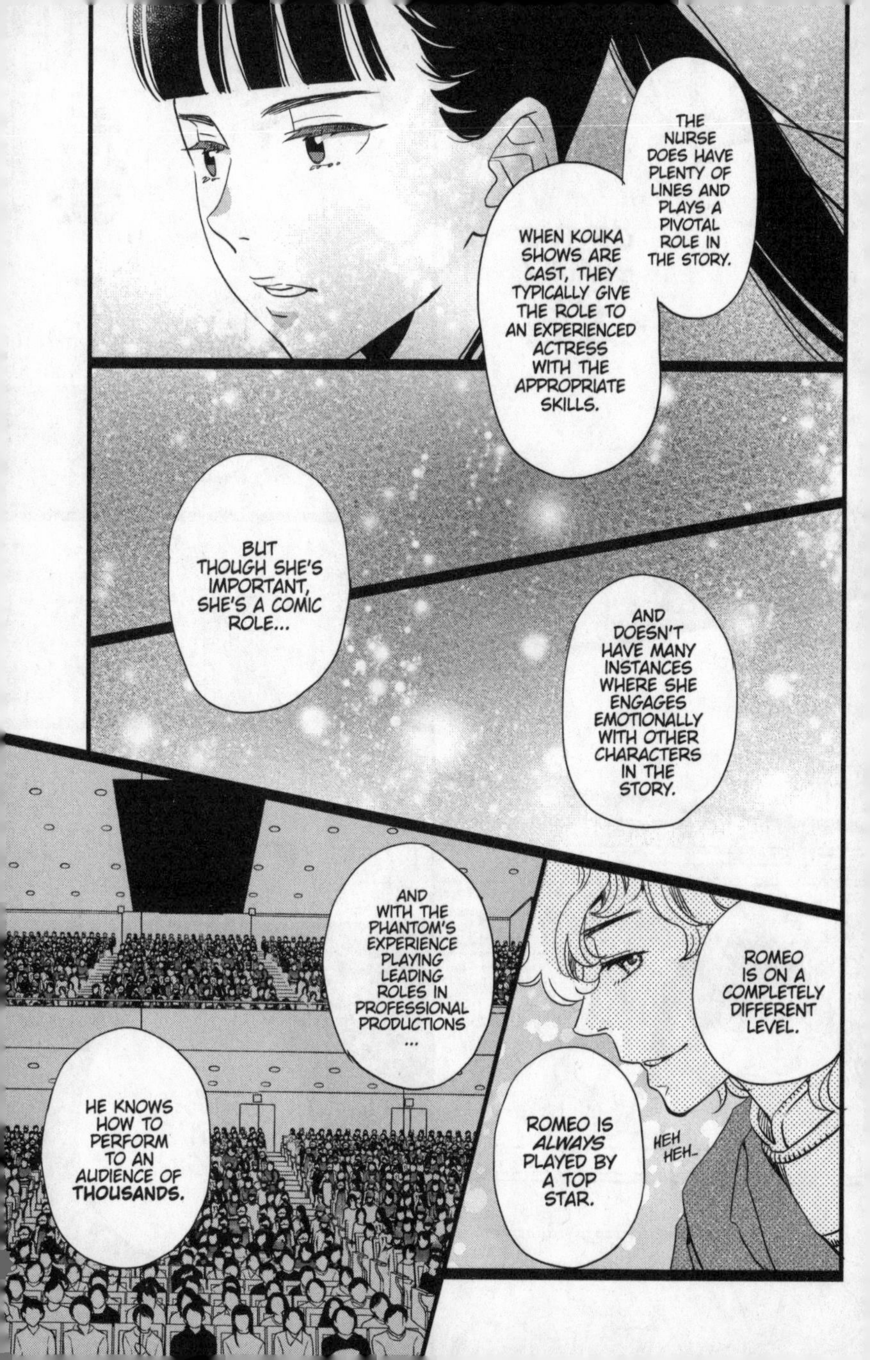
THE NURSE DOES HAVE PLENTY OF LINES AND PLAYS A PIVOTAL ROLE IN THE STORY.
WHEN KOUKA SHOWS ARE CAST, THEY TYPICALLY GIVE THE ROLE TO AN EXPERIENCED ACTRESS WITH THE APPROPRIATE SKILLS.
BUT THOUGH SHE'S IMPORTANT, SHE'S A COMIC ROLE...
AND DOESN'T HAVE MANY INSTANCES WHERE SHE ENGAGES EMOTIONALLY WITH OTHER CHARACTERS IN THE STORY.
ROMEO IS ON A COMPLETELY DIFFERENT LEVEL.
ROMEO IS *ALWAYS* PLAYED BY A TOP STAR.
HEH HEH..
AND WITH THE PHANTOM'S EXPERIENCE PLAYING LEADING ROLES IN PROFESSIONAL PRODUCTIONS ...
HE KNOWS HOW TO PERFORM TO AN AUDIENCE OF **THOUSANDS.**

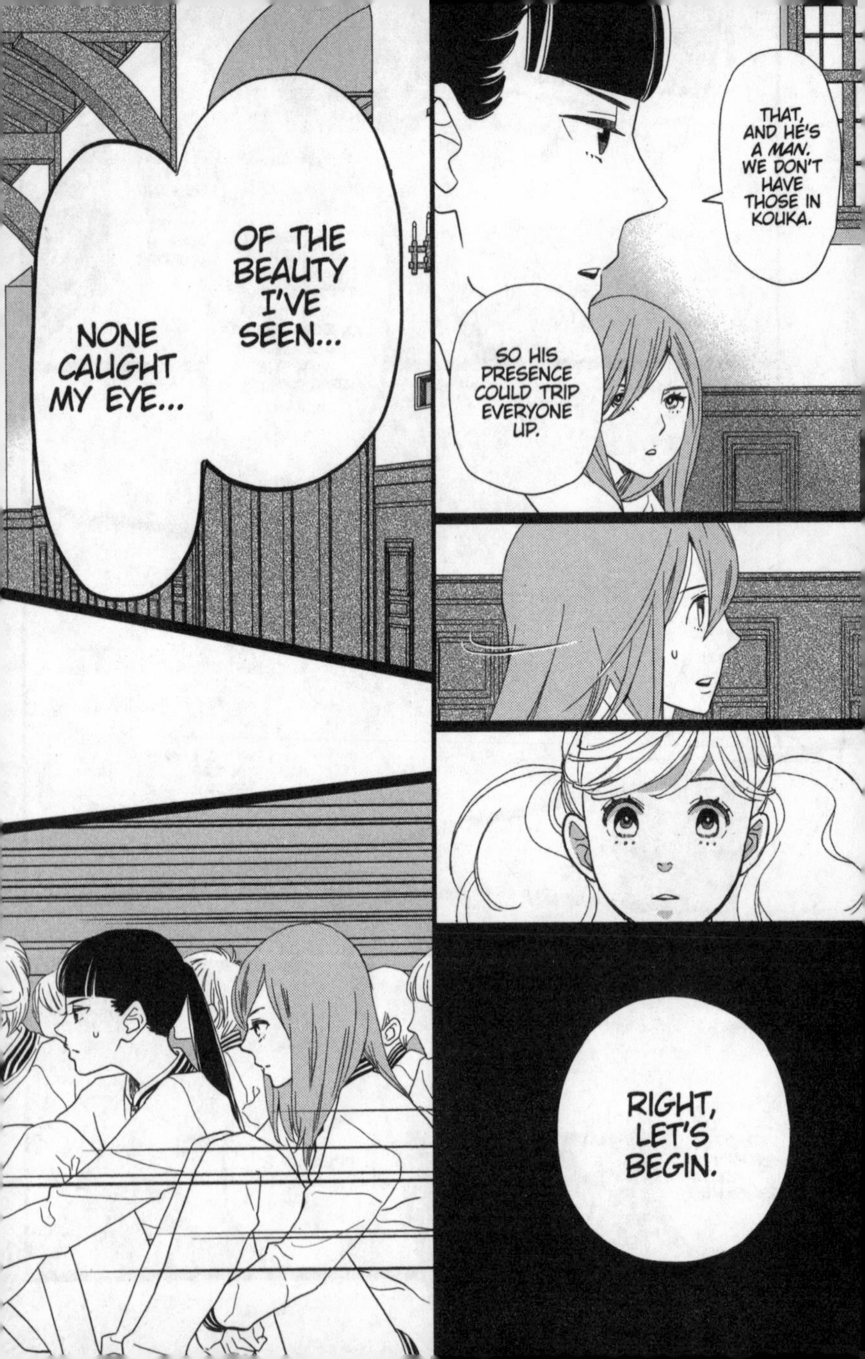
THAT, AND HE'S A *MAN*. WE DON'T HAVE THOSE IN KOUKA.
SO HIS PRESENCE COULD TRIP EVERYONE UP.
RIGHT, LET'S BEGIN.
OF THE BEAUTY I'VE SEEN...
NONE CAUGHT MY EYE...

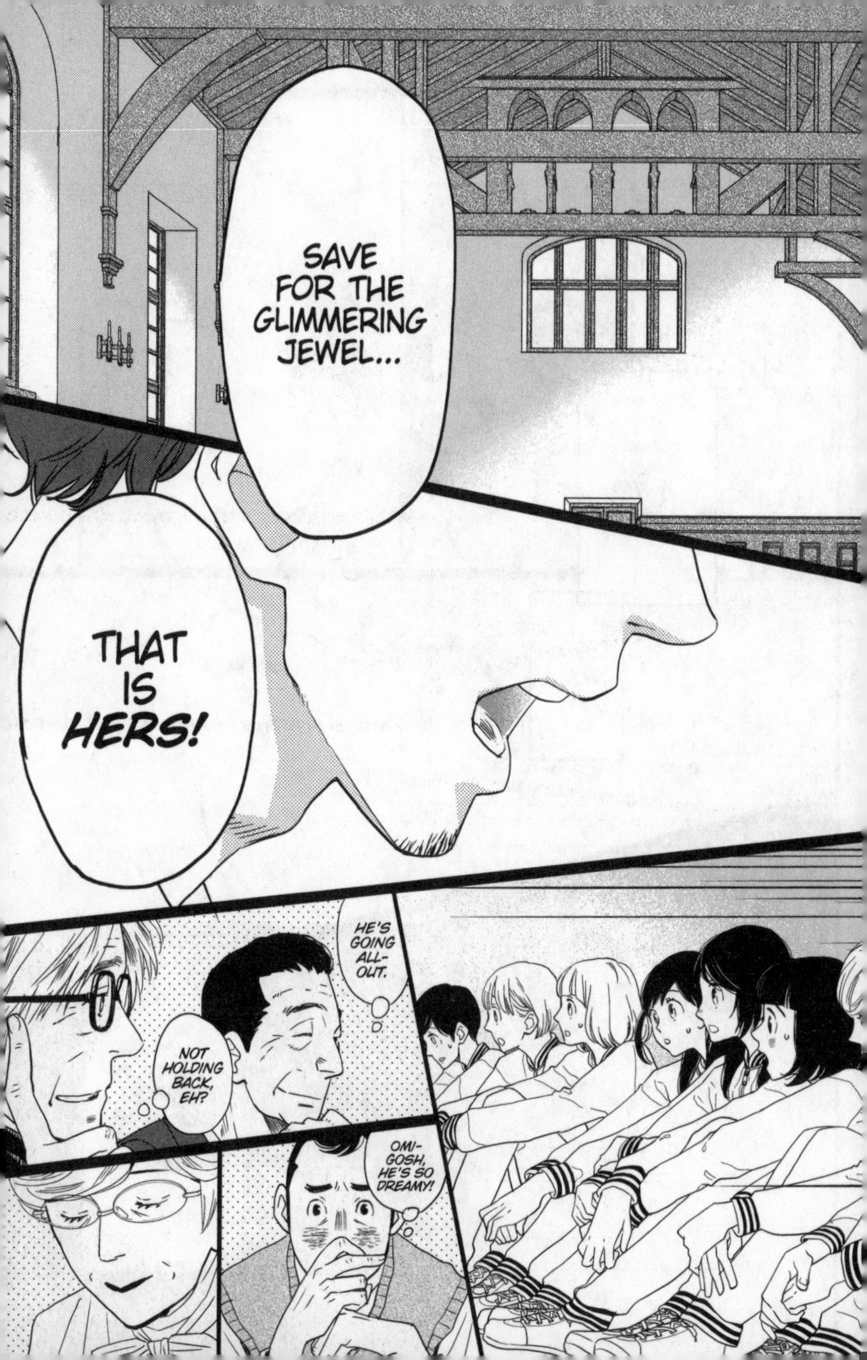
SAVE FOR THE GLIMMERING JEWEL...
THAT IS HERS!
HE'S GOING ALL-OUT.
NOT HOLDING BACK, EH?
OMI-GOSH, HE'S SO DREAMY!

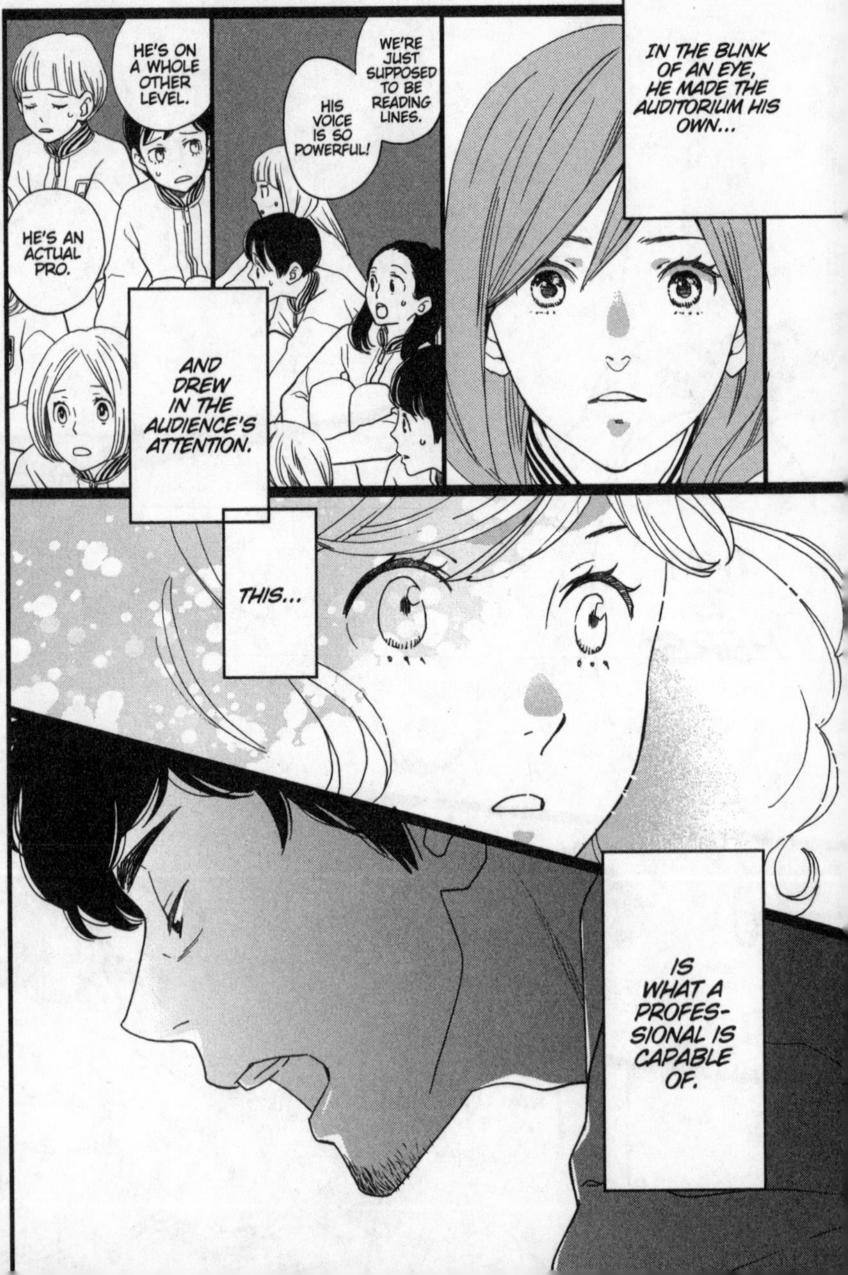
IN THE BLINK OF AN EYE, HE MADE THE AUDITORIUM HIS OWN...
WE'RE JUST SUPPOSED TO BE READING LINES.
HIS VOICE IS SO POWERFUL!
HE'S ON A WHOLE OTHER LEVEL.
HE'S AN ACTUAL PRO.
AND DREW IN THE AUDIENCE'S ATTENTION.
THIS...
IS WHAT A PROFES-SIONAL IS CAPABLE OF.

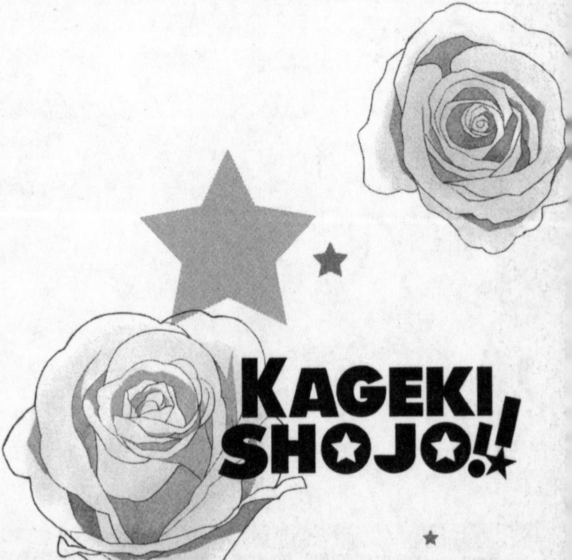
KAGEKI SHOJO!!

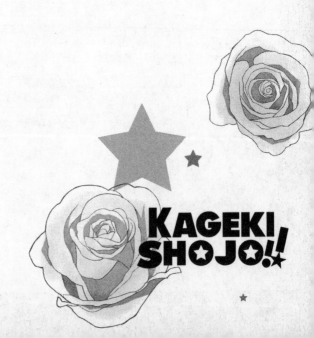

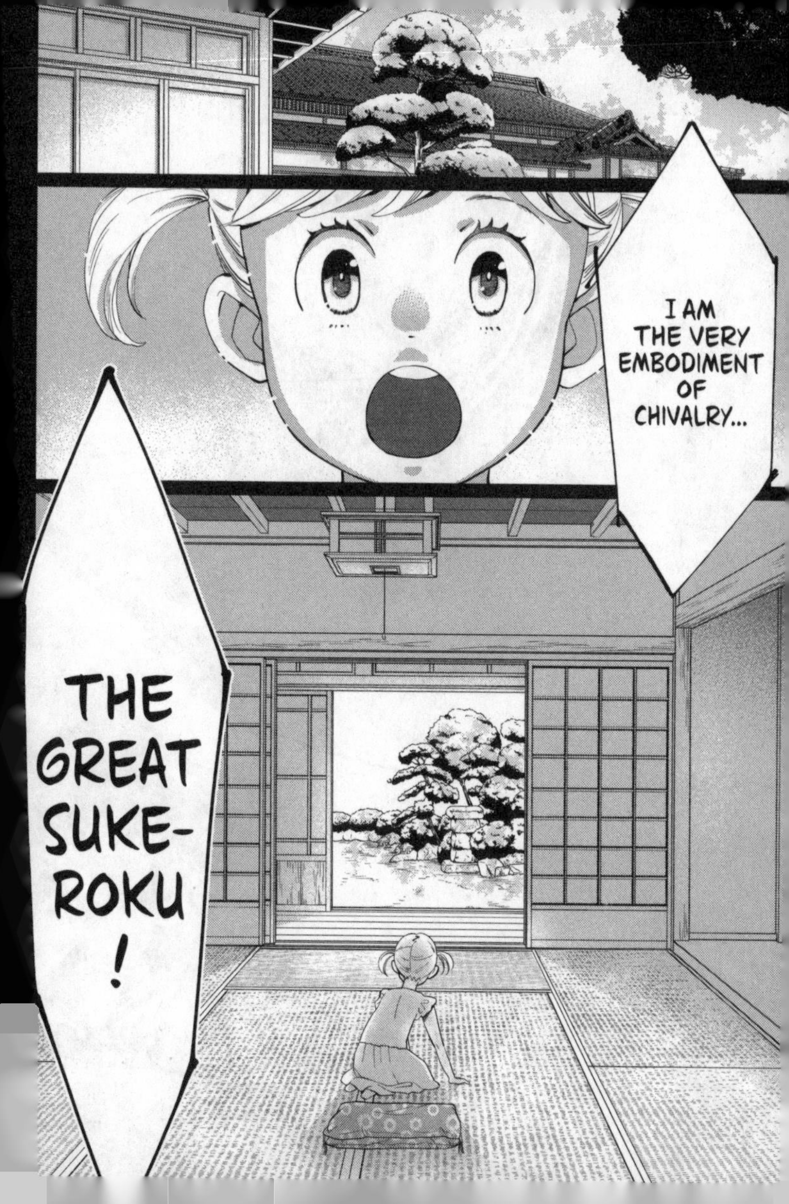
I AM THE VERY EMBODIMENT OF CHIVALRY...
THE GREAT SUKE-ROKU!

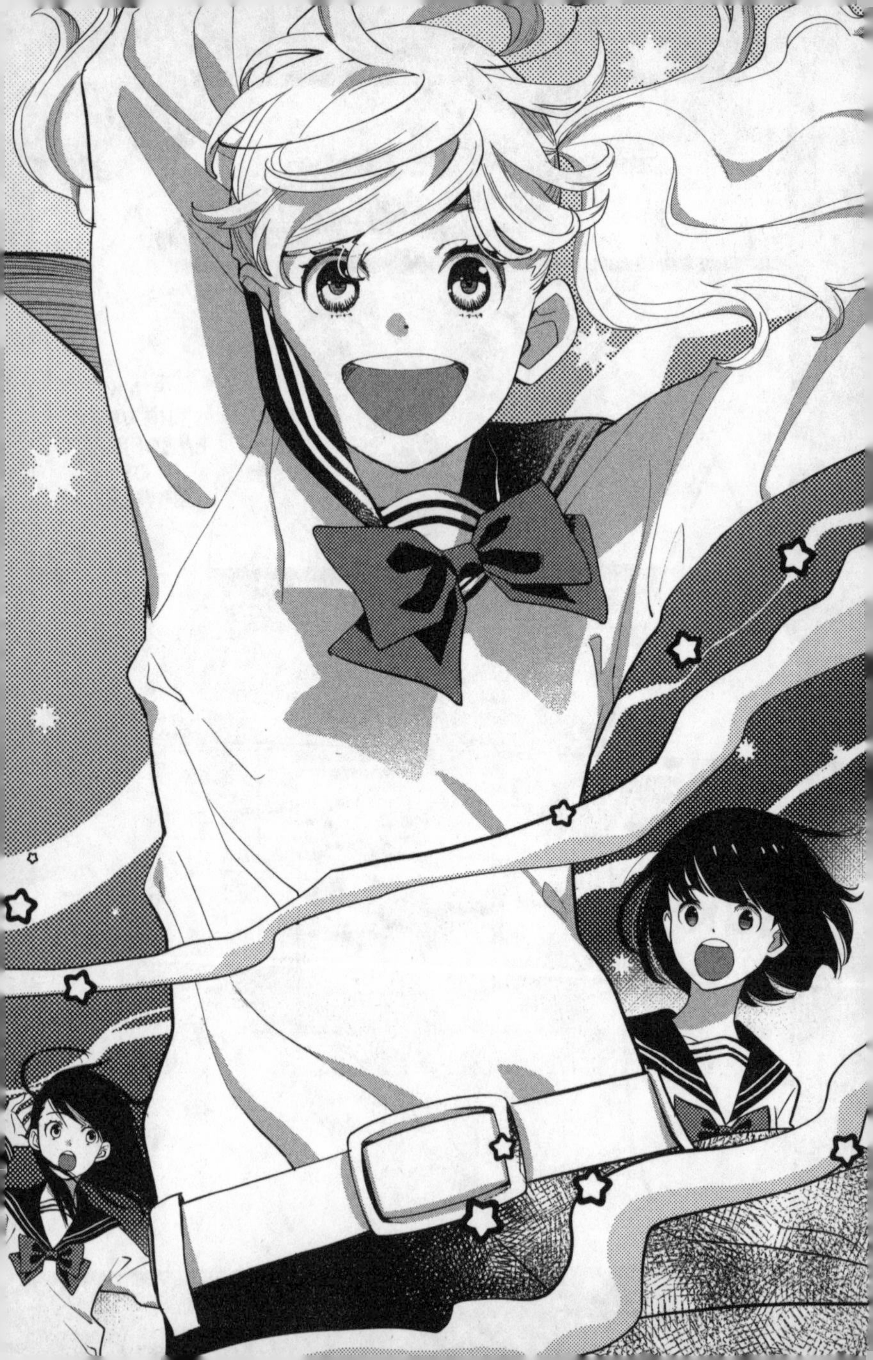

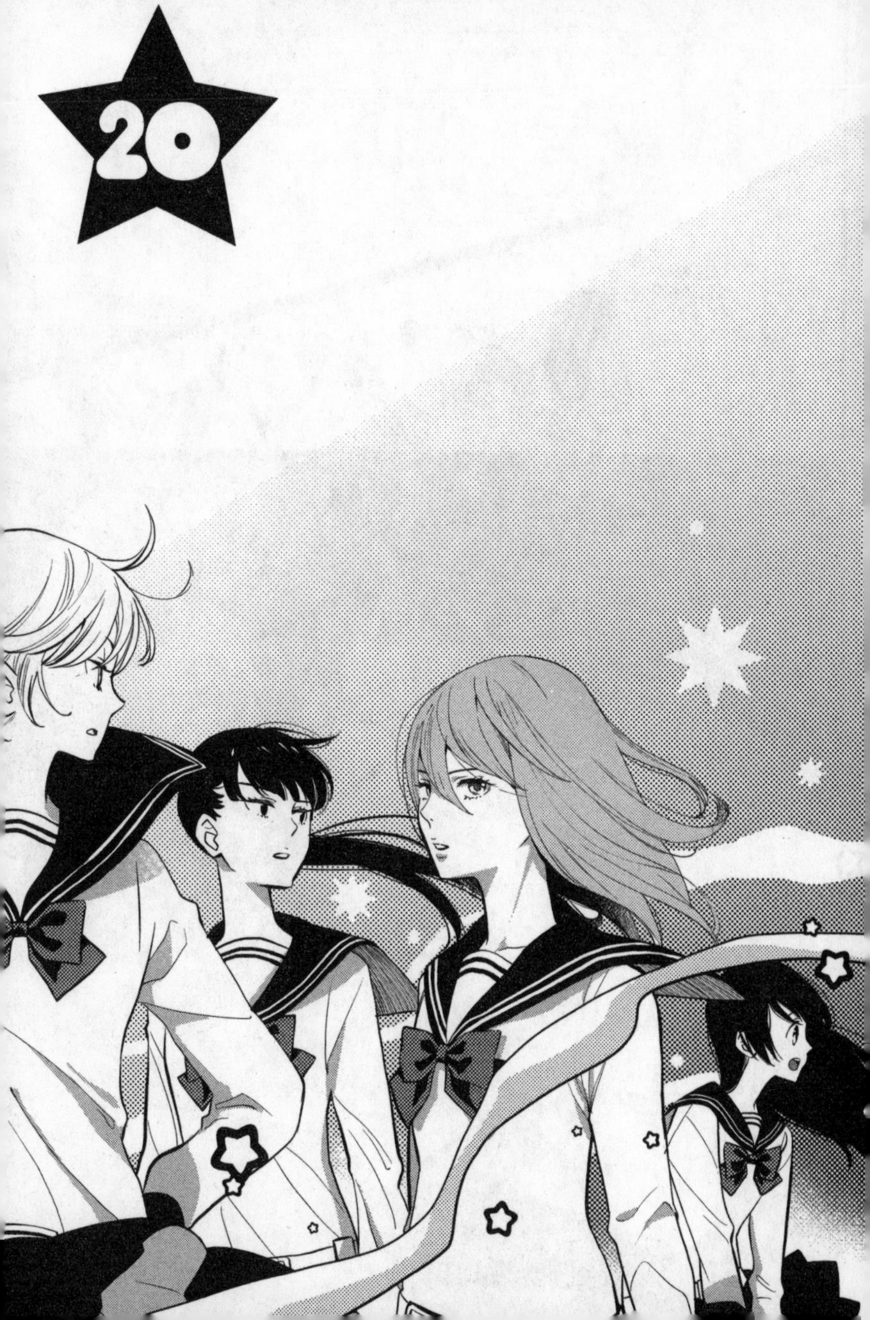
20

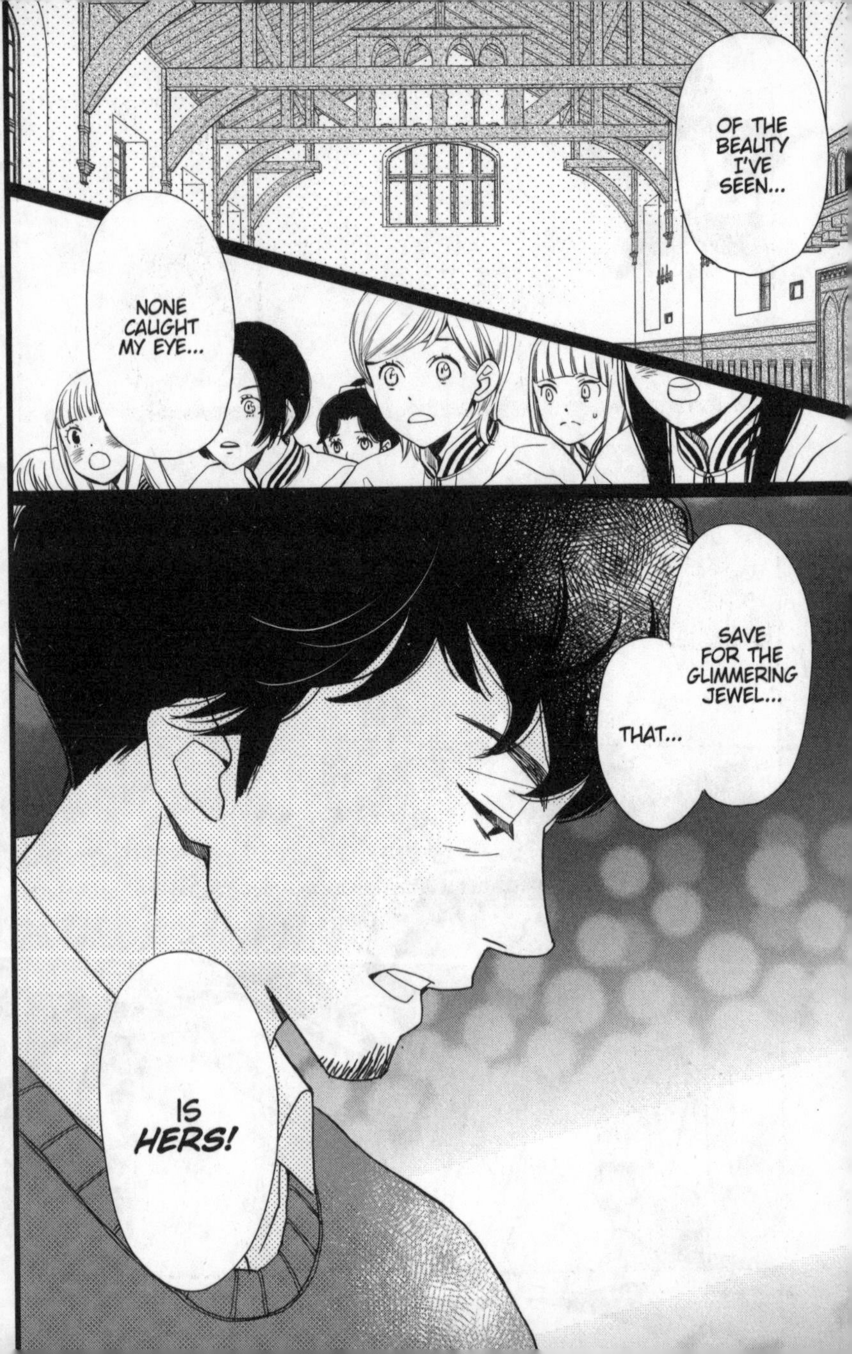
OF THE BEAUTY I'VE SEEN...
NONE CAUGHT MY EYE...
SAVE FOR THE GLIMMERING JEWEL...
THAT...
IS HERS!

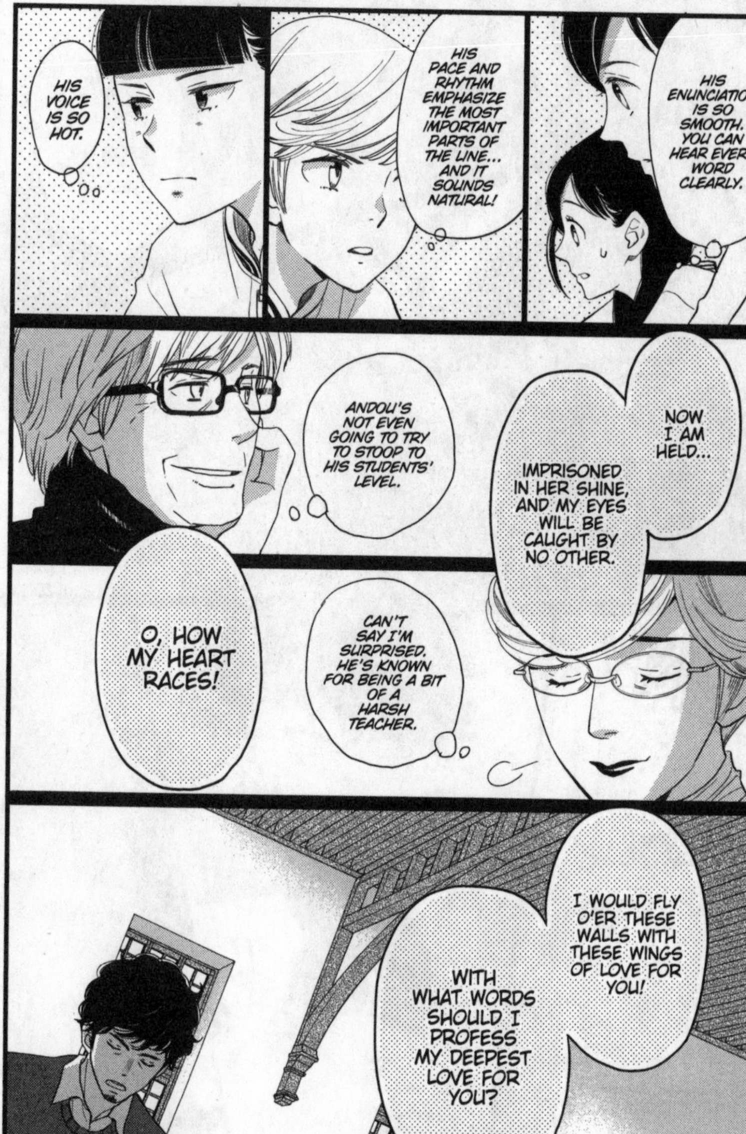
HIS ENUNCIATION IS SO SMOOTH. YOU CAN HEAR EVERY WORD CLEARLY.
HIS PACE AND RHYTHM EMPHASIZE THE MOST IMPORTANT PARTS OF THE LINE... AND IT SOUNDS NATURAL!
HIS VOICE IS SO HOT.
NOW I AM HELD...
IMPRISONED IN HER SHINE, AND MY EYES WILL BE CAUGHT BY NO OTHER.
ANDOU'S NOT EVEN GOING TO TRY TO STOOP TO HIS STUDENTS' LEVEL.
CAN'T SAY I'M SURPRISED. HE'S KNOWN FOR BEING A BIT OF A HARSH TEACHER.
O, HOW MY HEART RACES!
I WOULD FLY O'ER THESE WALLS WITH THESE WINGS OF LOVE FOR YOU!
WITH WHAT WORDS SHOULD I PROFESS MY DEEPEST LOVE FOR YOU?

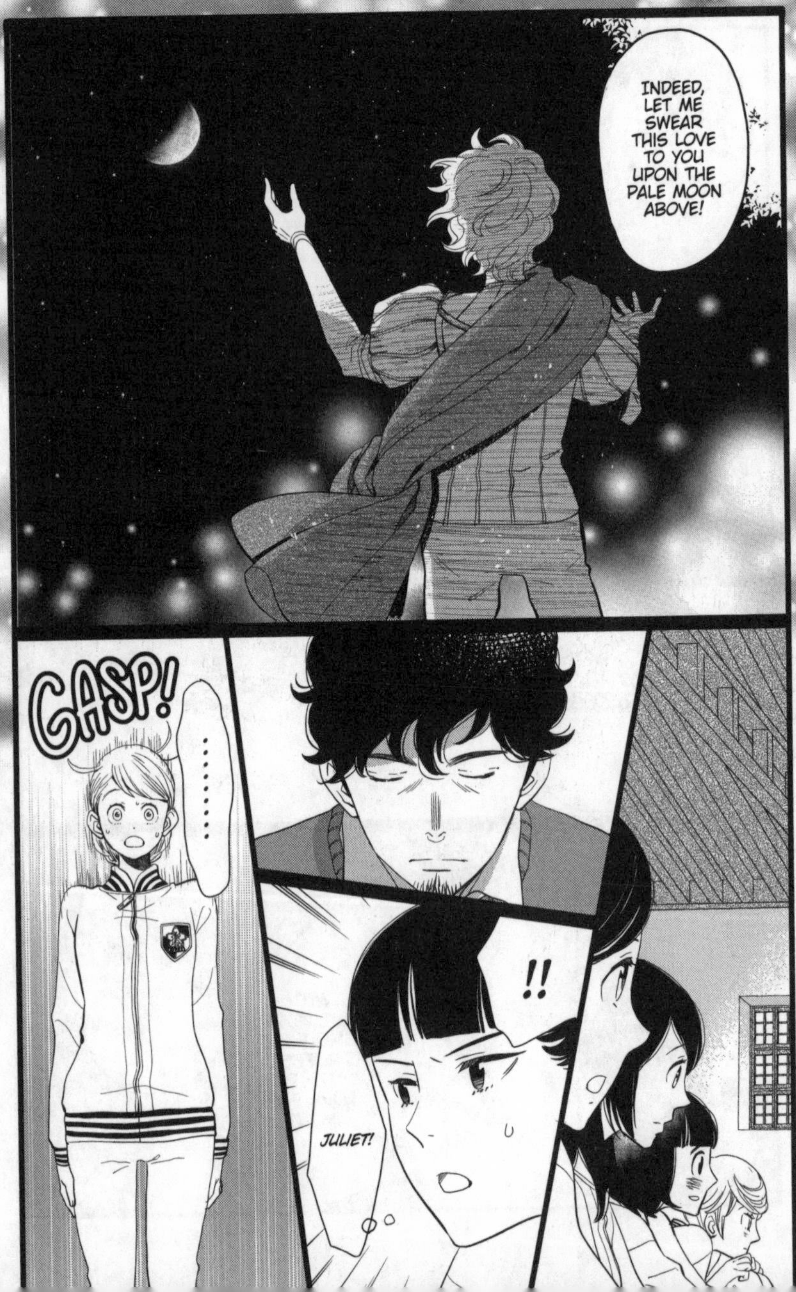
INDEED, LET ME SWEAR THIS LOVE TO YOU UPON THE PALE MOON ABOVE!
!!
JULIET!
GASP!
......

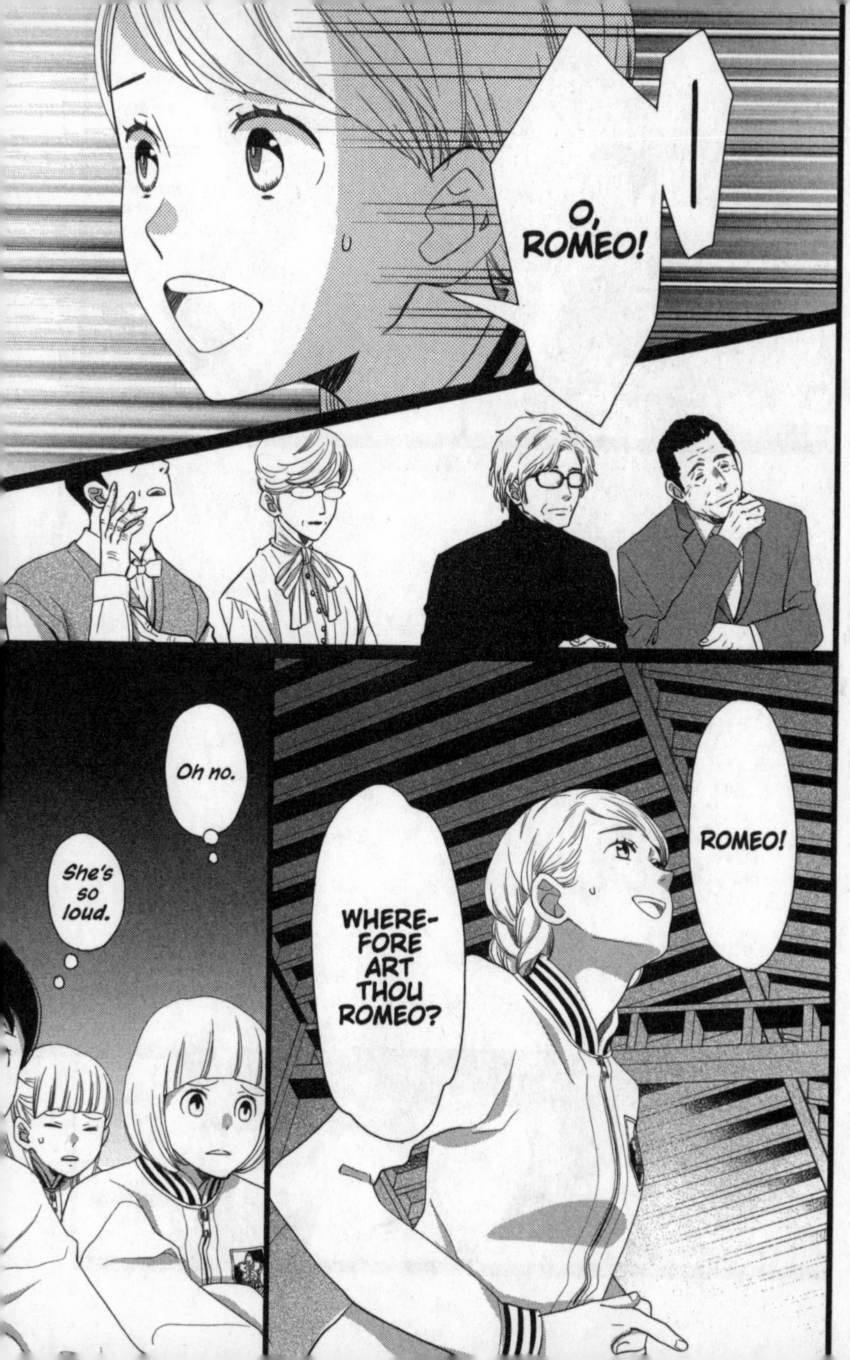
O, ROMEO!
ROMEO!
WHERE-FORE ART THOU ROMEO?
Oh no.
She's so loud.

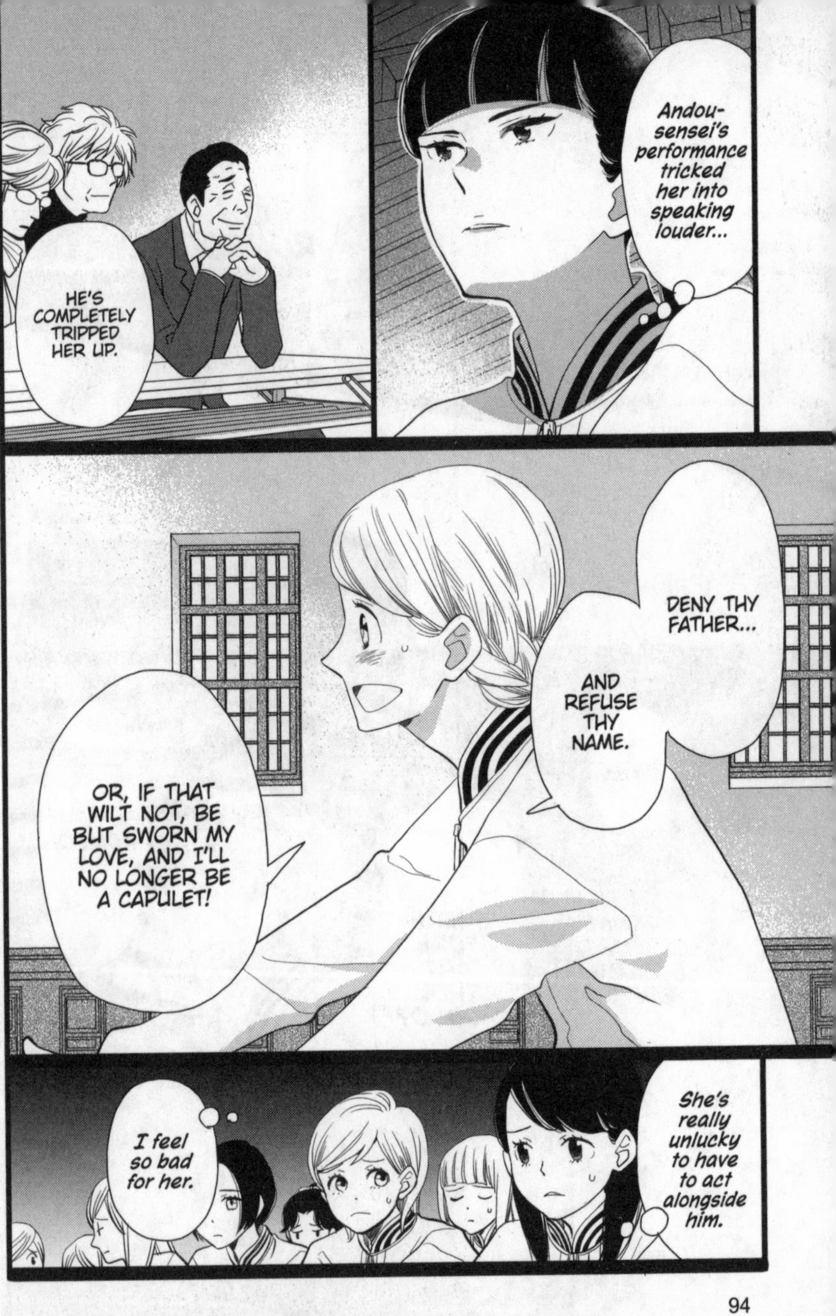
Andou-sensei's performance tricked her into speaking louder...
HE'S COMPLETELY TRIPPED HER UP.
DENY THY FATHER...
AND REFUSE THY NAME.
OR, IF THAT WILT NOT, BE BUT SWORN MY LOVE, AND I'LL NO LONGER BE A CAPULET!
She's really unlucky to have to act alongside him.
I feel so bad for her.

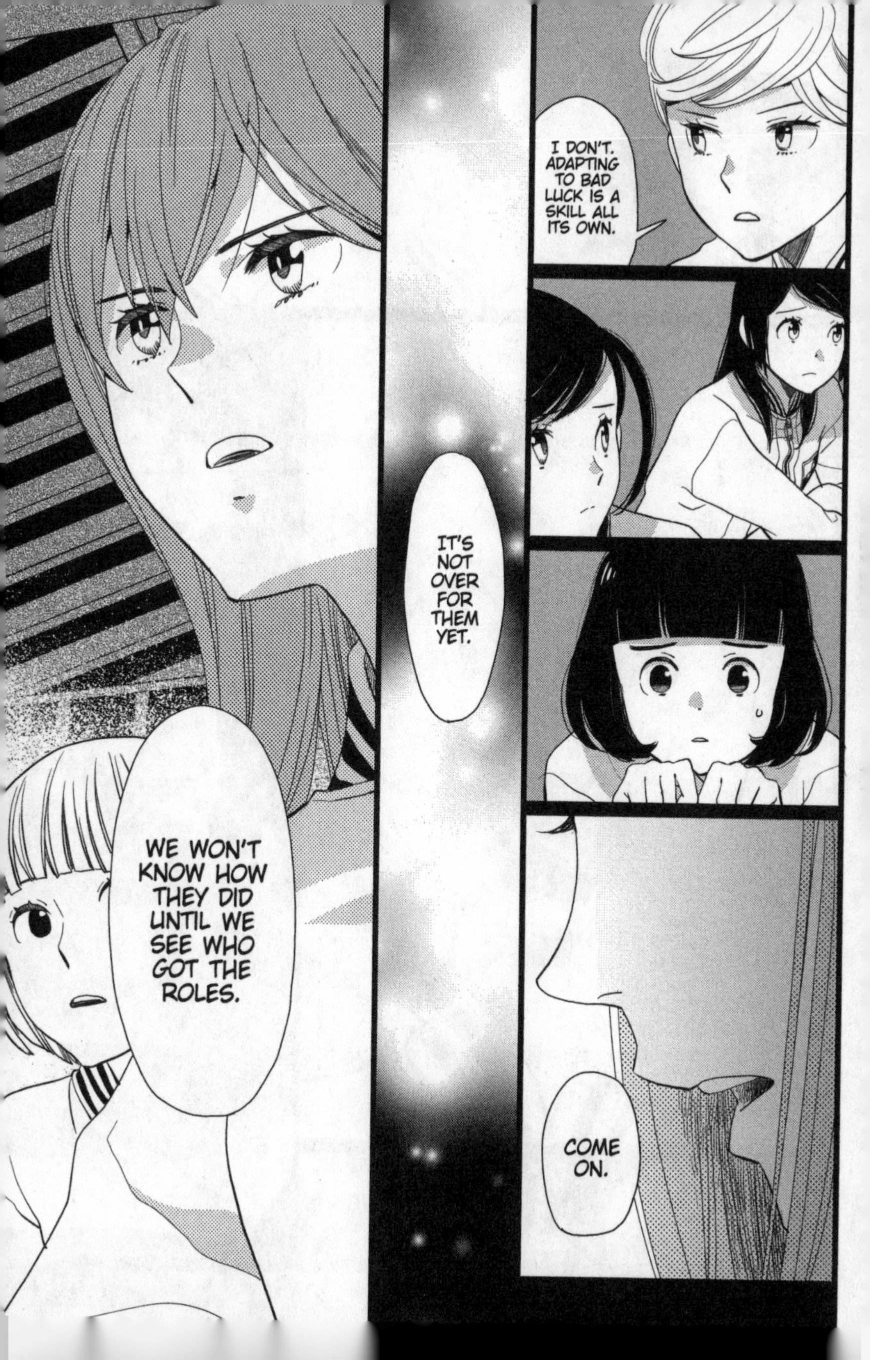
I DON'T. ADAPTING TO BAD LUCK IS A SKILL ALL ITS OWN.
COME ON.
IT'S NOT OVER FOR THEM YET.
WE WON'T KNOW HOW THEY DID UNTIL WE SEE WHO GOT THE ROLES.

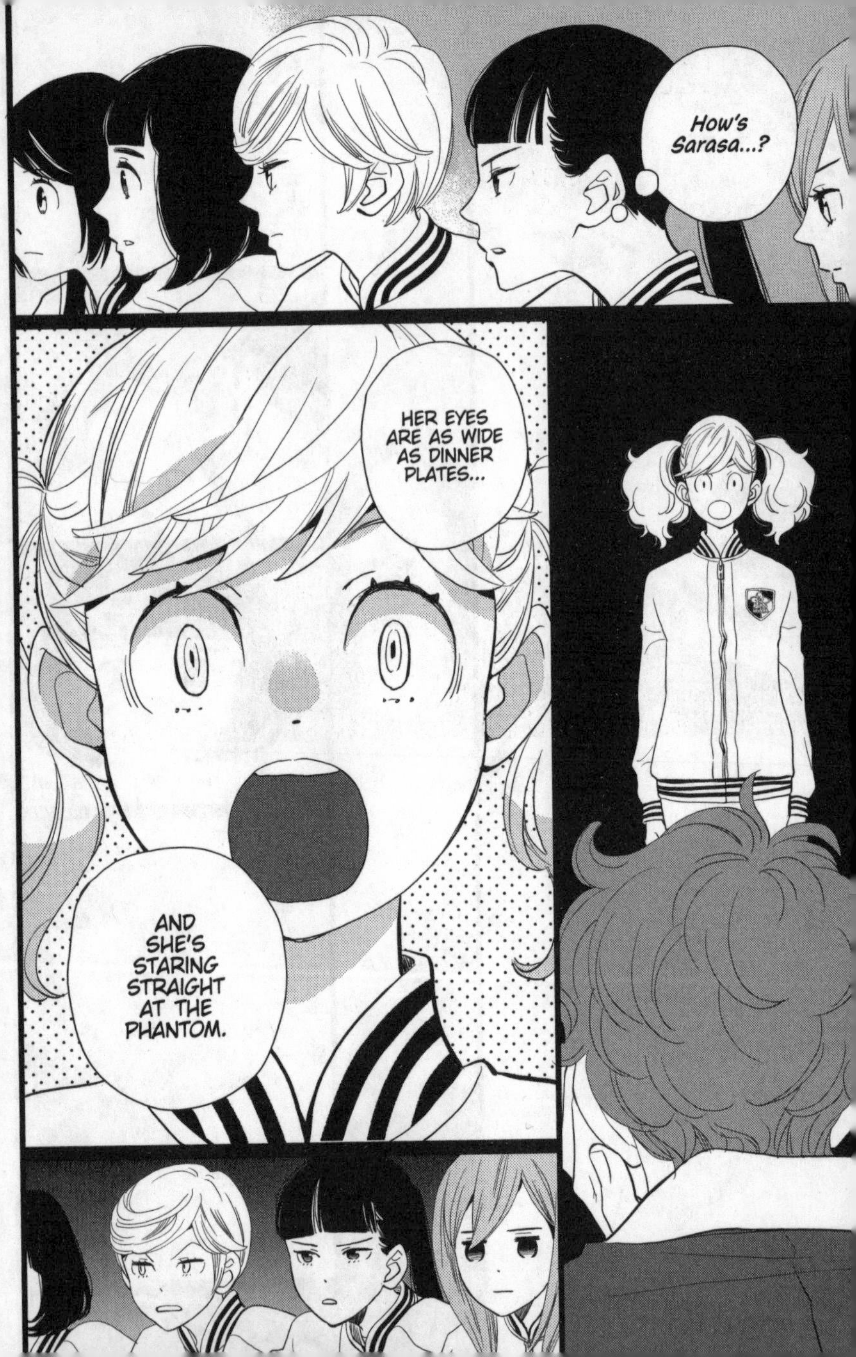
How's Sarasa...?
HER EYES ARE AS WIDE AS DINNER PLATES...
AND SHE'S STARING STRAIGHT AT THE PHANTOM.

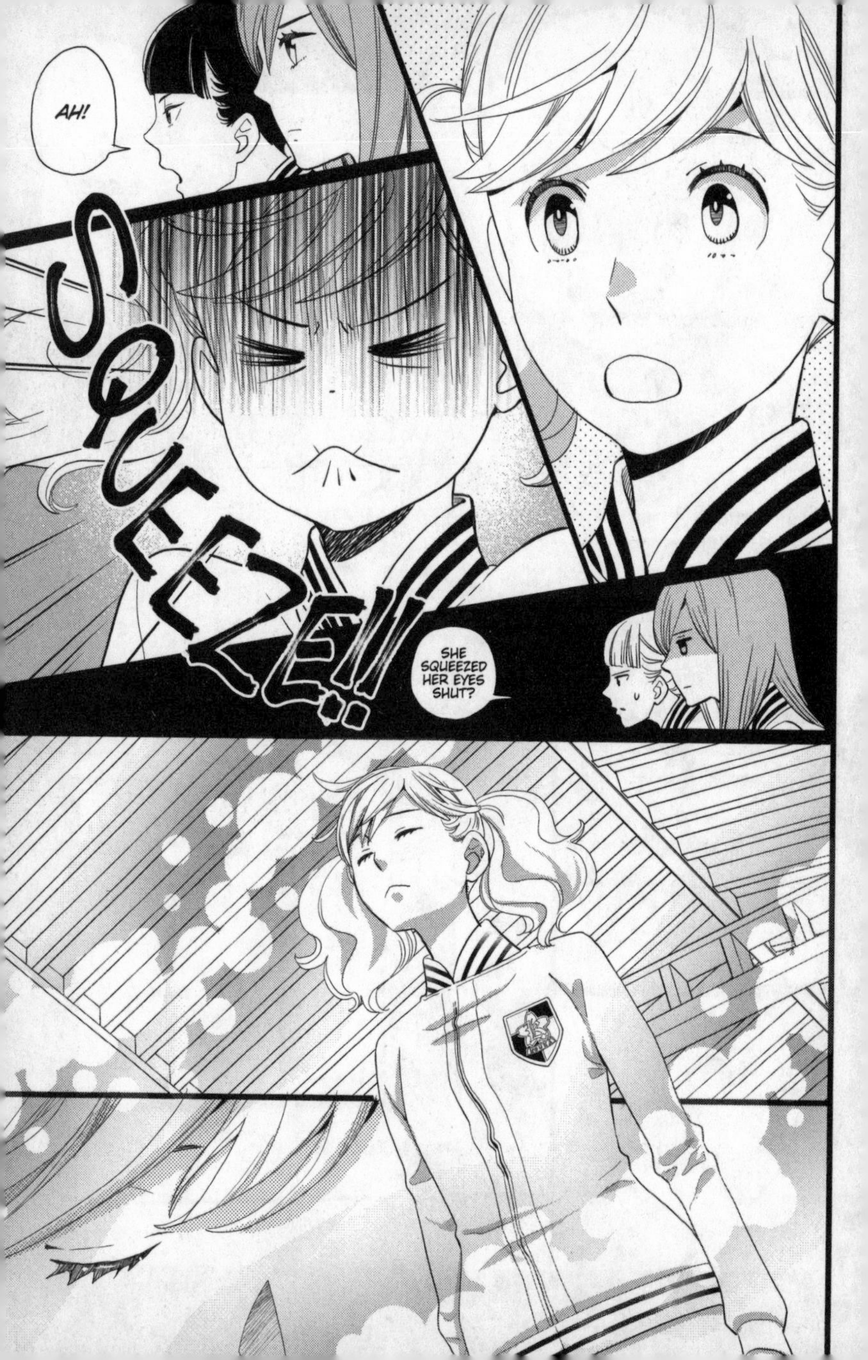
AH!
SQUEEZE!!
SHE SQUEEZED HER EYES SHUT?

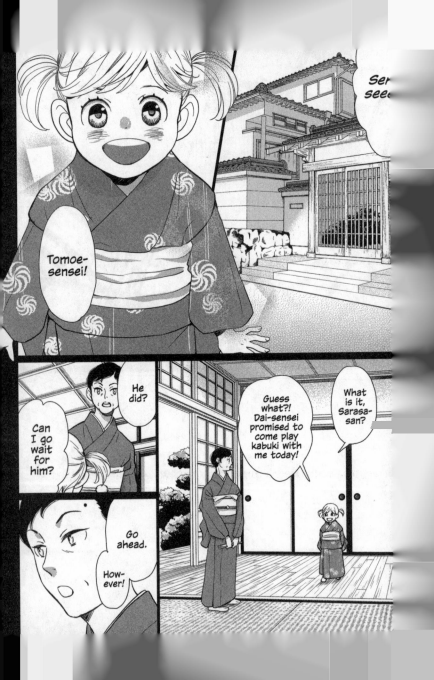

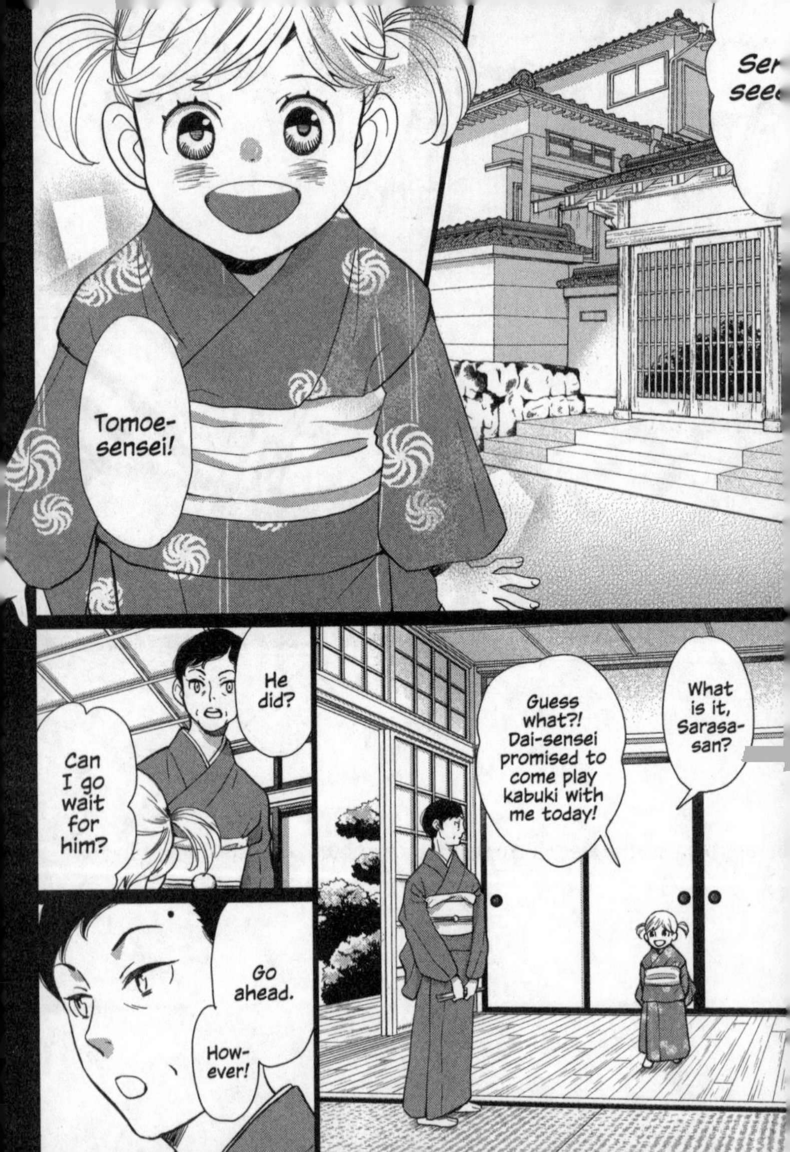
Ser seee
Tomoe-sensei!
What is it, Sarasa-san?
Guess what?! Dai-sensei promised to come play kabuki with me today!
He did?
Can I go wait for him?
Go ahead.
How-ever!

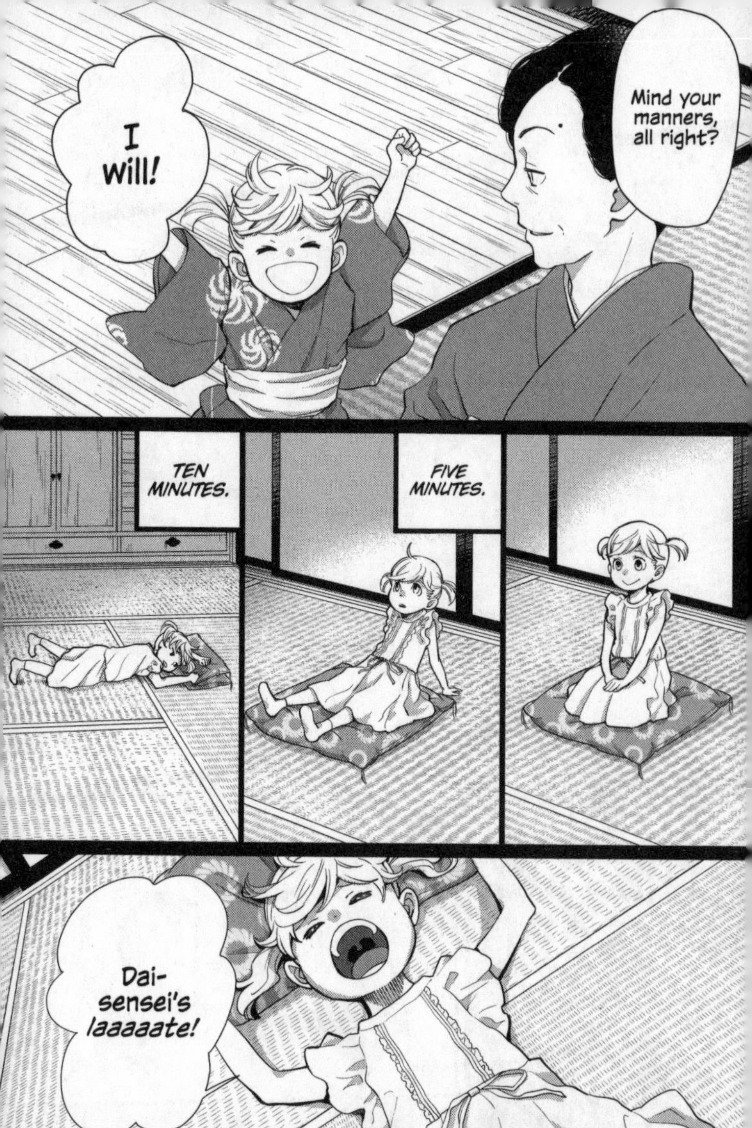
Mind your manners, all right?
I Will!
FIVE MINUTES.
TEN MINUTES.
Dai-sensei's laaaaate!

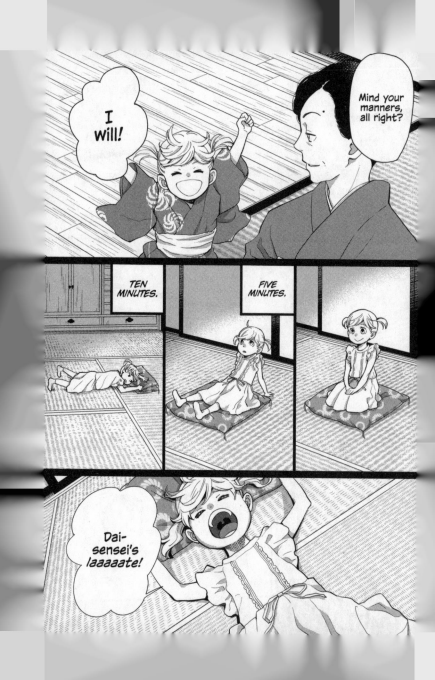

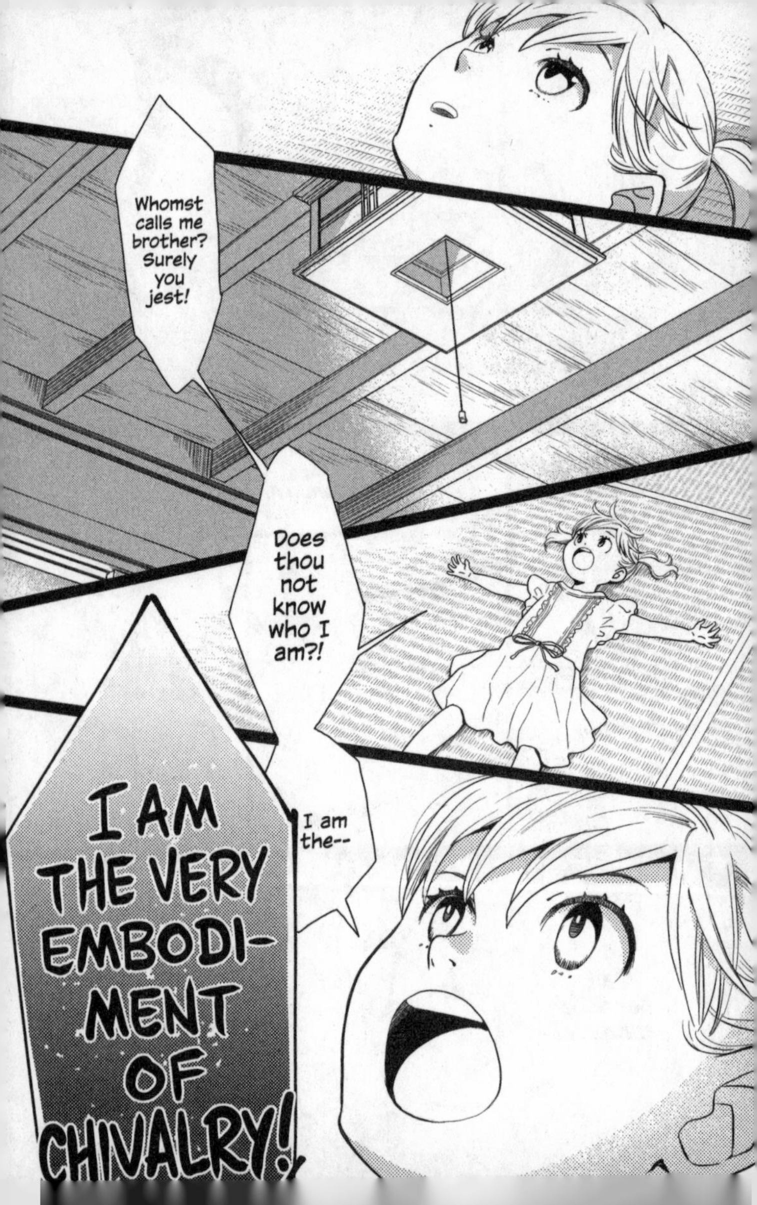
Whomst calls me brother? Surely you jest!
Does thou not know who I am?!
I am the--
I AM THE VERY EMBODI-MENT OF CHIVALRY!

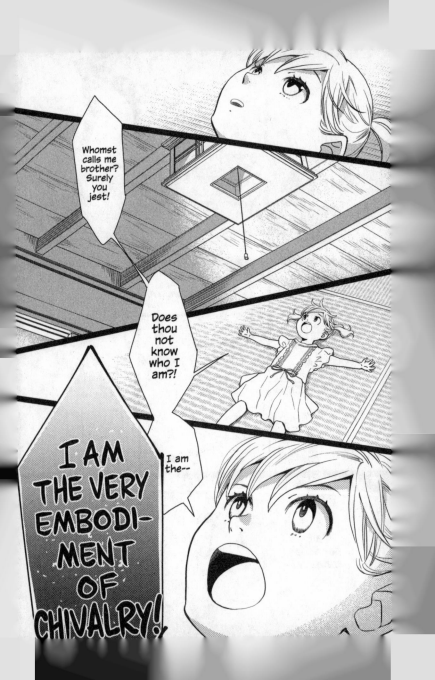

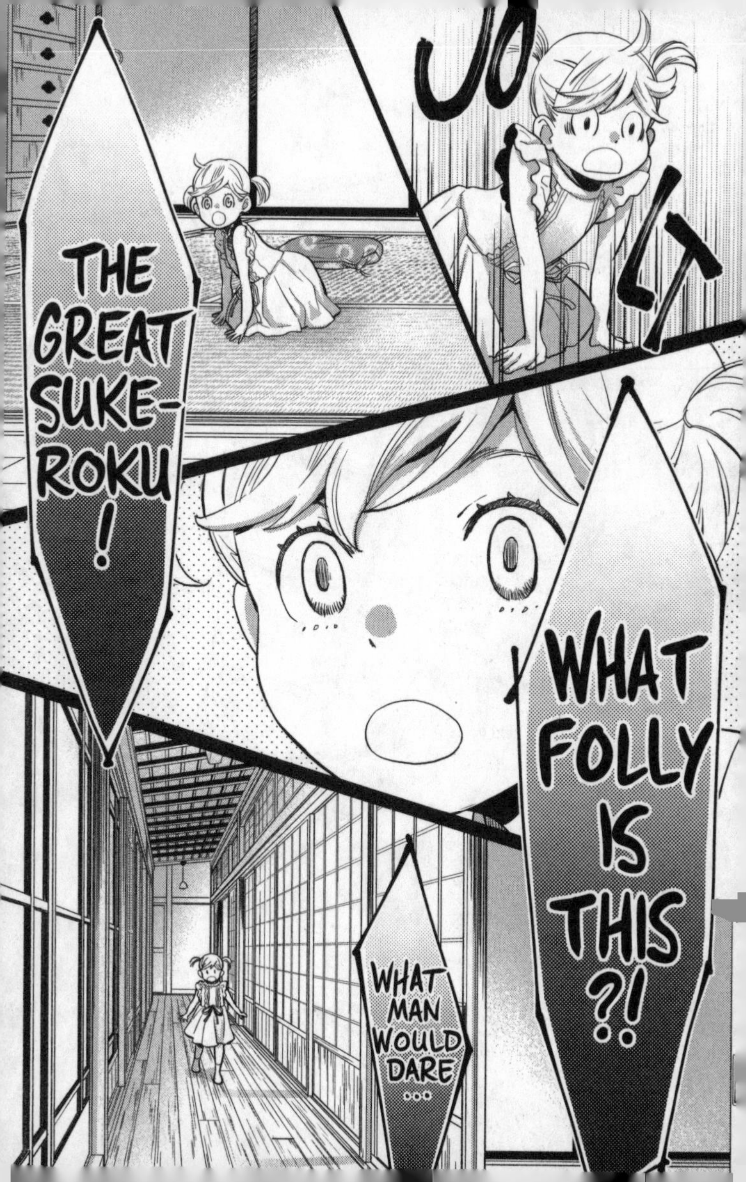
JOLT
THE GREAT SUKE-ROKU!
WHAT FOLLY IS THIS?!
WHAT MAN WOULD DARE...

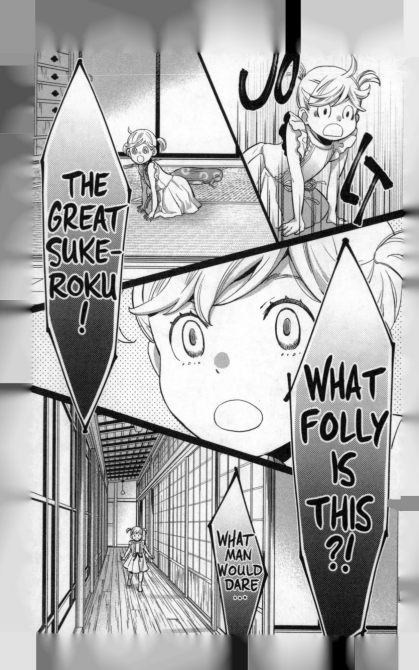

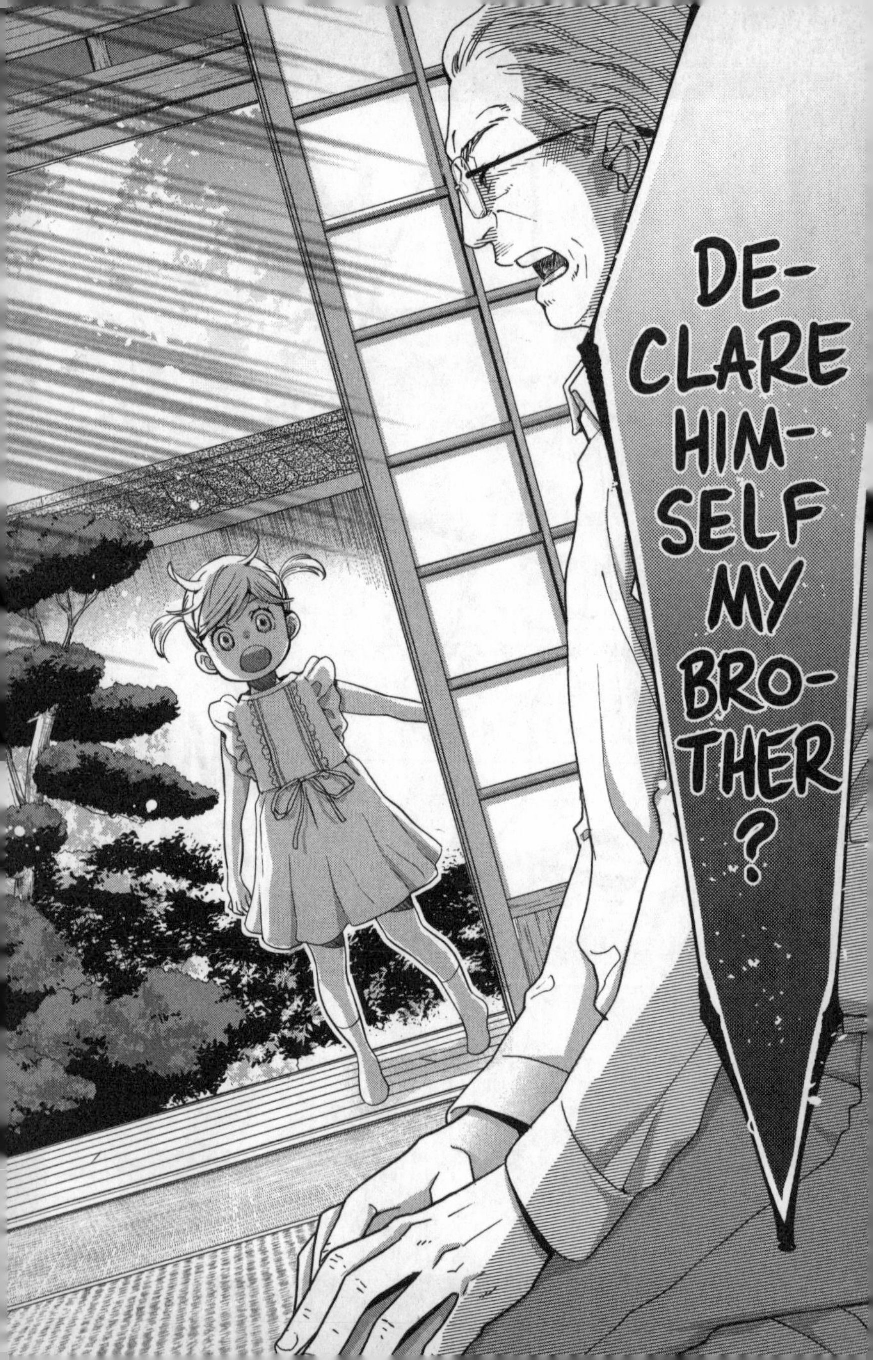
DE-CLARE HIM-SELF MY BRO-THER?

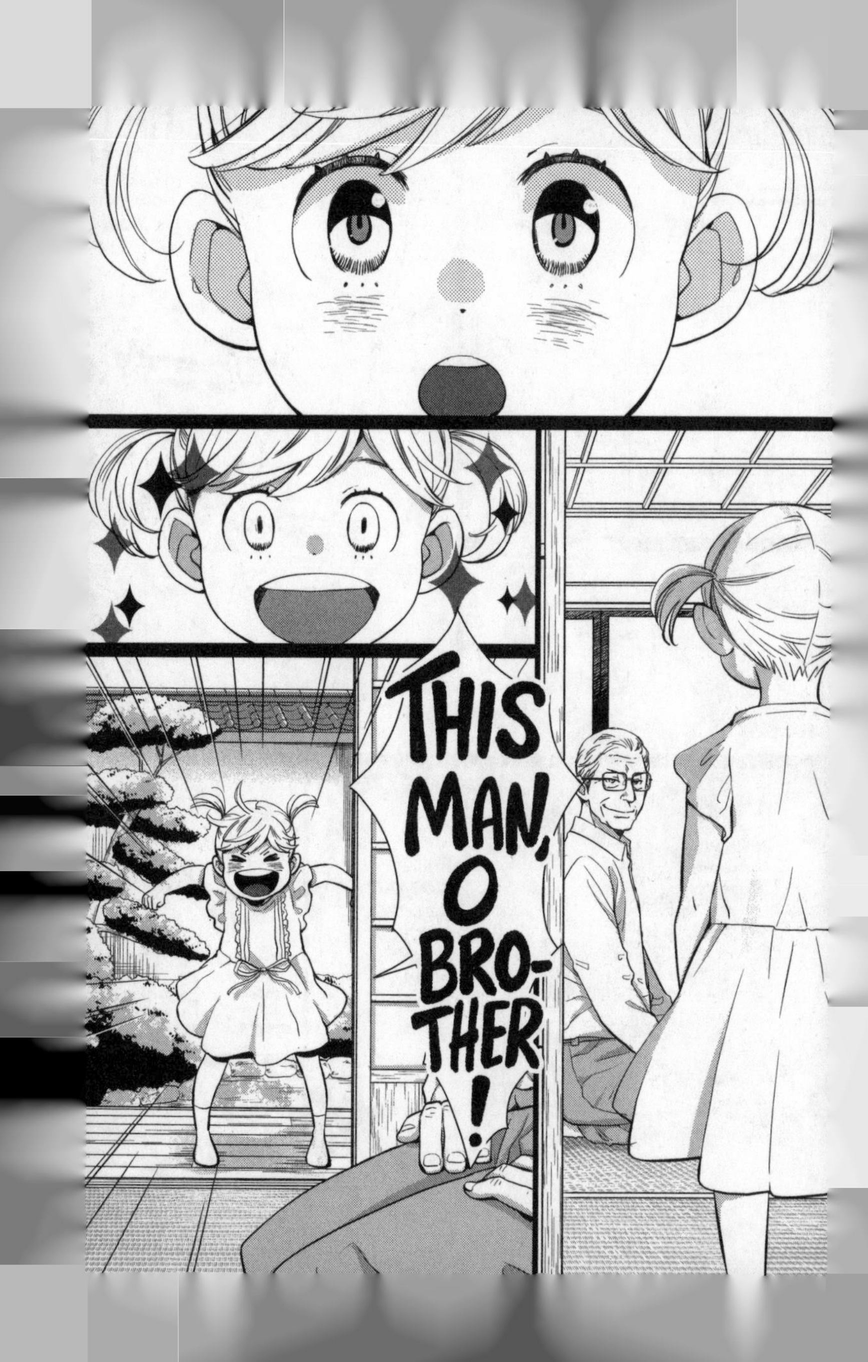
THIS MAN, O BRO-THER!

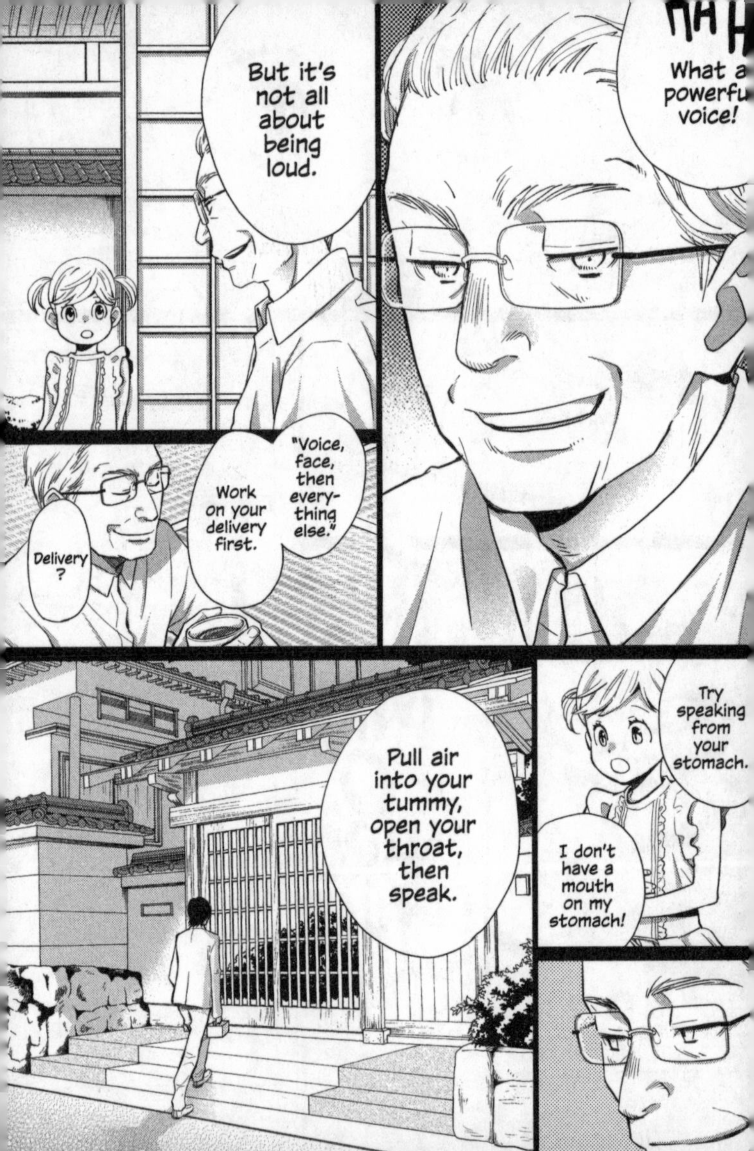
What a powerfu voice!
But it's not all about being loud.
"Voice, face, then every-thing else."
Work on your delivery first.
Delivery?
Try speaking from your stomach.
I don't have a mouth on my stomach!
Pull air into your tummy, open your throat, then speak.

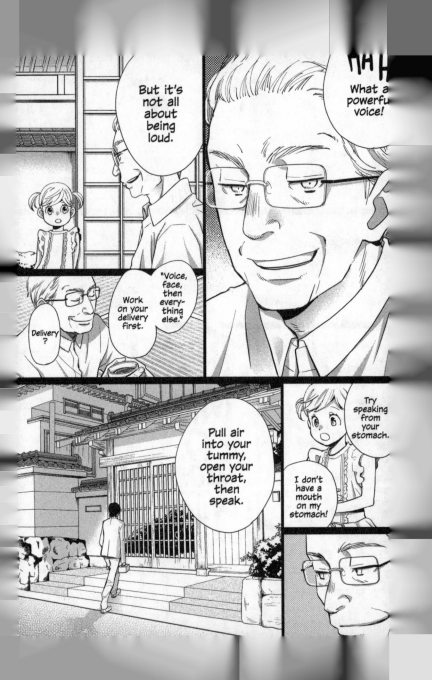

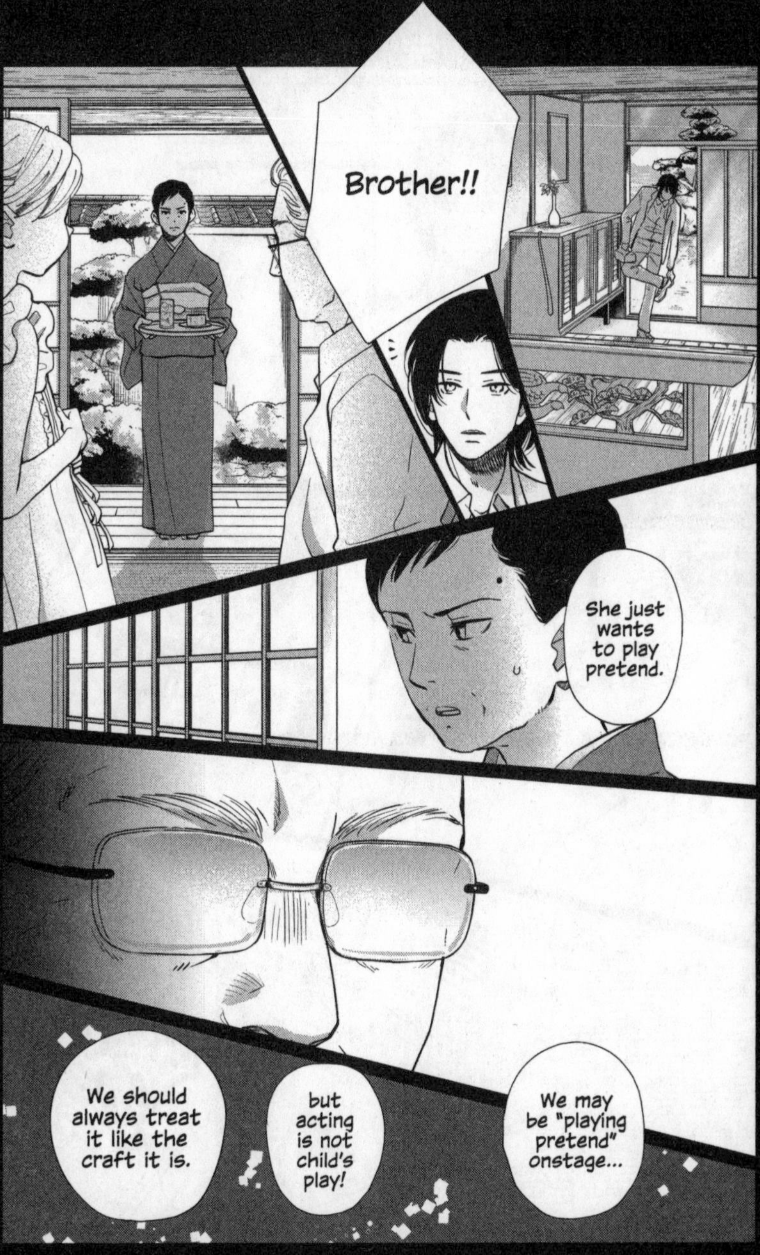
Brother!!
She just wants to play pretend.
We may be "playing pretend" onstage...
but acting is not child's play!
We should always treat it like the craft it is.

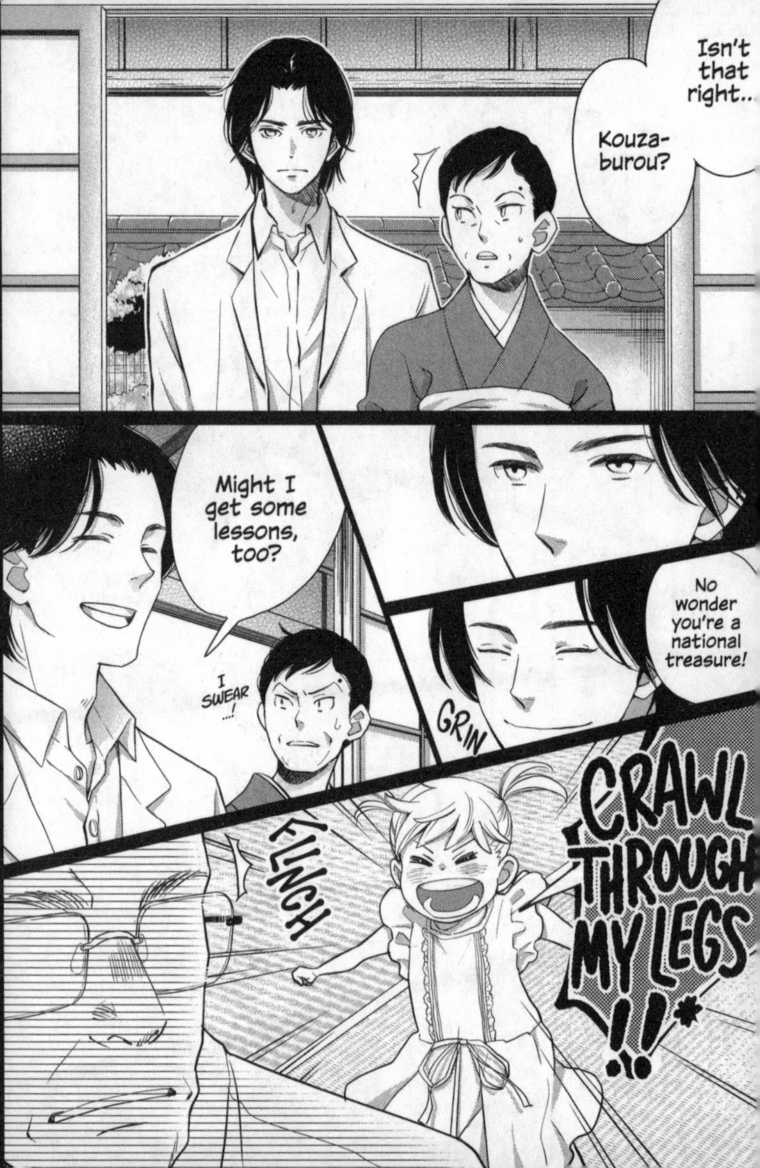
Isn't that right...
Kouza-burou?
No wonder you're a national treasure!
GRIN
Might I get some lessons, too?
I SWEAR...!
CRAWL THROUGH MY LEGS!!*
FLINCH

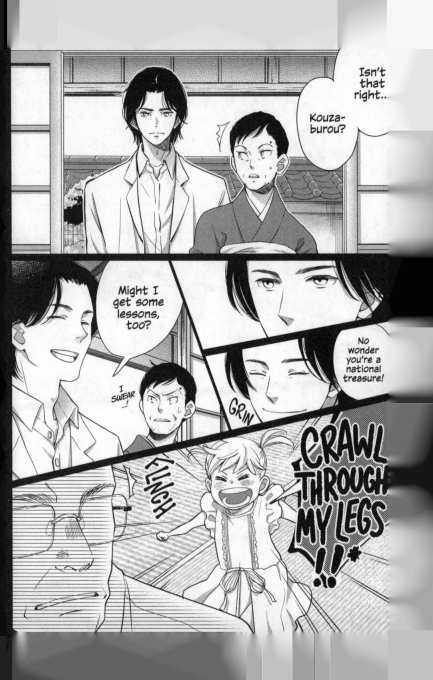

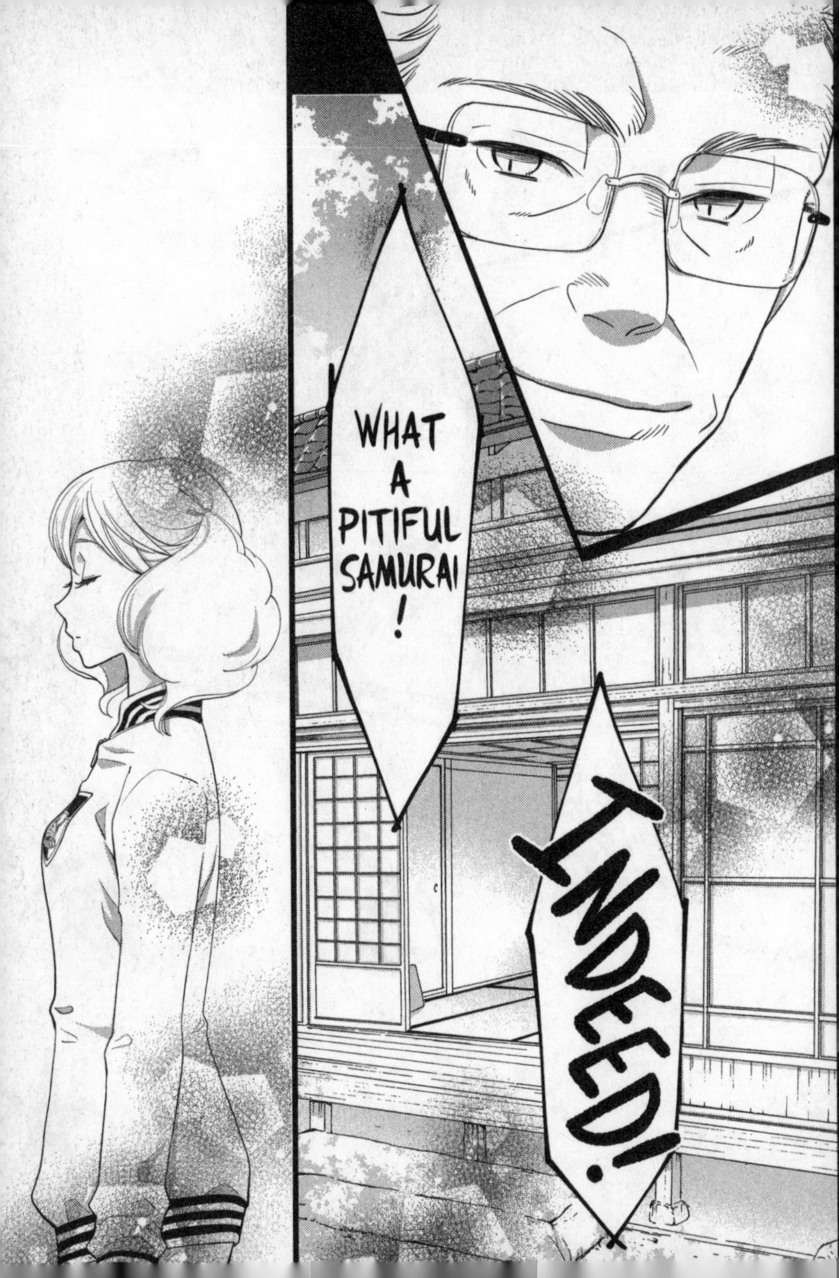
WHAT A PITIFUL SAMURAI!
INDEED!

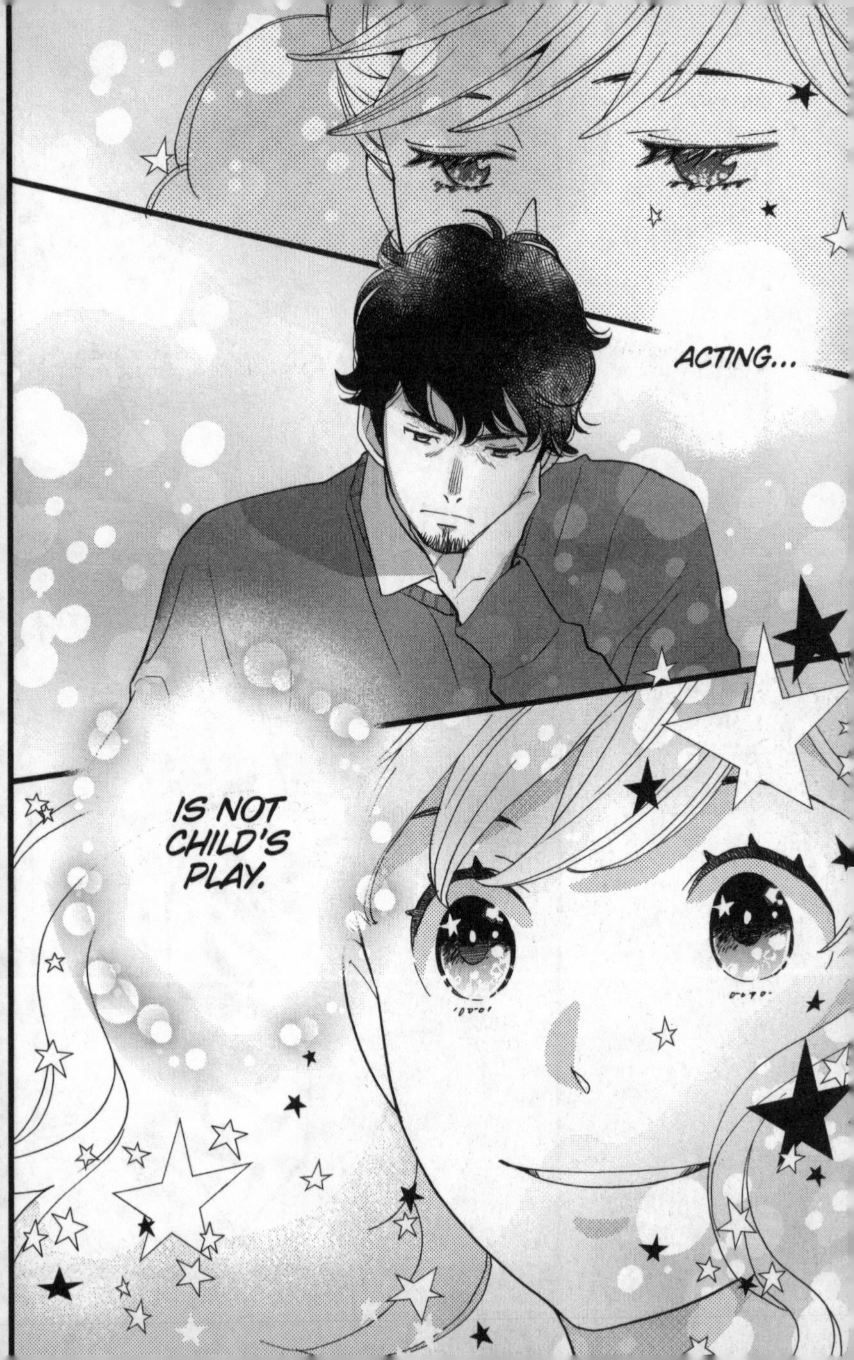
ACTING...
IS NOT CHILD'S PLAY.

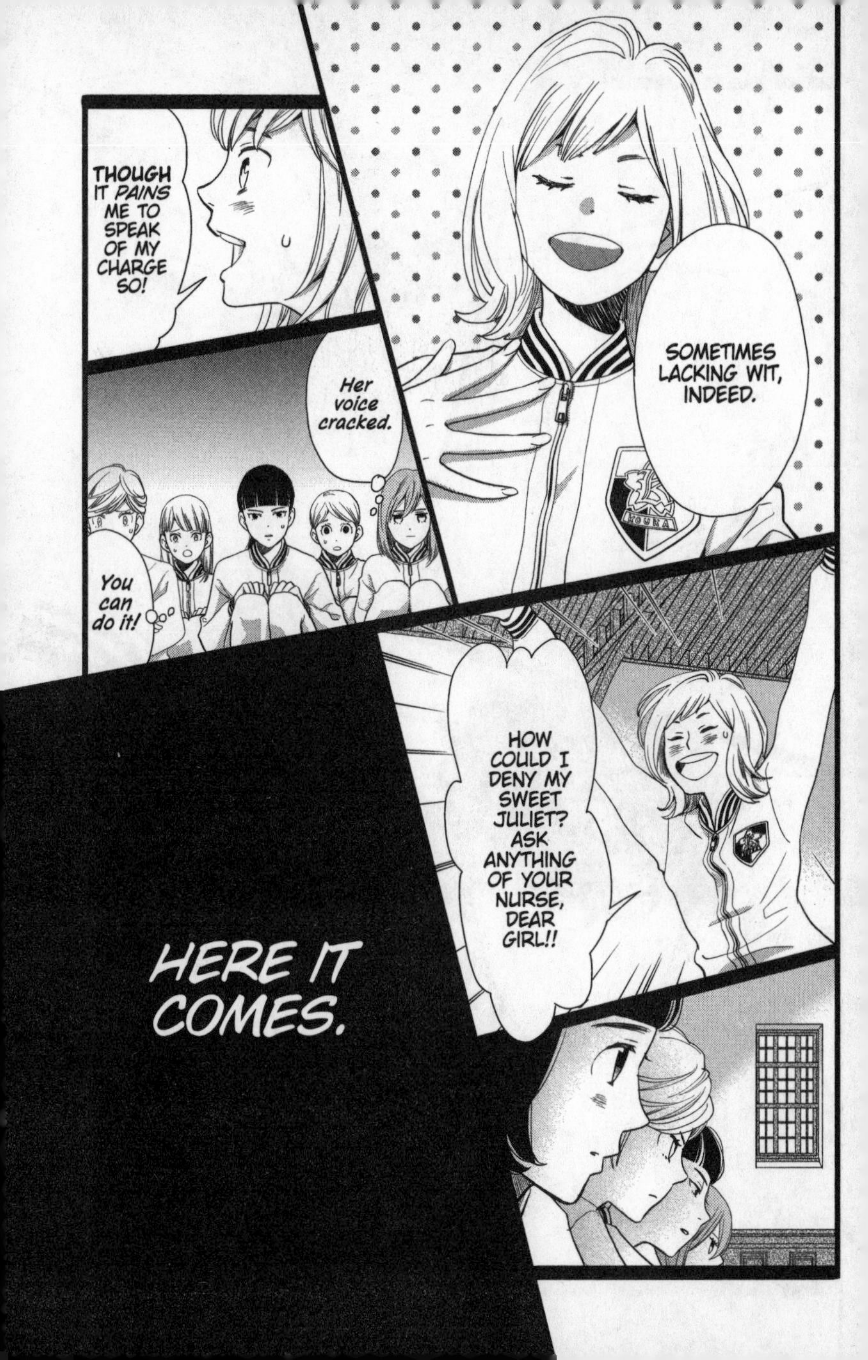
SOMETIMES LACKING WIT, INDEED.
THOUGH IT *PAINS* ME TO SPEAK OF MY CHARGE SO!
Her voice cracked.
You can do it!
HOW COULD I DENY MY SWEET JULIET? ASK ANYTHING OF YOUR NURSE, DEAR GIRL!!
HERE IT COMES.

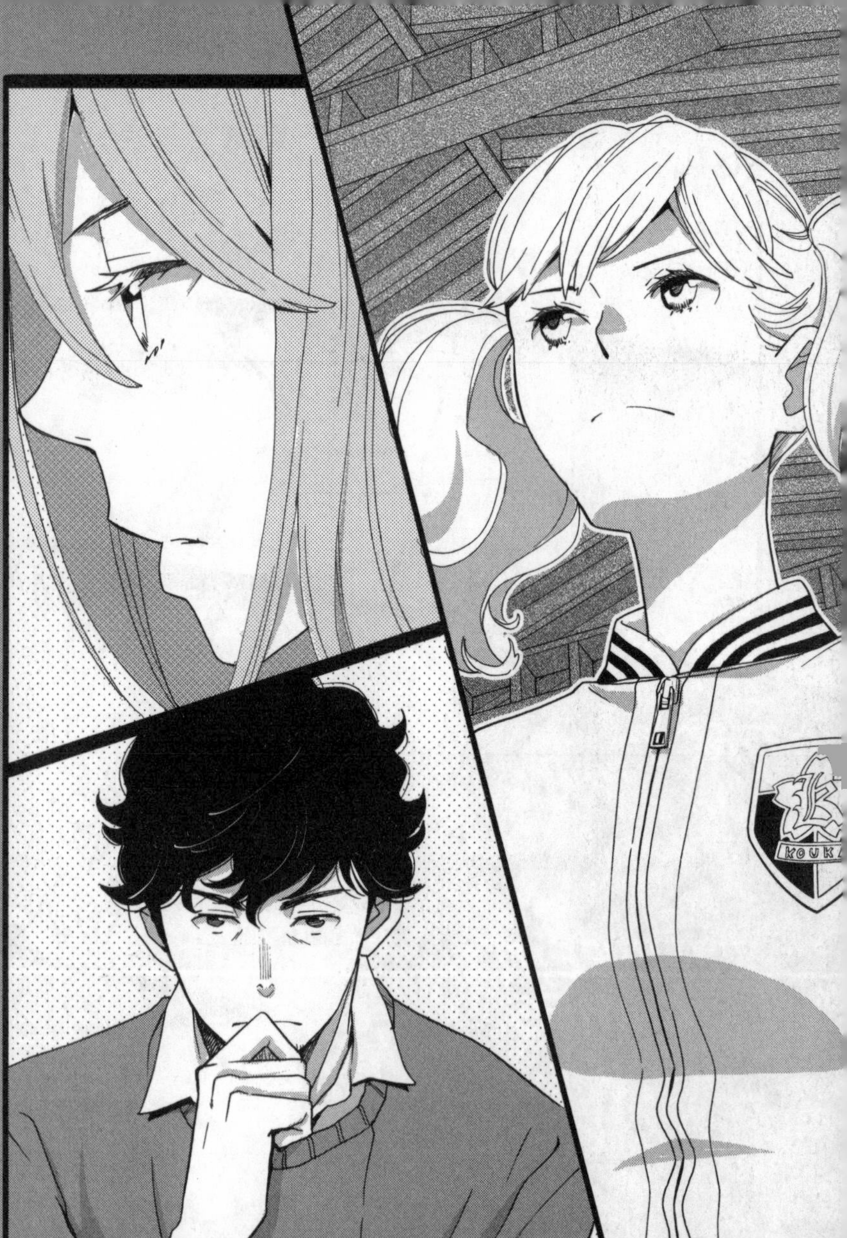

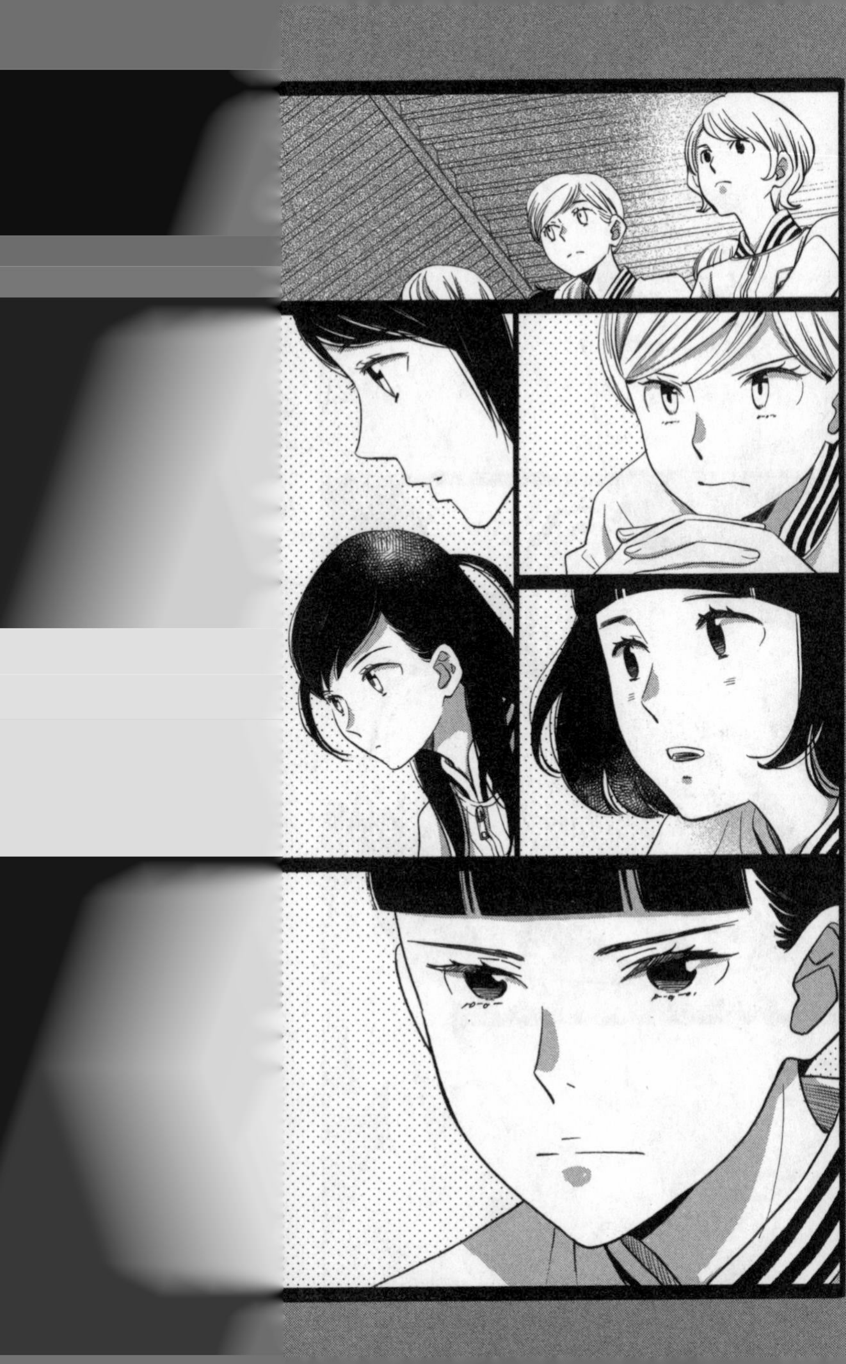

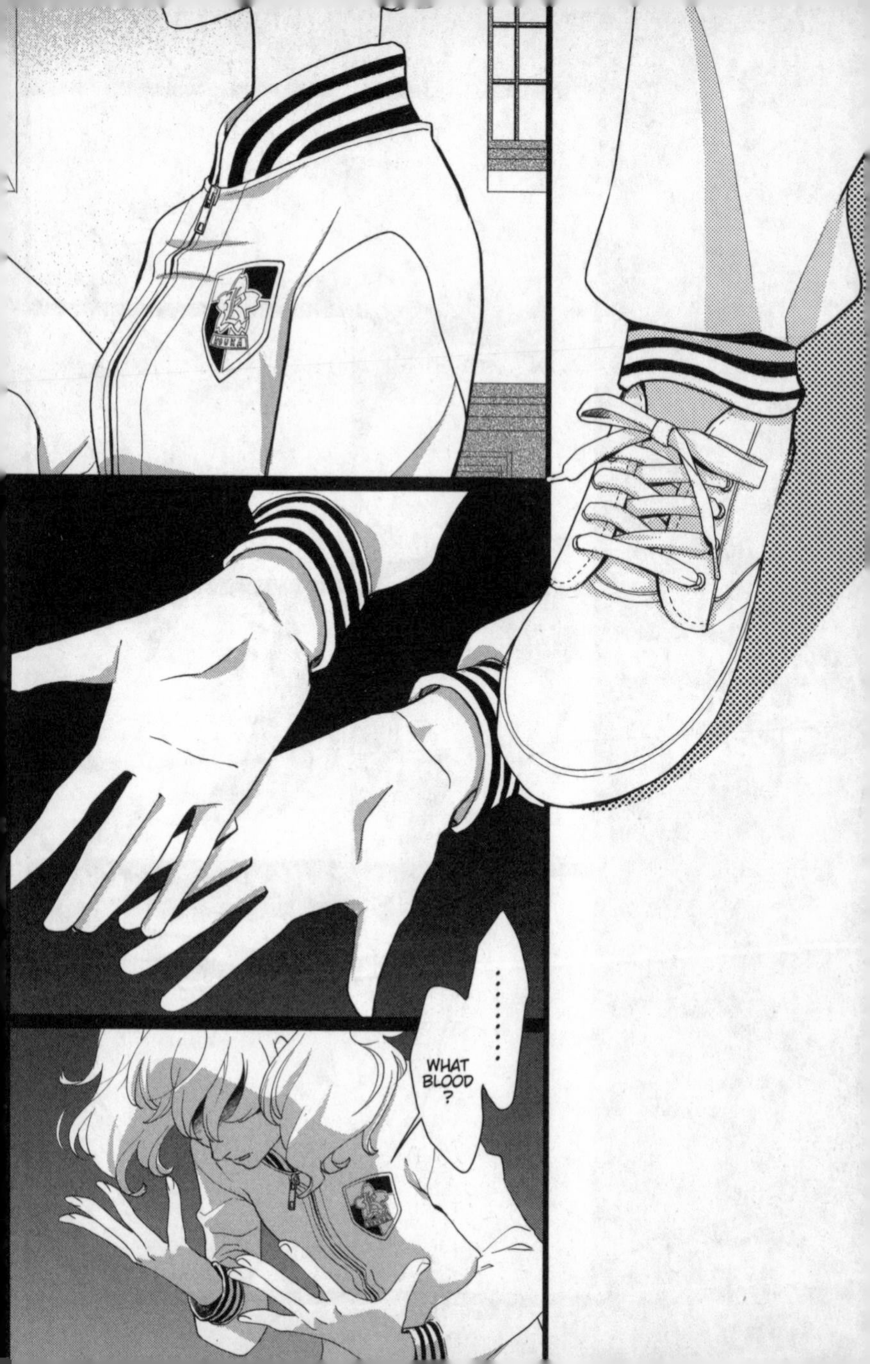
......
WHAT BLOOD?

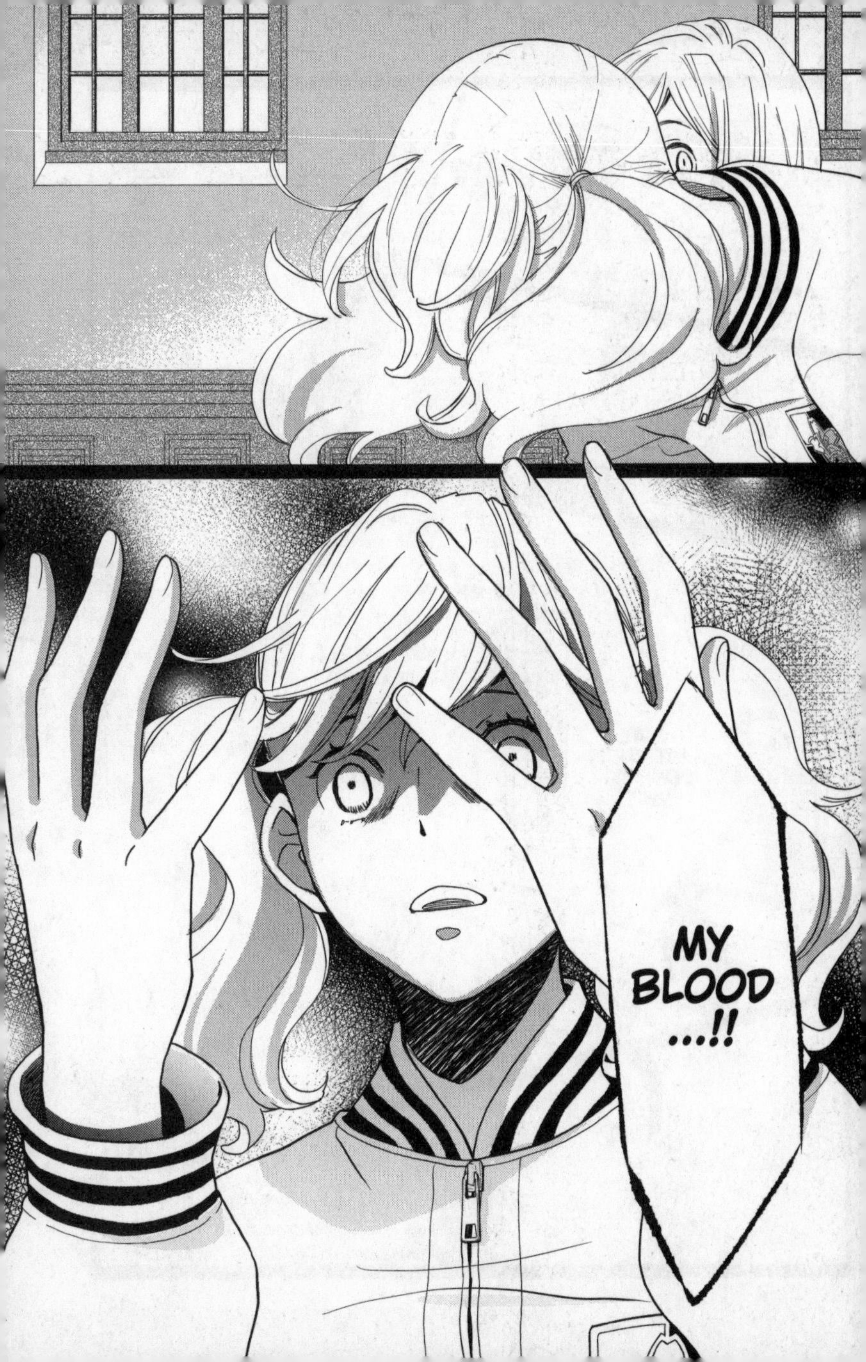
MY BLOOD ...!!

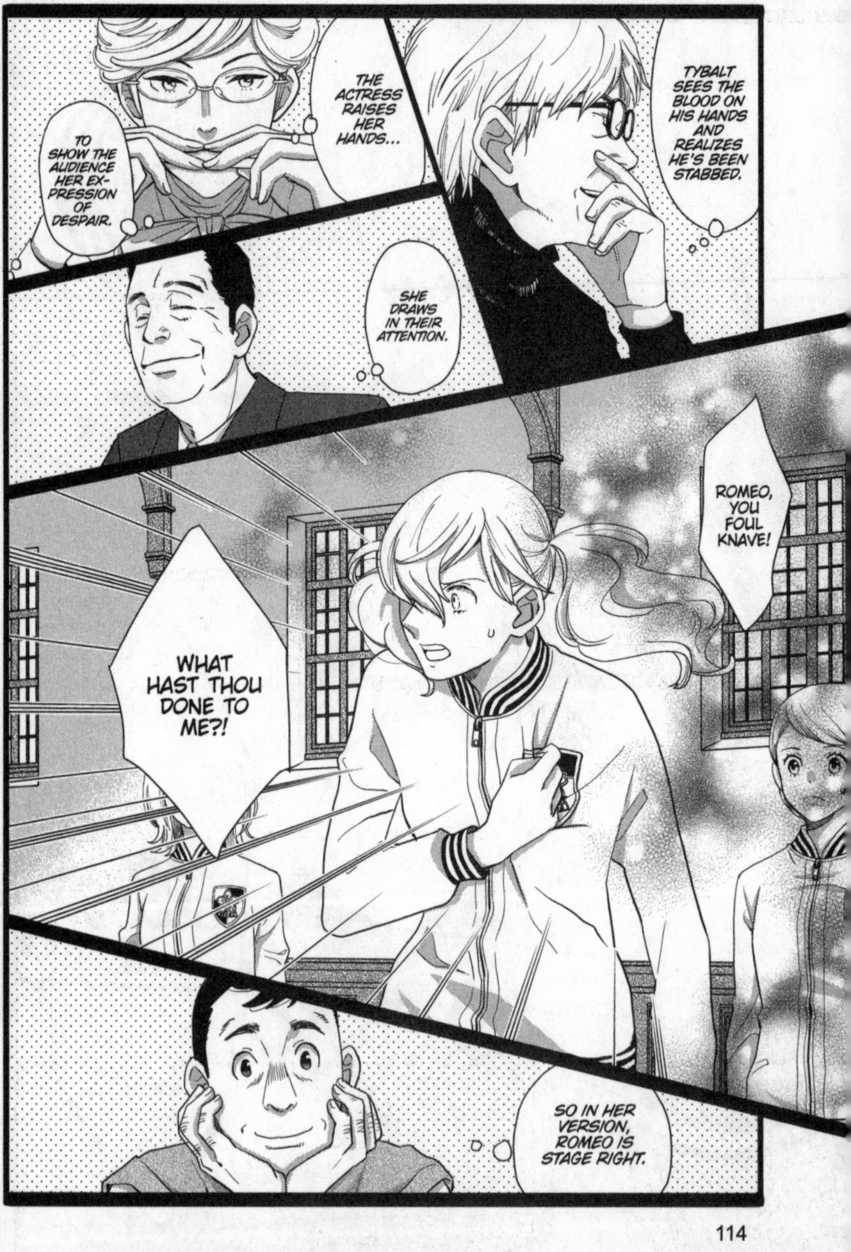
TYBALT SEES THE BLOOD ON HIS HANDS AND REALIZES HE'S BEEN STABBED.
THE ACTRESS RAISES HER HANDS...
TO SHOW THE AUDIENCE HER EX-PRESSION OF DESPAIR.
SHE DRAWS IN THEIR ATTENTION.
ROMEO, YOU FOUL KNAVE!
WHAT HAST THOU DONE TO ME?!
SO IN HER VERSION, ROMEO IS STAGE RIGHT.

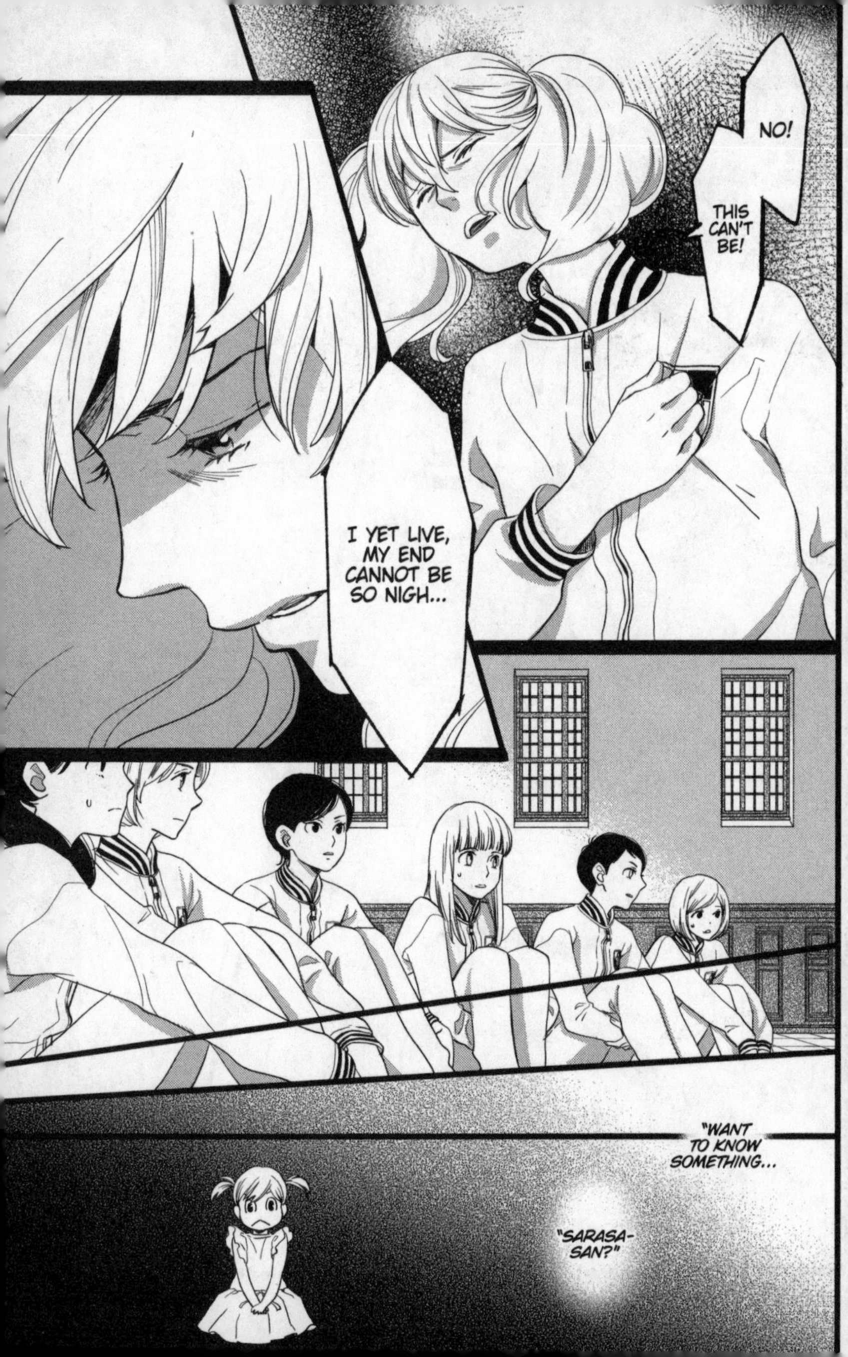
NO!
THIS CAN'T BE!
I YET LIVE, MY END CANNOT BE SO NIGH...
"WANT TO KNOW SOMETHING...
"SARASA-SAN?"

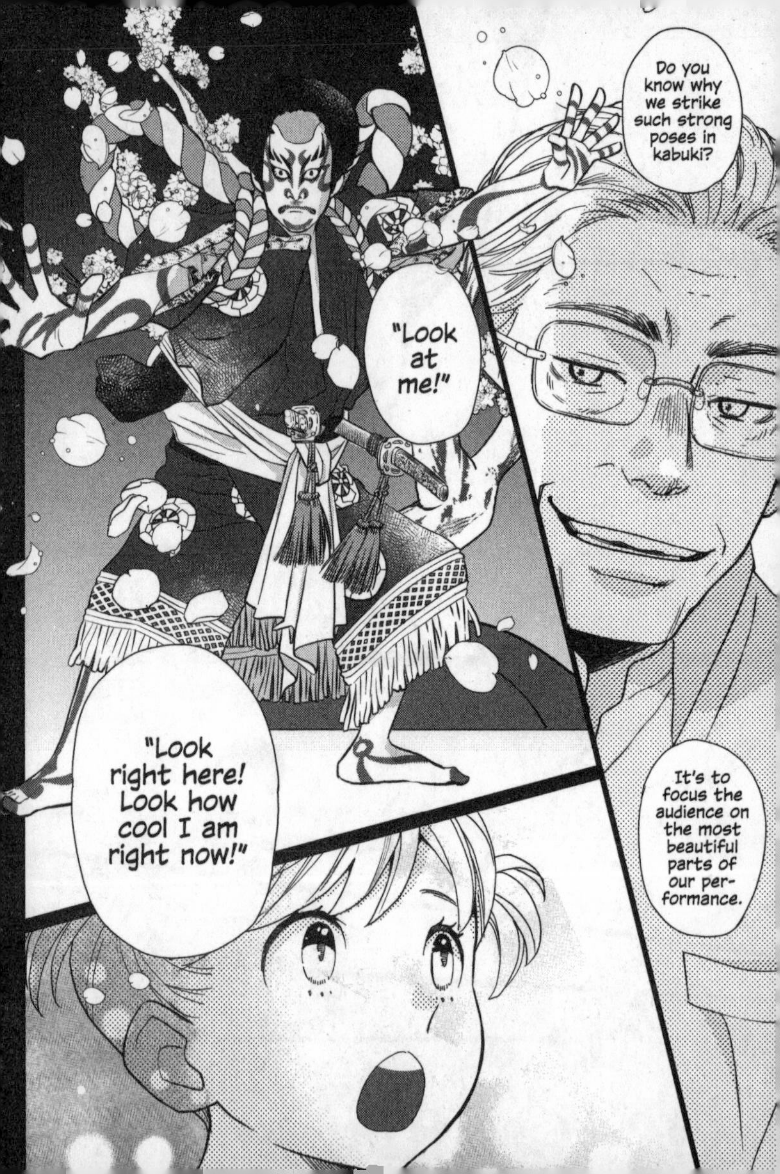
Do you know why we strike such strong poses in kabuki?
It's to focus the audience on the most beautiful parts of our per- formance.
"Look at me!"
"Look right here! Look how cool I am right now!"

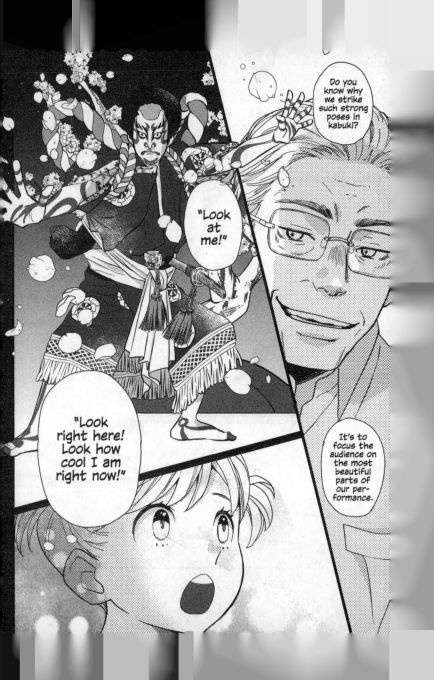

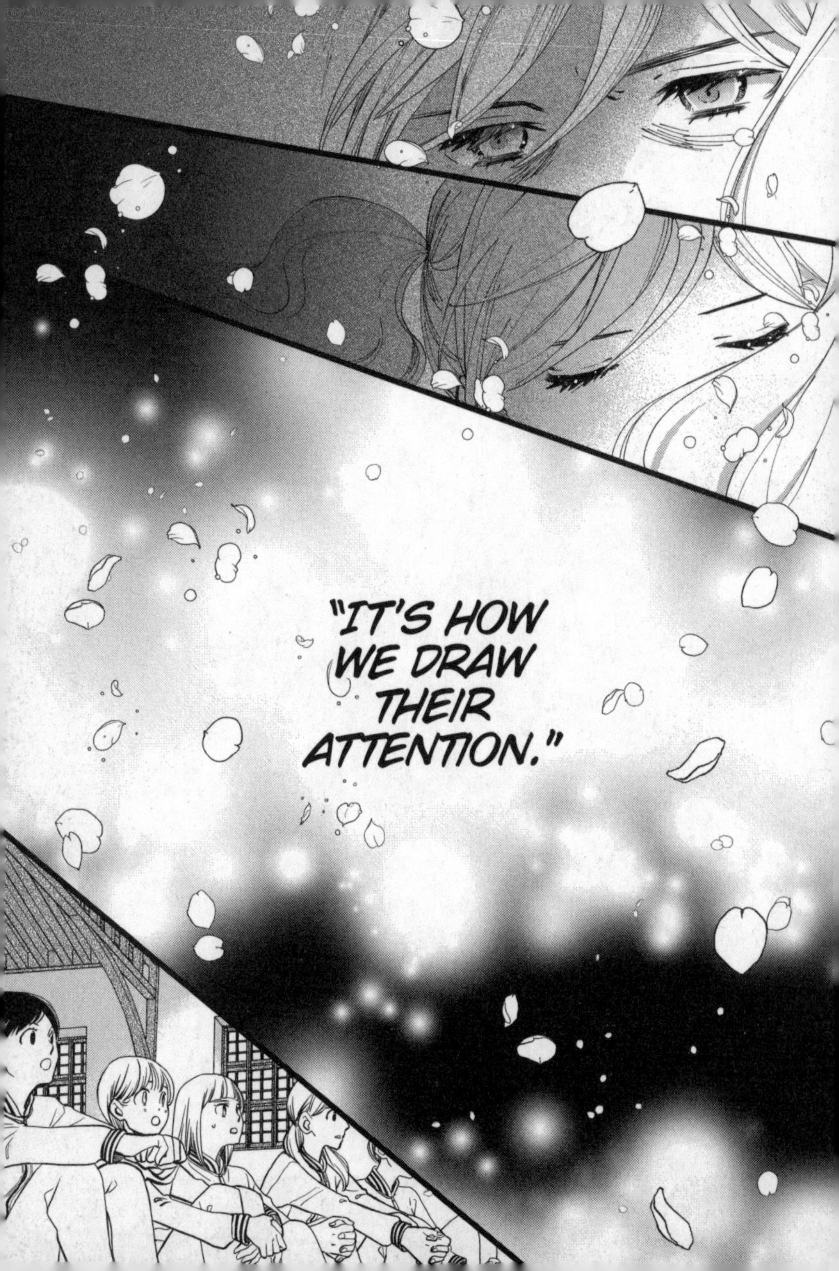
"IT'S HOW WE DRAW THEIR ATTENTION."

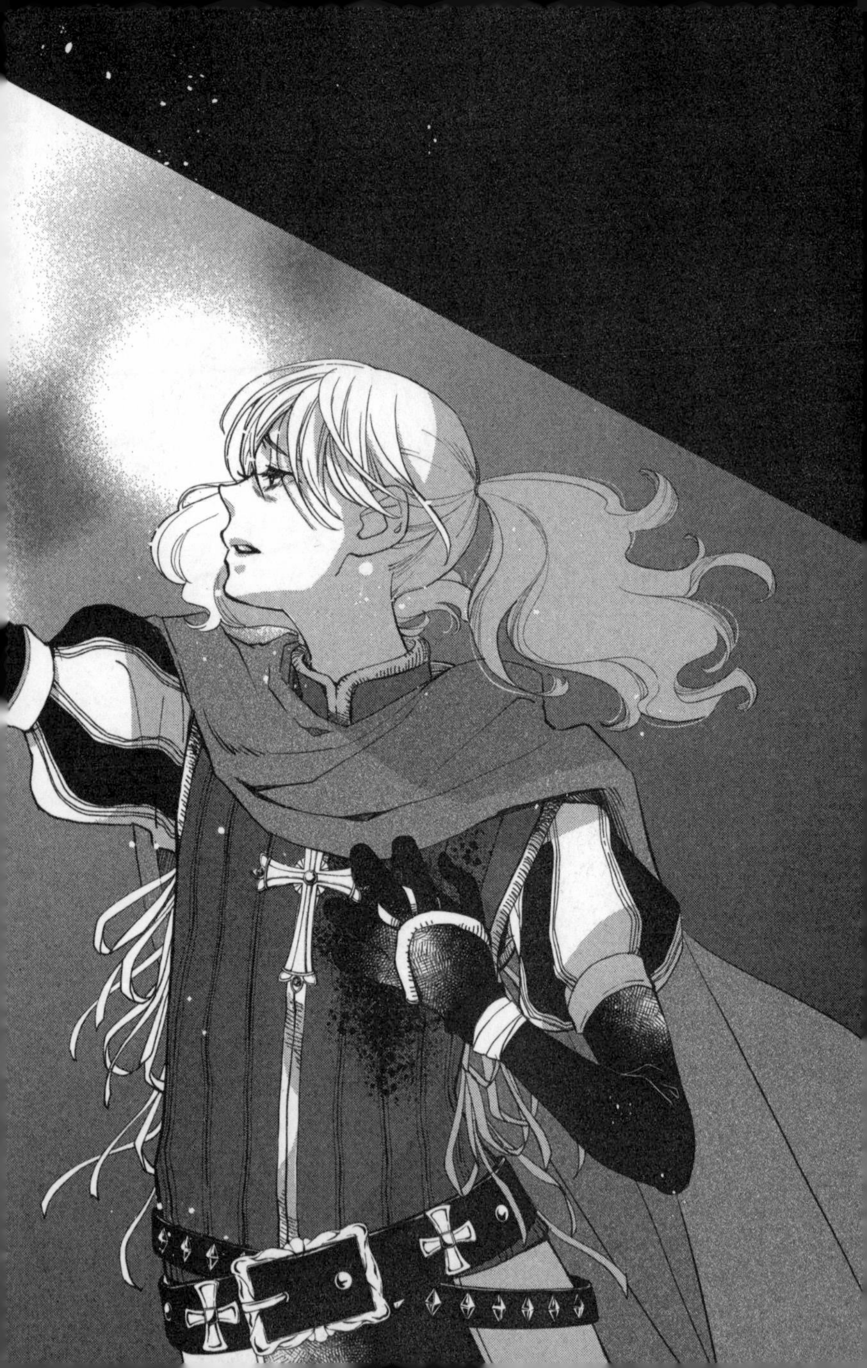

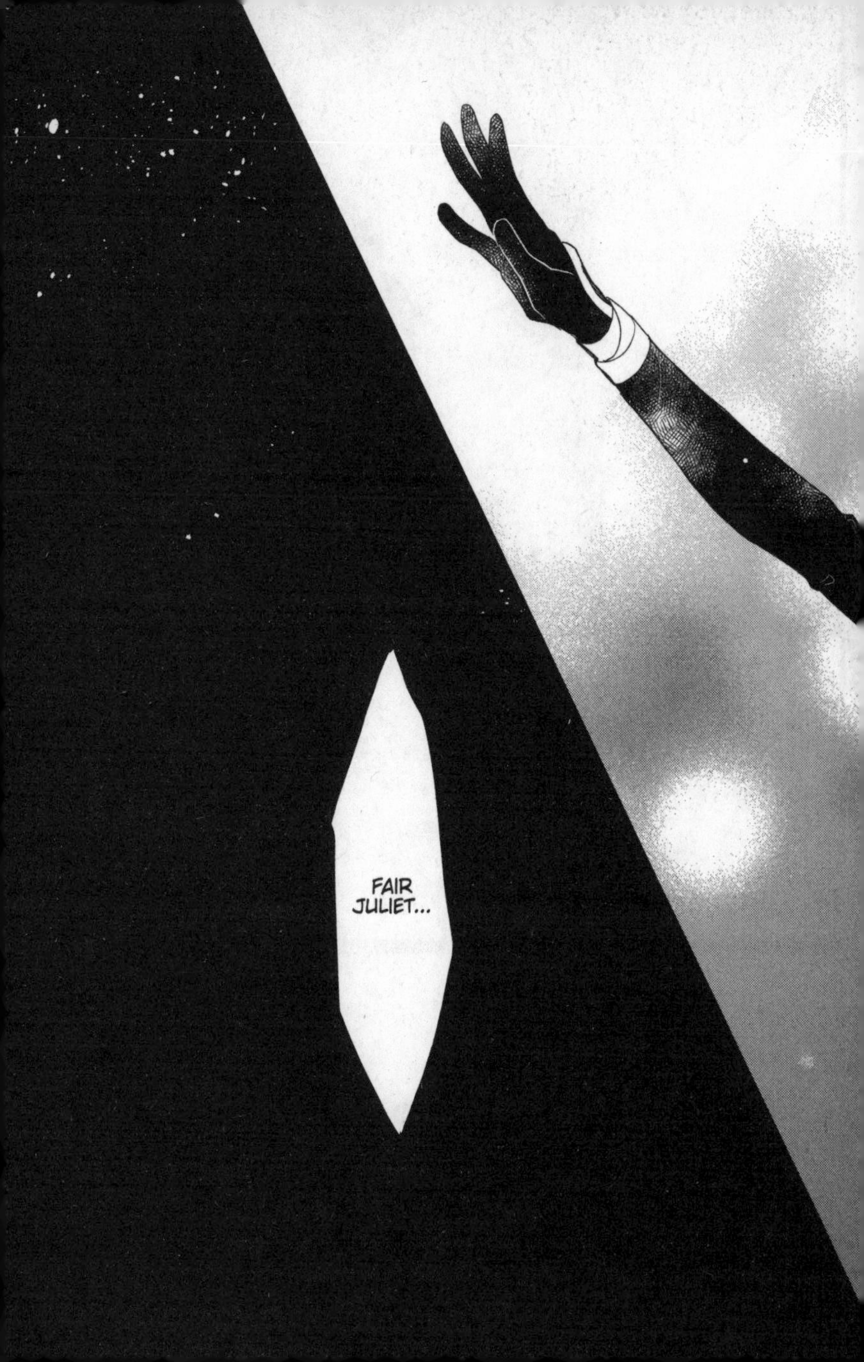
FAIR
JULIET...

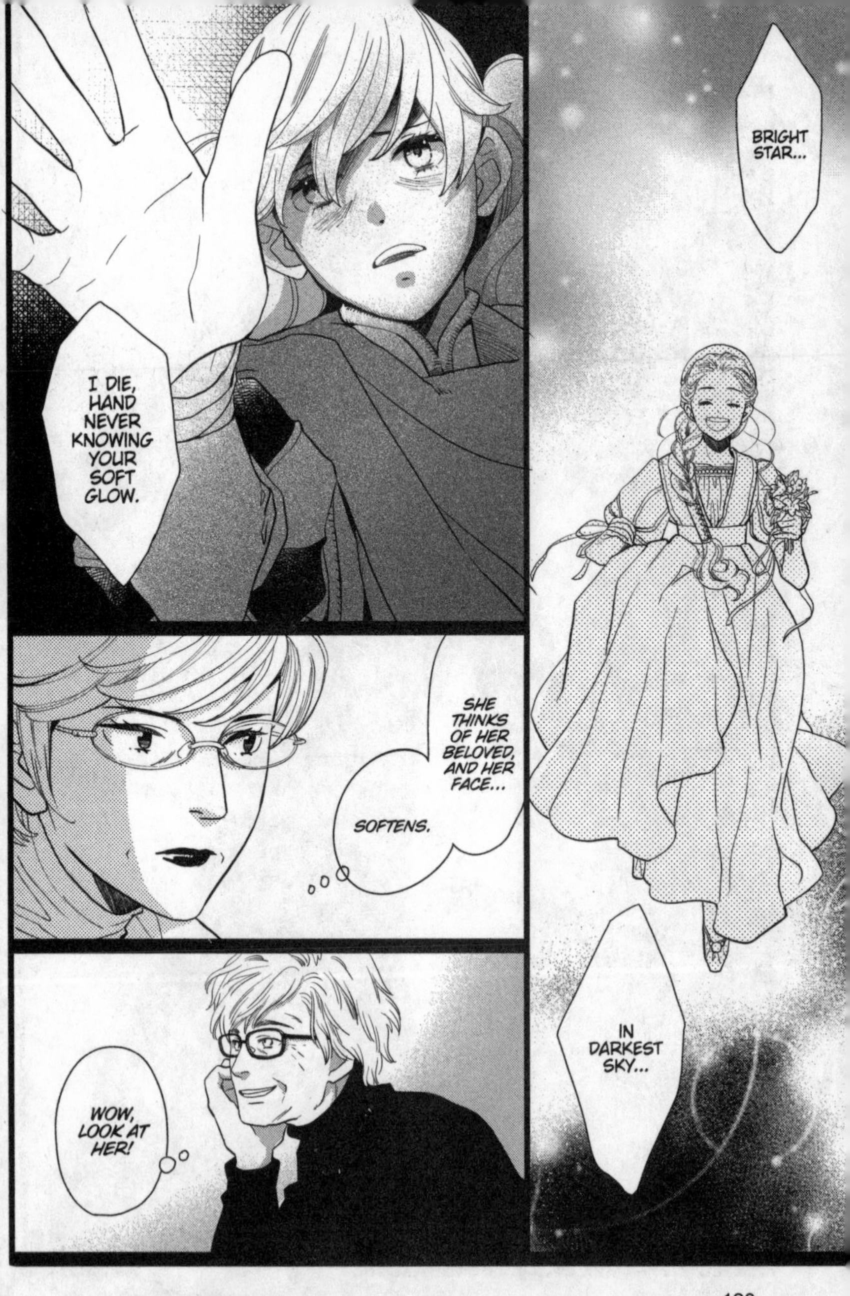
BRIGHT STAR...
IN DARKEST SKY...
I DIE, HAND NEVER KNOWING YOUR SOFT GLOW.
SHE THINKS OF HER BELOVED, AND HER FACE...
SOFTENS.
WOW, LOOK AT HER!

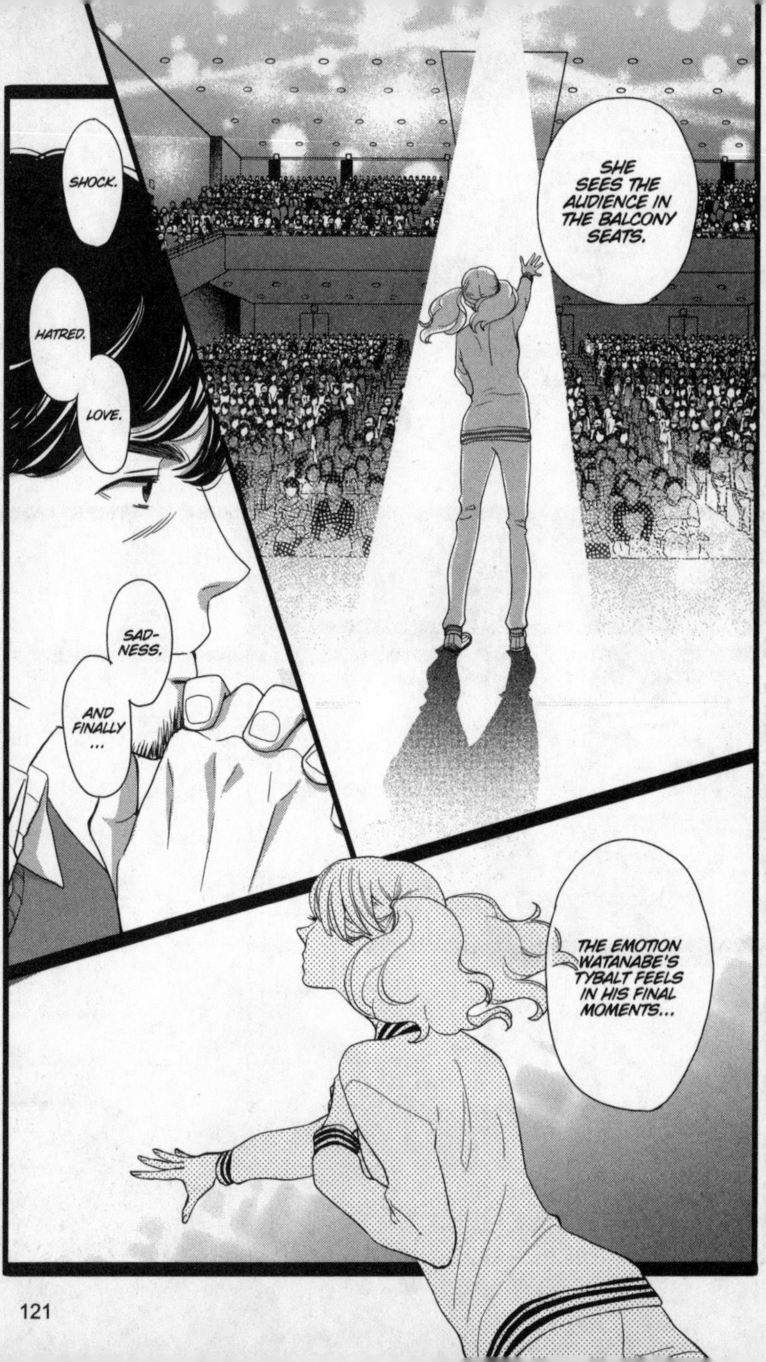
SHE SEES THE AUDIENCE IN THE BALCONY SEATS.
SHOCK.
HATRED.
LOVE.
SAD-NESS.
AND FINALLY ...
THE EMOTION WATANABE'S TYBALT FEELS IN HIS FINAL MOMENTS...

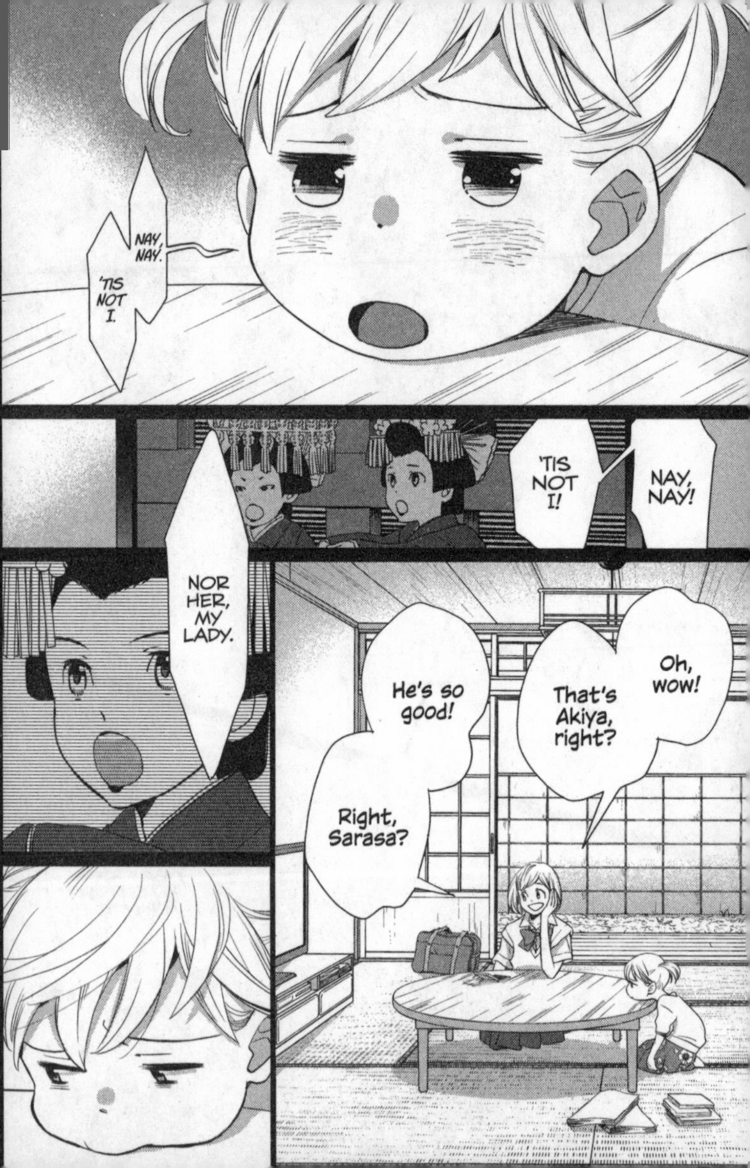
NAY, NAY.
'TIS NOT I.
NAY, NAY!
'TIS NOT I!
NOR HER, MY LADY.
Oh, wow!
That's Akiya, right?
He's so good!
Right, Sarasa?

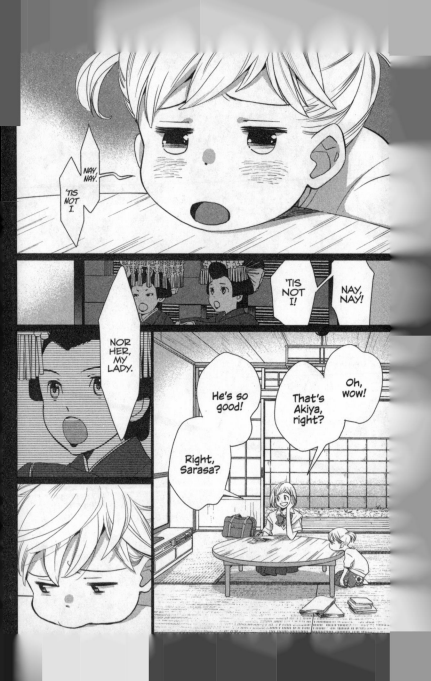

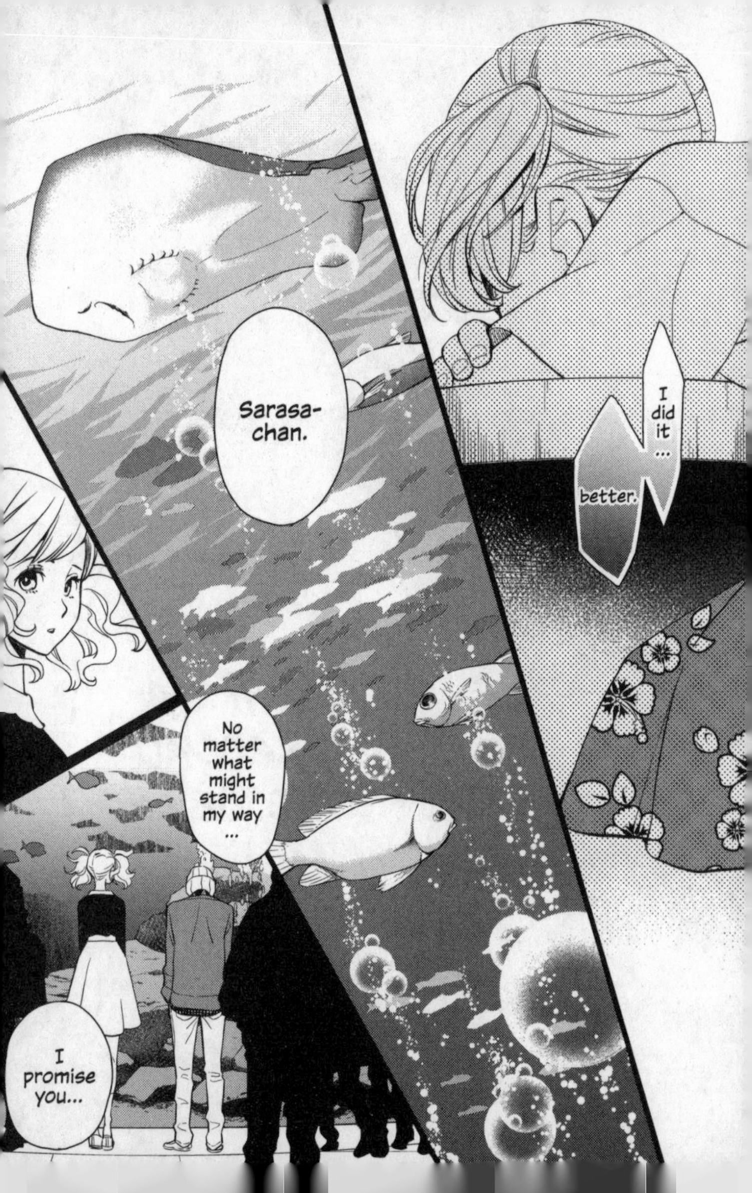
I did it... better.
Sarasa-chan.
No matter what might stand in my way...
I promise you...

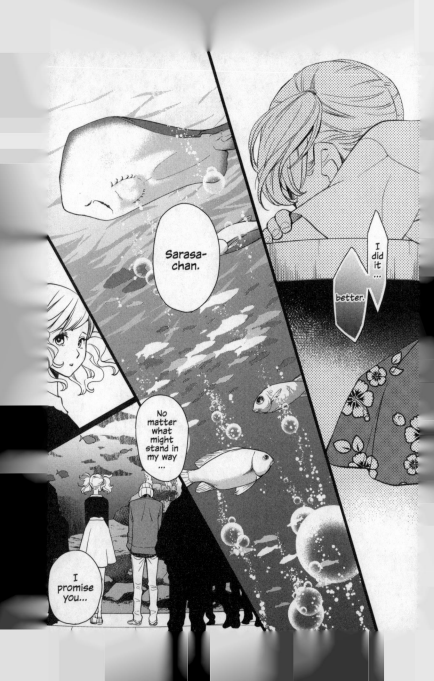

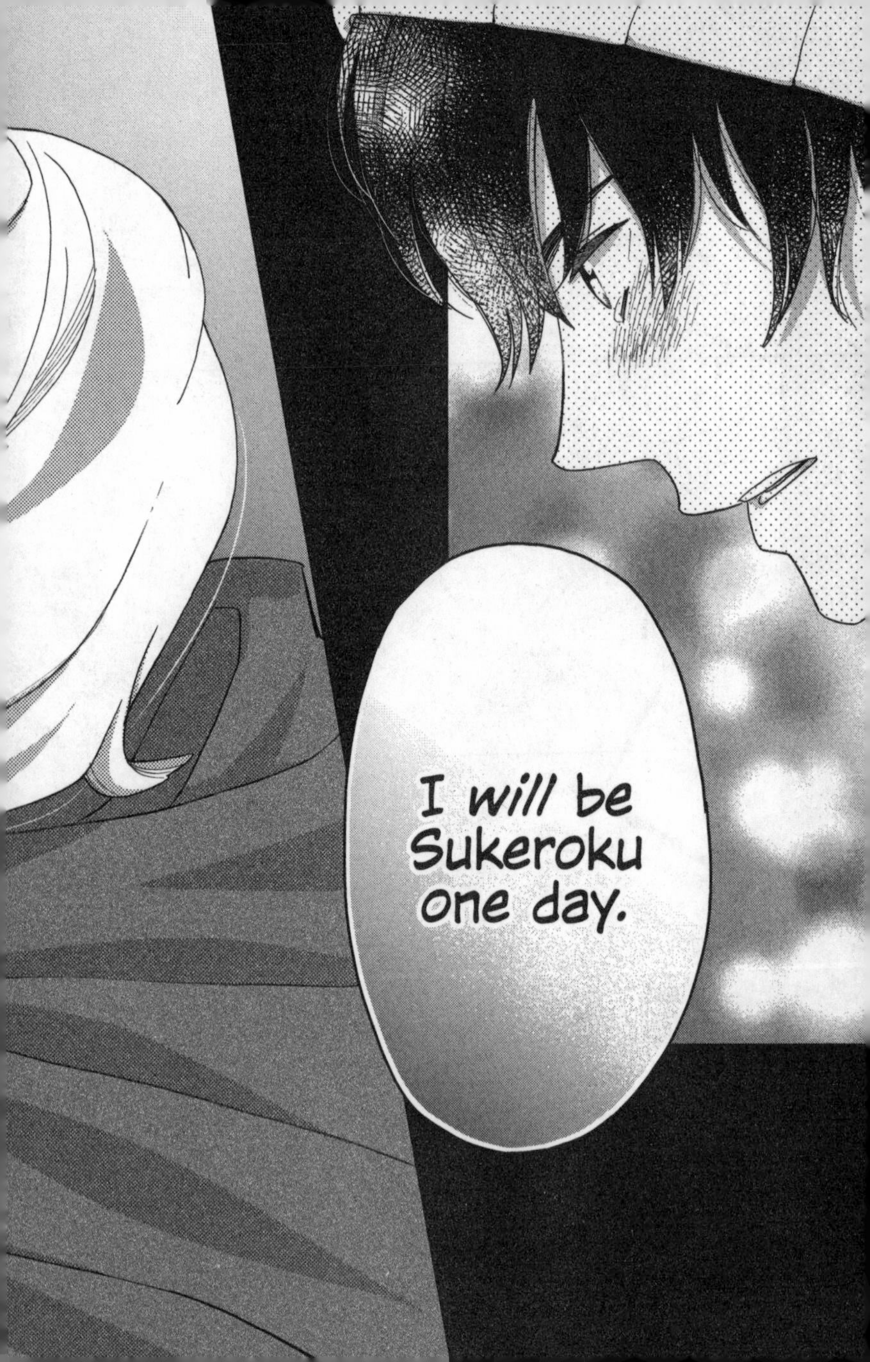
I *will* be Sukeroku one day.

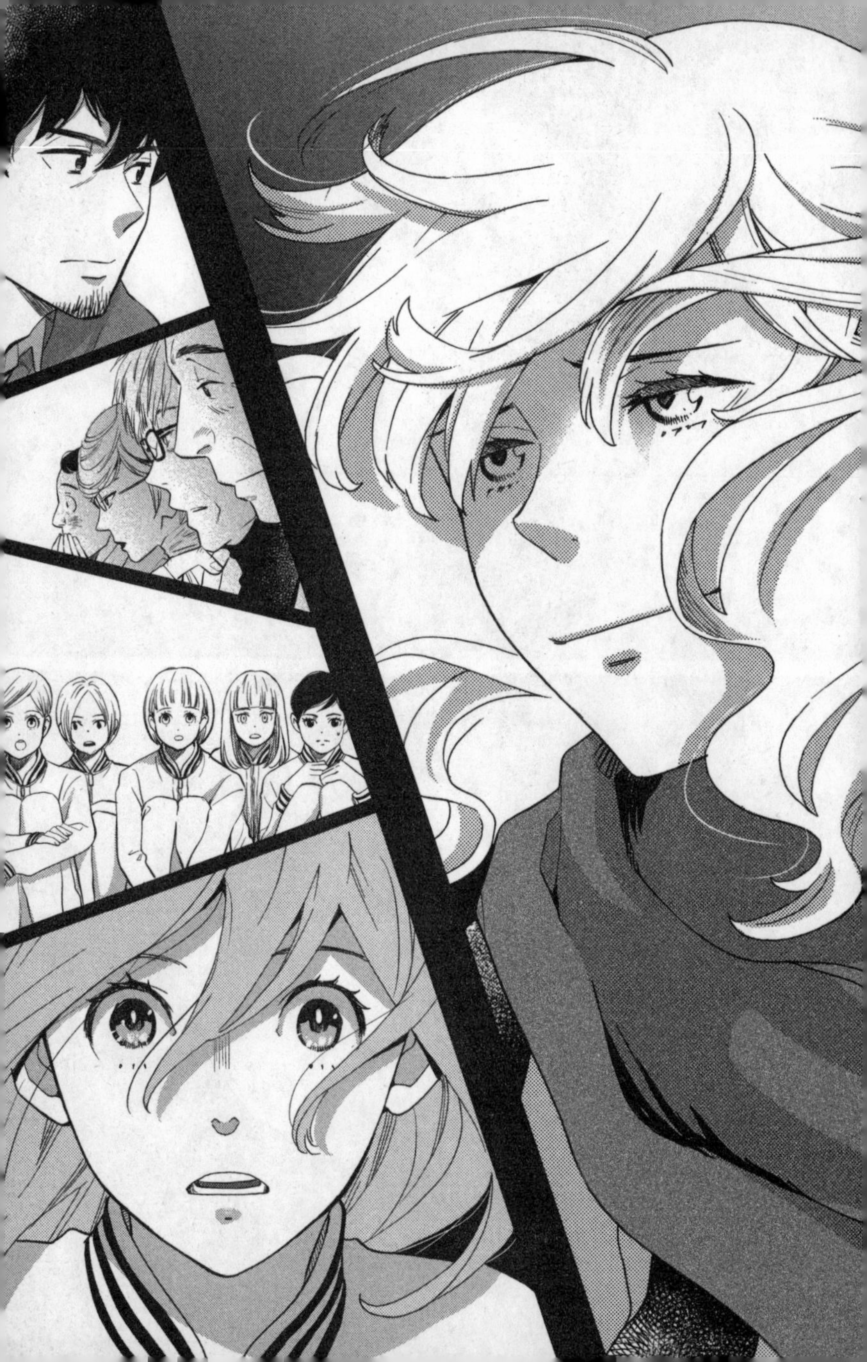

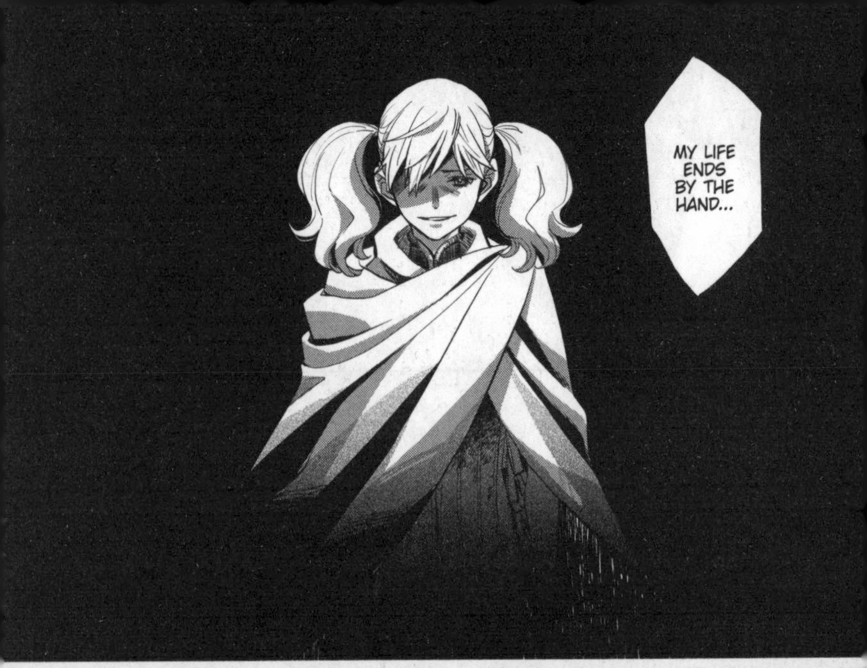
MY LIFE ENDS BY THE HAND...
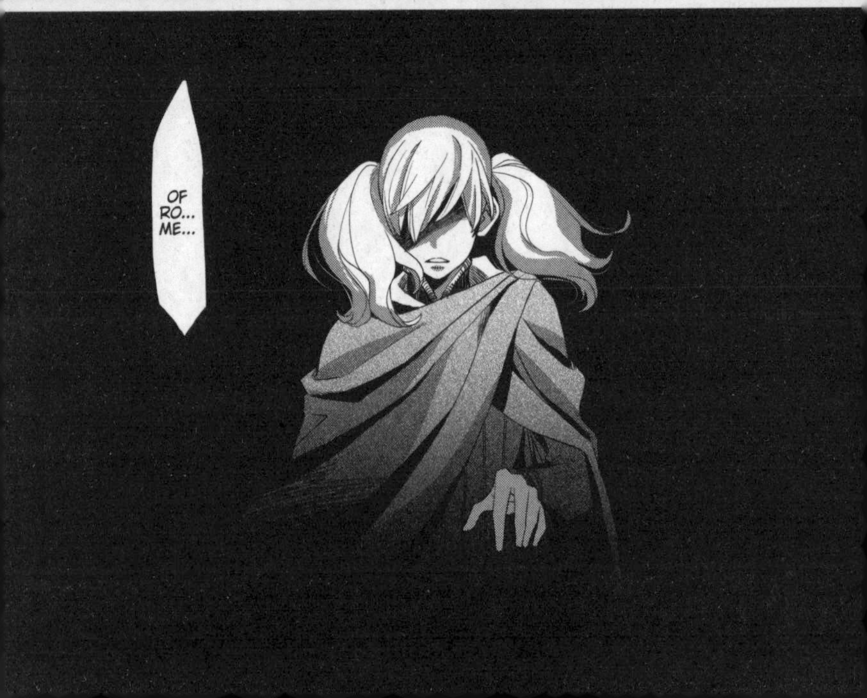
OF RO... ME...

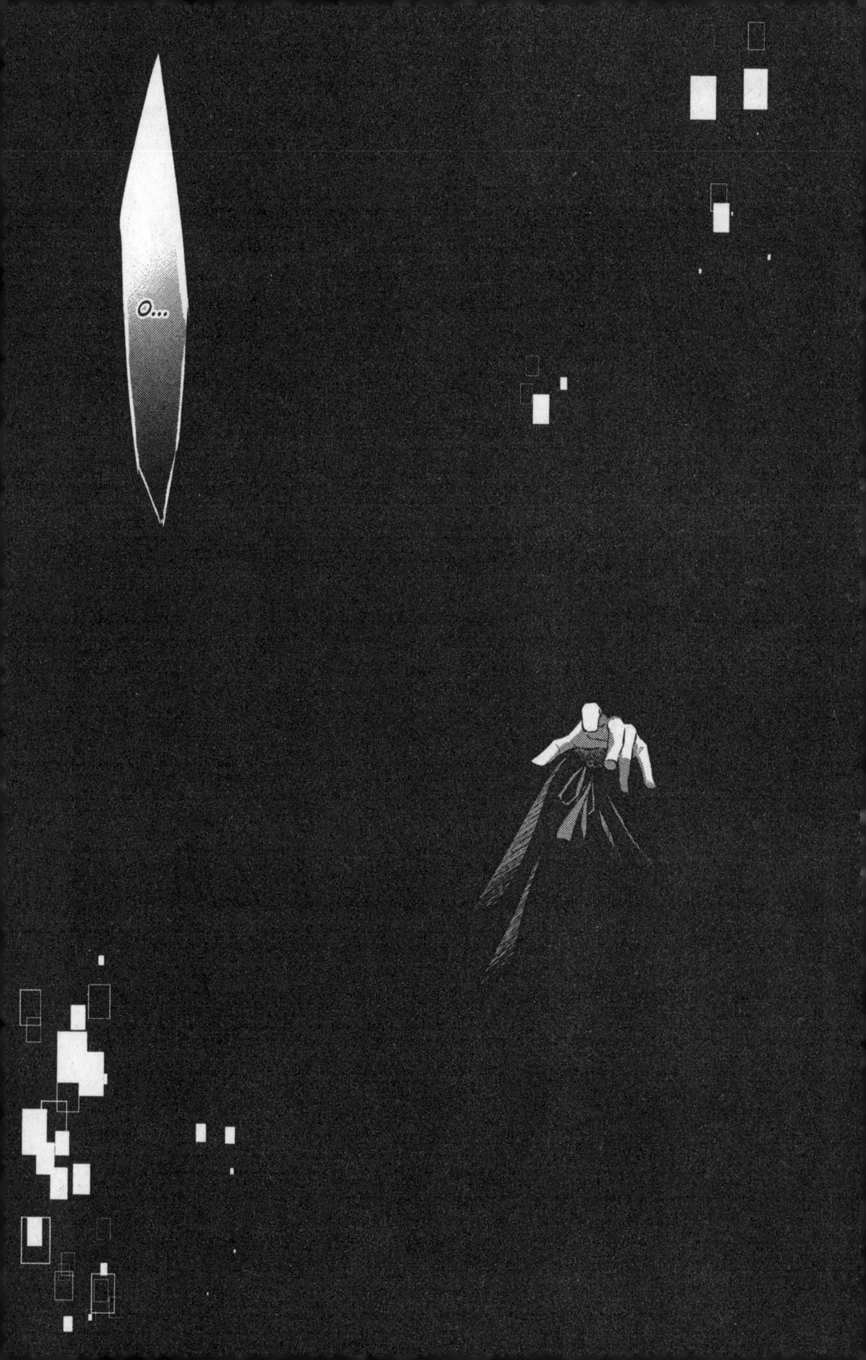
O...

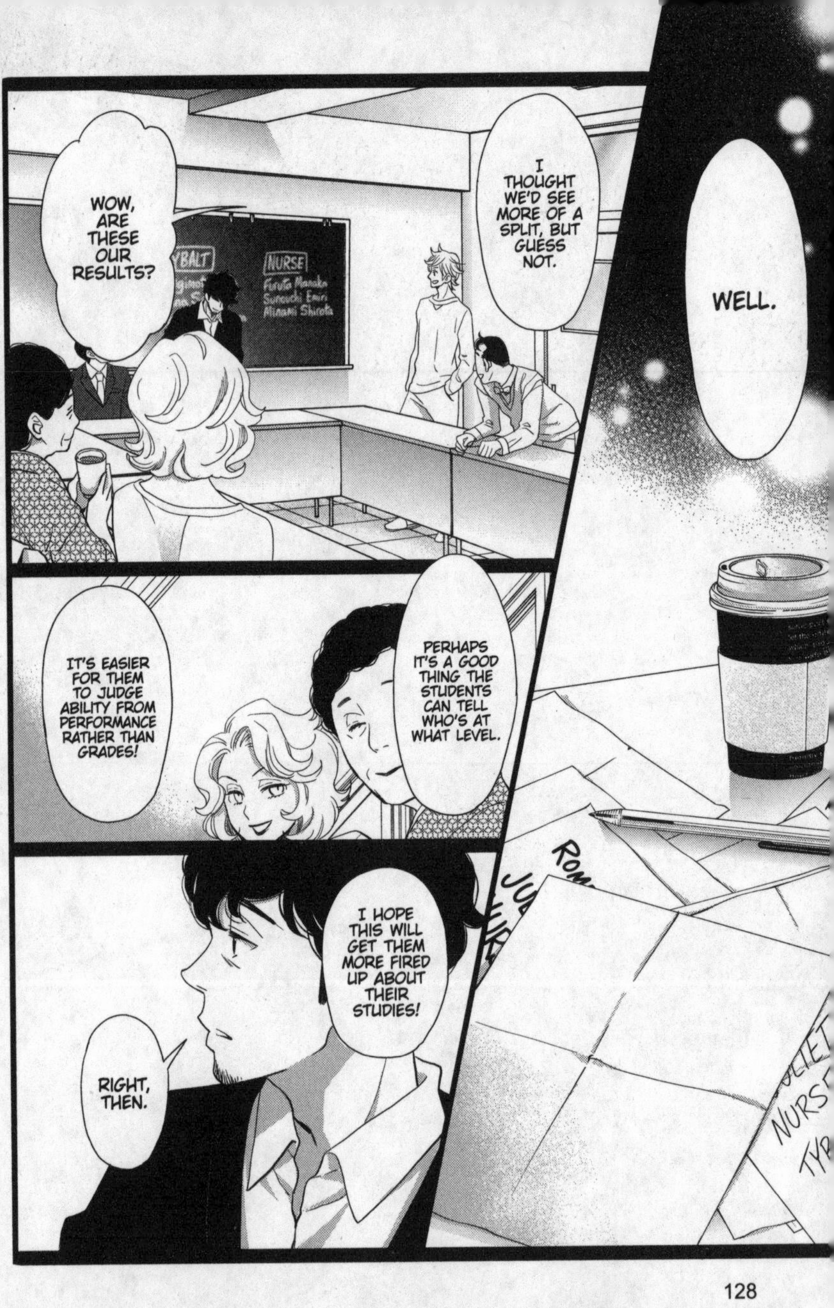
WELL.
I THOUGHT WE'D SEE MORE OF A SPLIT, BUT GUESS NOT.
WOW, ARE THESE OUR RESULTS?
NURSE
PERHAPS IT'S A GOOD THING THE STUDENTS CAN TELL WHO'S AT WHAT LEVEL.
IT'S EASIER FOR THEM TO JUDGE ABILITY FROM PERFORMANCE RATHER THAN GRADES!
I HOPE THIS WILL GET THEM MORE FIRED UP ABOUT THEIR STUDIES!
RIGHT, THEN.

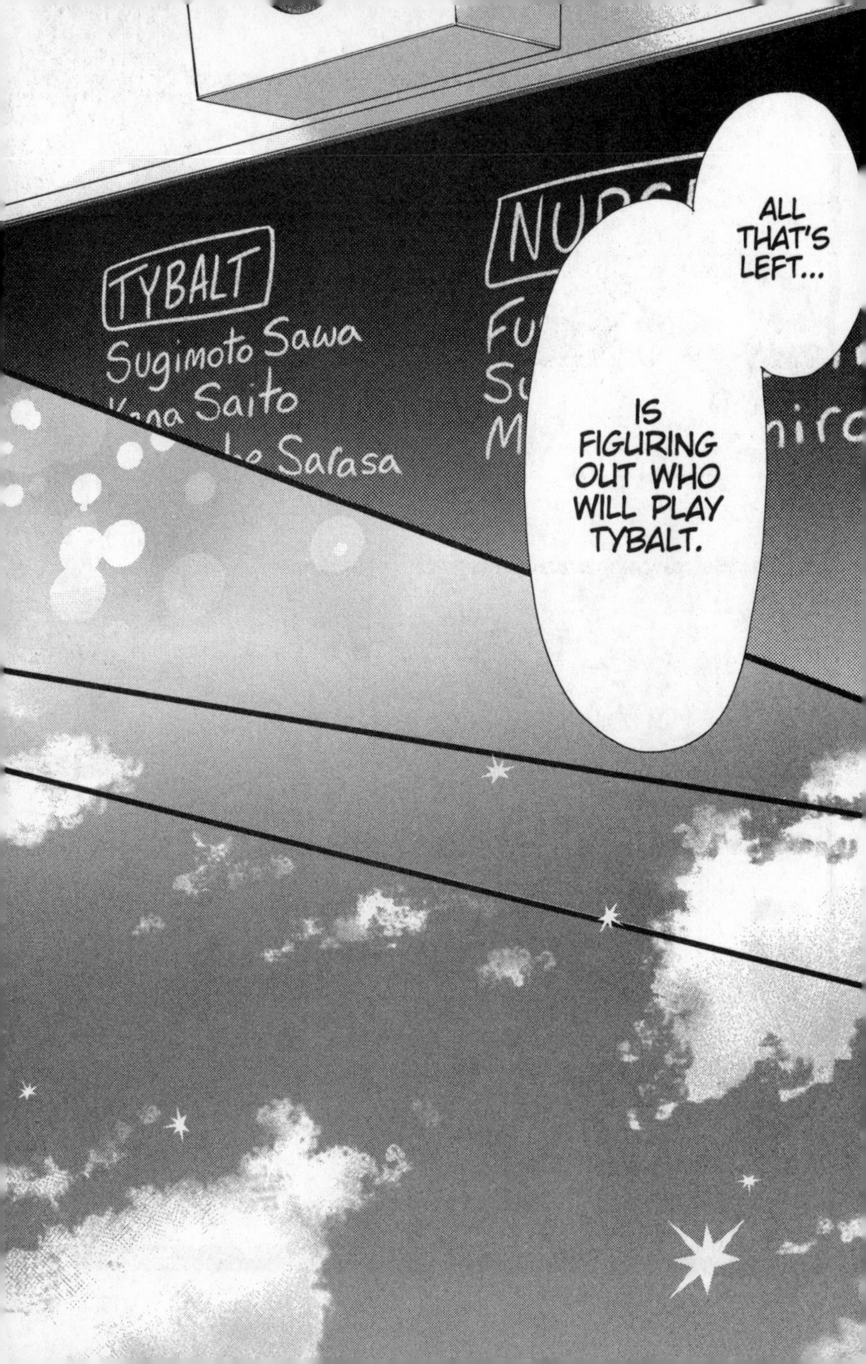
ALL THAT'S LEFT...
IS FIGURING OUT WHO WILL PLAY TYBALT.
TYBALT
Sugimoto Sawa

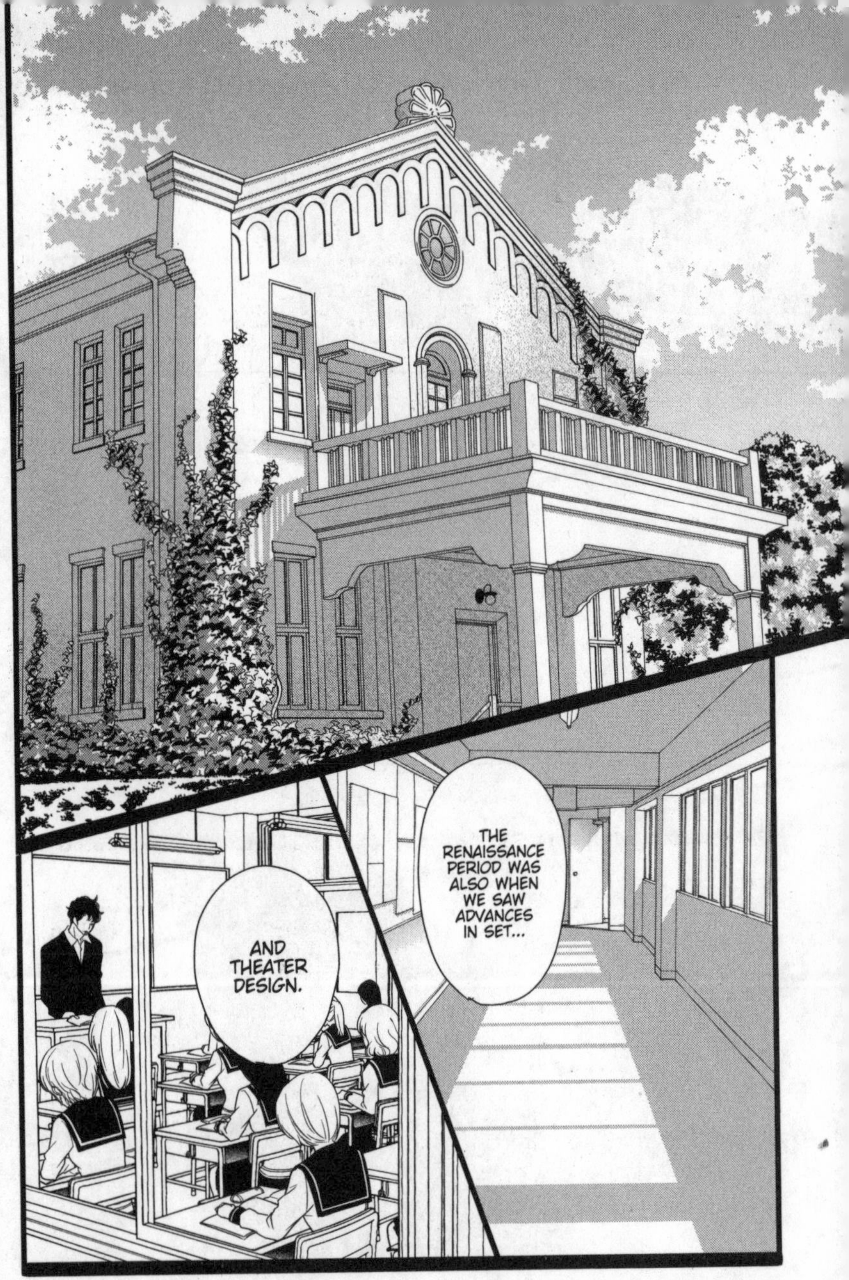
THE RENAISSANCE PERIOD WAS ALSO WHEN WE SAW ADVANCES IN SET...
AND THEATER DESIGN.

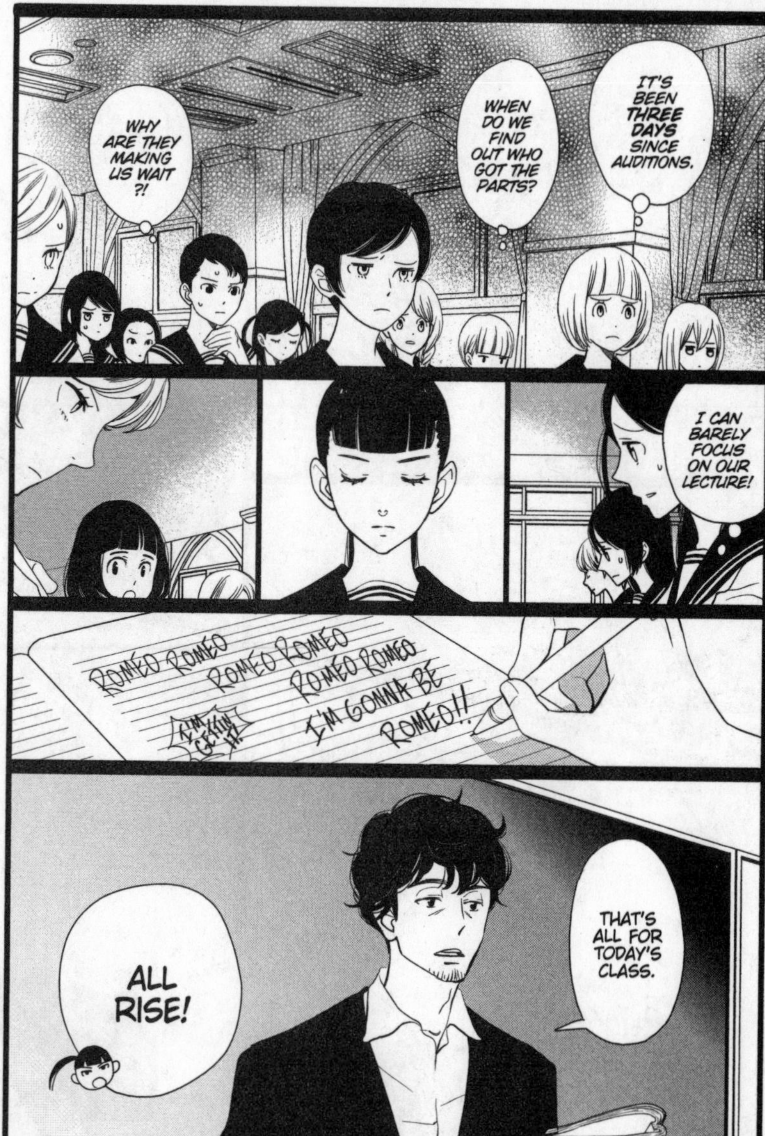
IT'S BEEN THREE DAYS SINCE AUDITIONS.
WHEN DO WE FIND OUT WHO GOT THE PARTS?
WHY ARE THEY MAKING US WAIT ?!
I CAN BARELY FOCUS ON OUR LECTURE!
ROMEO ROMEO ROMEO ROMEO ROMEO ROMEO
I'M GONNA BE ROMEO!!
I'M GETTIN IT!
THAT'S ALL FOR TODAY'S CLASS.
ALL RISE!

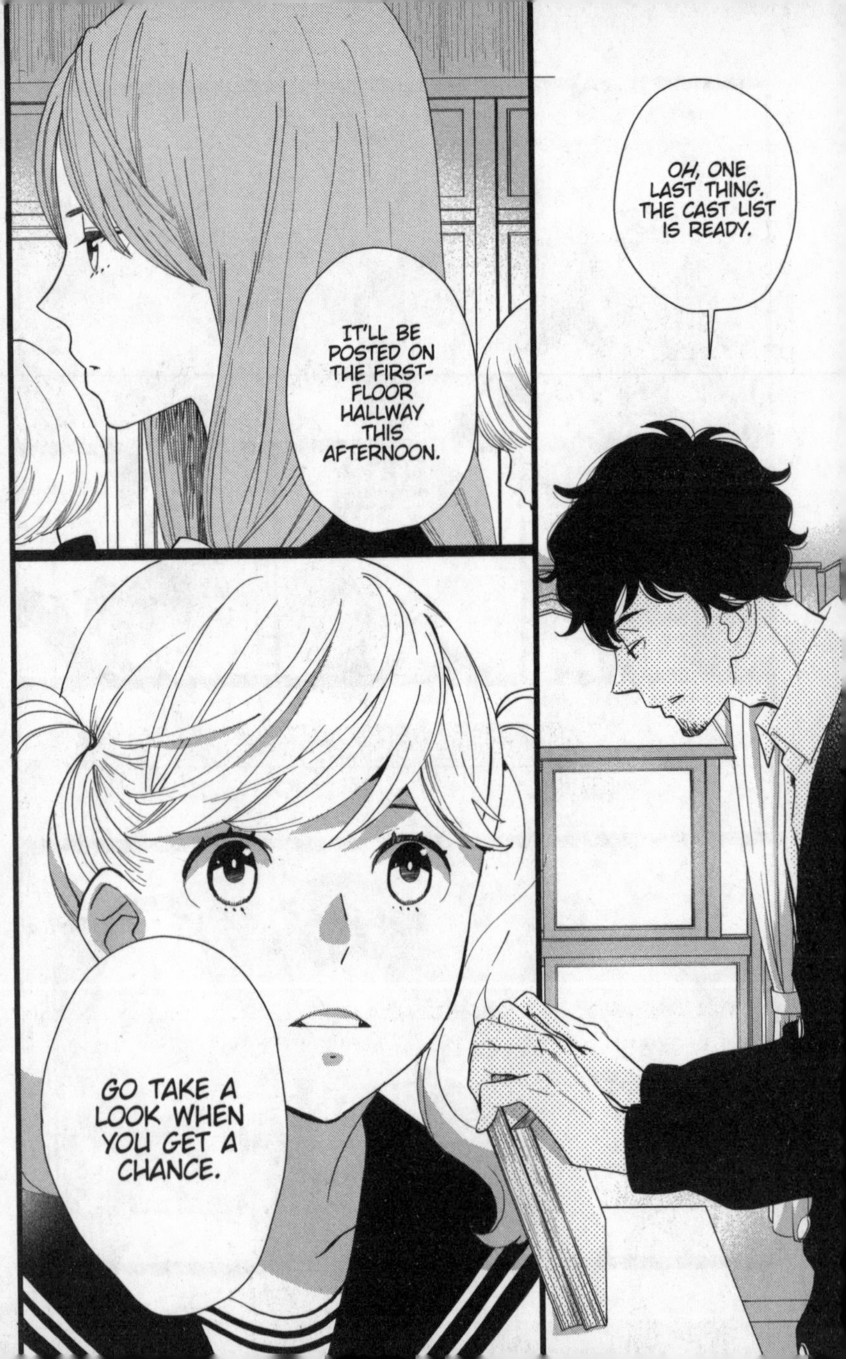
OH, ONE LAST THING. THE CAST LIST IS READY.
IT'LL BE POSTED ON THE FIRST-FLOOR HALLWAY THIS AFTERNOON.
GO TAKE A LOOK WHEN YOU GET A CHANCE.

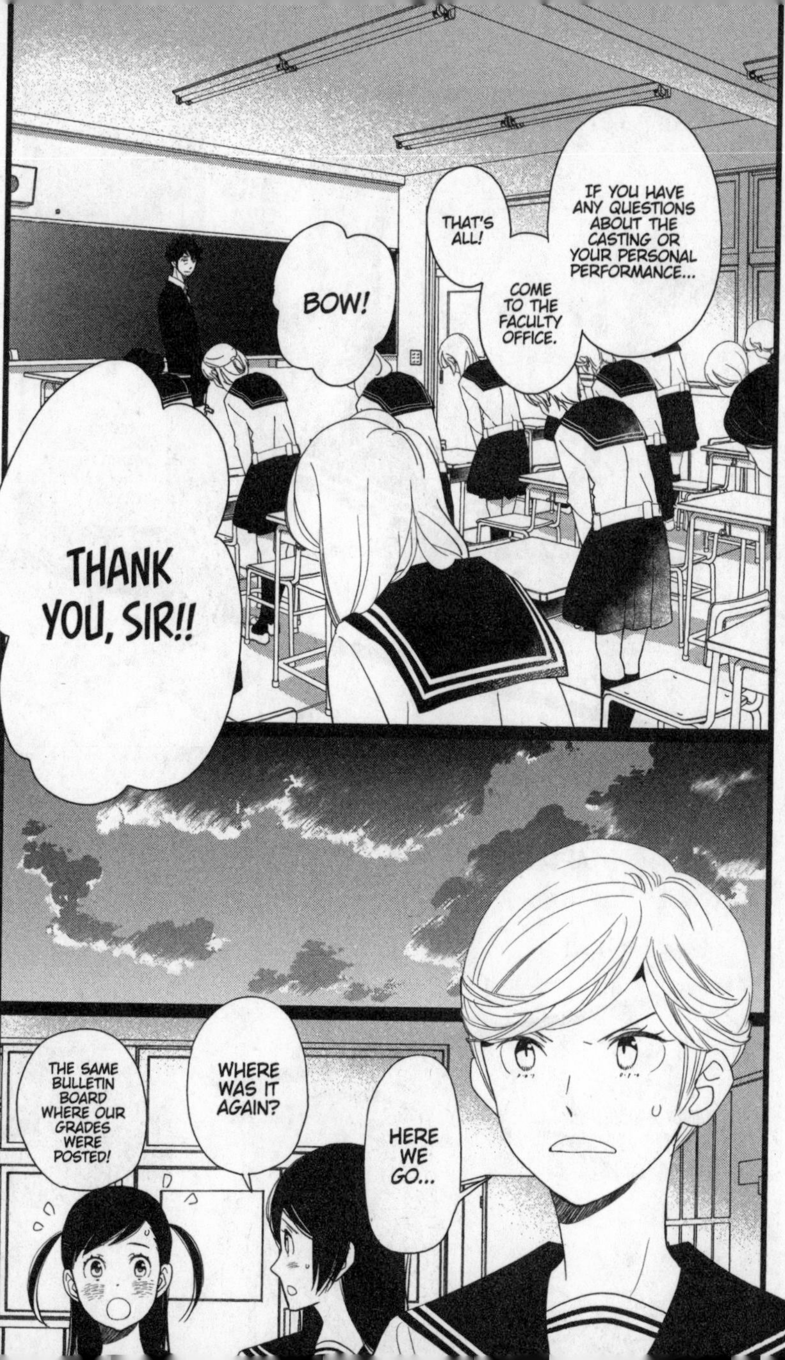
IF YOU HAVE ANY QUESTIONS ABOUT THE CASTING OR YOUR PERSONAL PERFORMANCE...
COME TO THE FACULTY OFFICE.
THAT'S ALL!
BOW!
THANK YOU, SIR!!
HERE WE GO...
WHERE WAS IT AGAIN?
THE SAME BULLETIN BOARD WHERE OUR GRADES WERE POSTED!

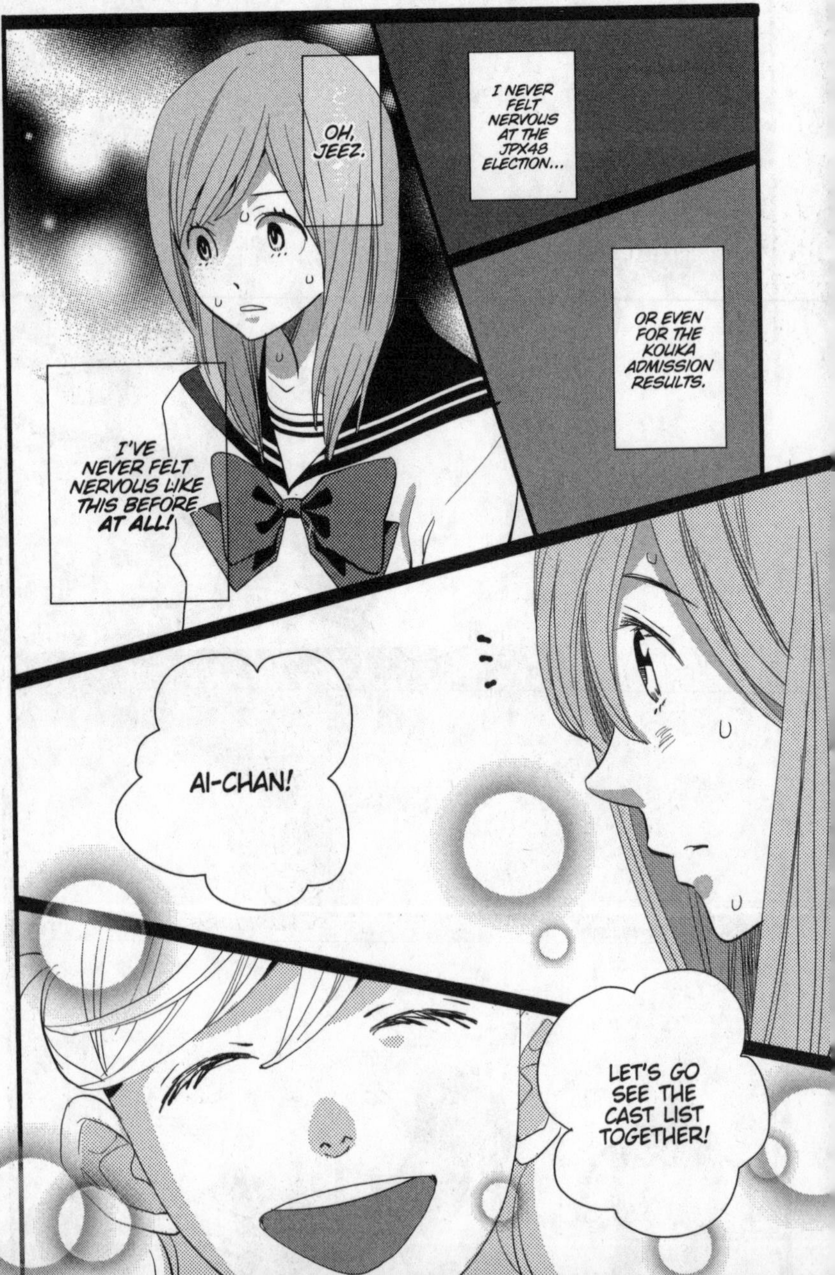
I NEVER FELT NERVOUS AT THE JPX48 ELECTION...
OR EVEN FOR THE KOUKA ADMISSION RESULTS.
OH, JEEZ.
I'VE NEVER FELT NERVOUS LIKE THIS BEFORE AT ALL!
...
AI-CHAN!
LET'S GO SEE THE CAST LIST TOGETHER!

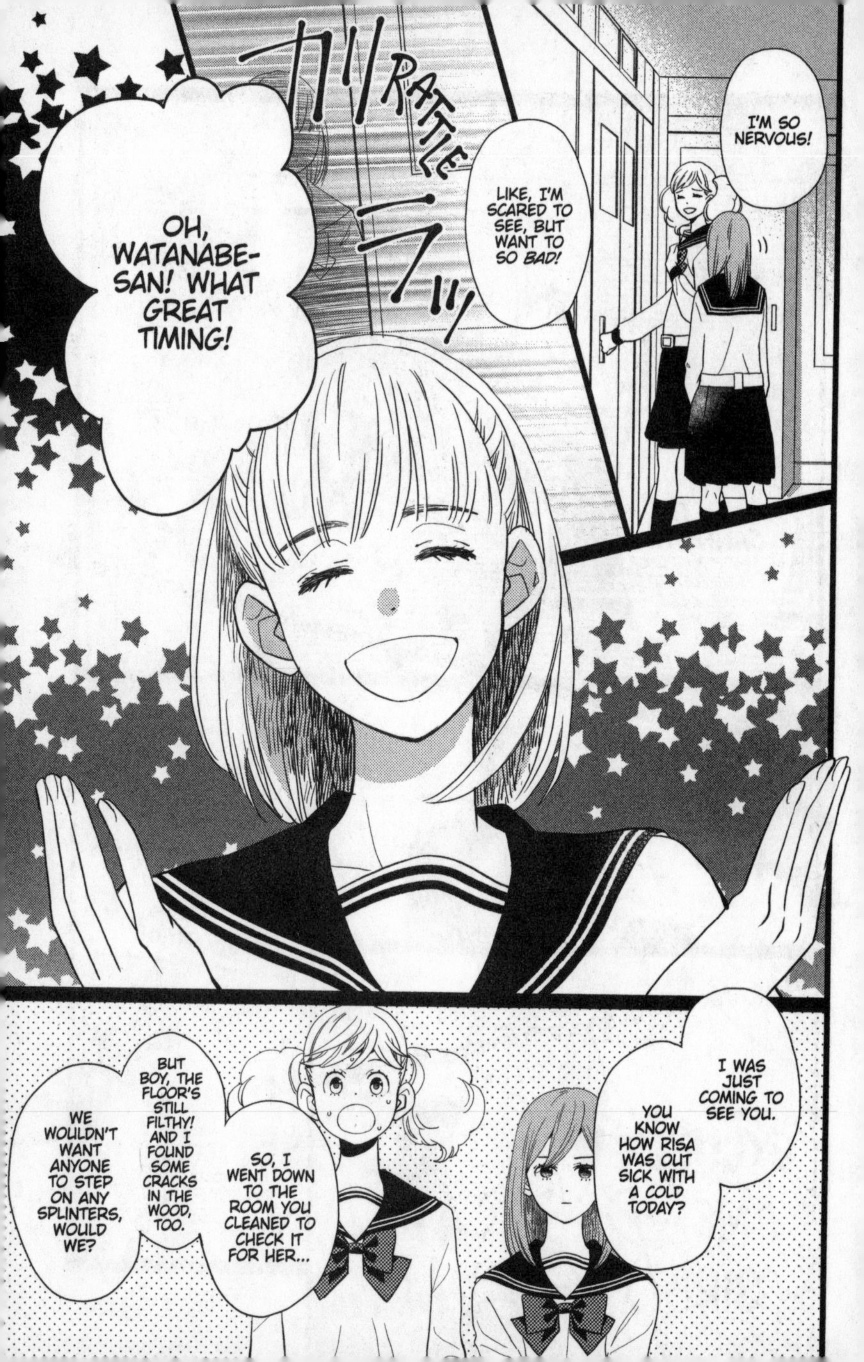
I'M SO NERVOUS!
LIKE, I'M SCARED TO SEE, BUT WANT TO SO *BAD!*
RATTLE
OH, WATANABE-SAN! WHAT GREAT TIMING!
I WAS JUST COMING TO SEE YOU.
YOU KNOW HOW RISA WAS OUT SICK WITH A COLD TODAY?
SO, I WENT DOWN TO THE ROOM YOU CLEANED TO CHECK IT FOR HER...
BUT BOY, THE FLOOR'S STILL FILTHY! AND I FOUND SOME CRACKS IN THE WOOD, TOO.
WE WOULDN'T WANT ANYONE TO STEP ON ANY SPLINTERS, WOULD WE?

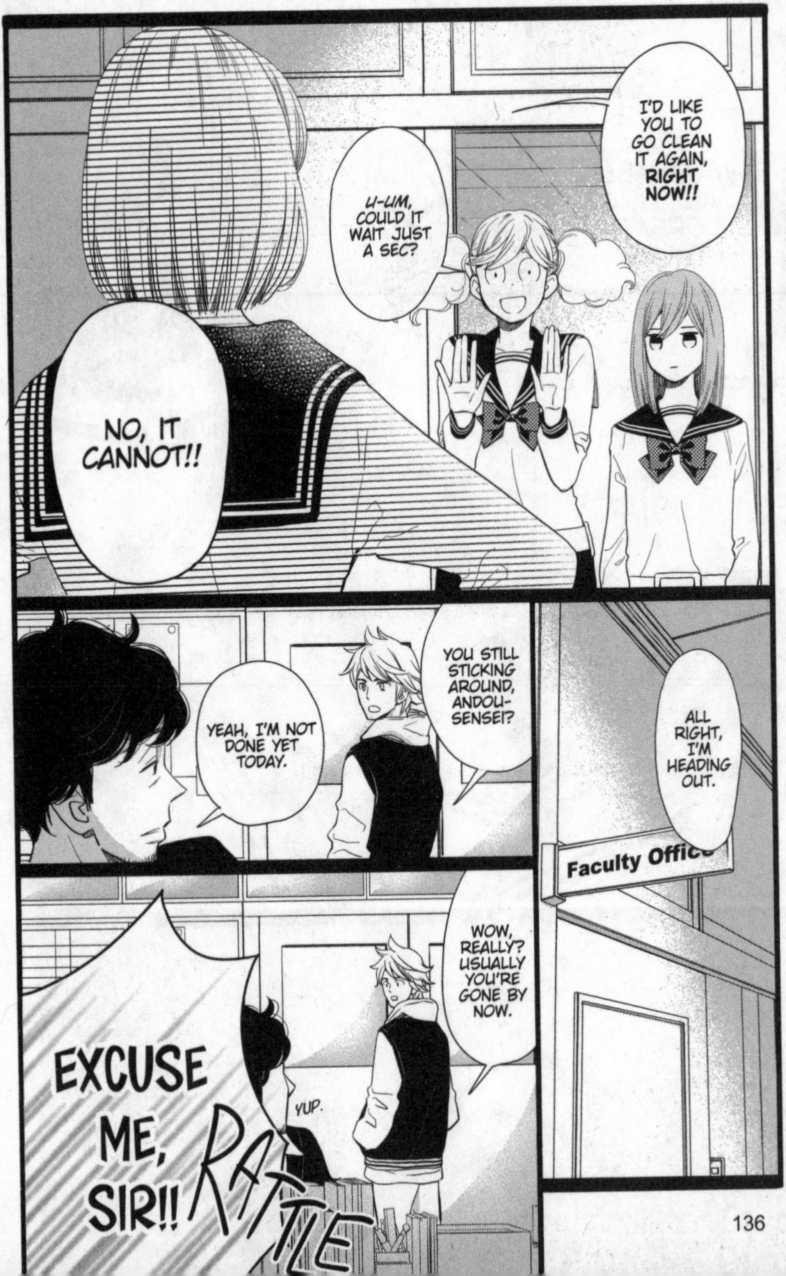
I'D LIKE YOU TO GO CLEAN IT AGAIN, RIGHT NOW!!
U-UM, COULD IT WAIT JUST A SEC?
NO, IT CANNOT!!
ALL RIGHT, I'M HEADING OUT.
Faculty Office
YOU STILL STICKING AROUND, ANDOU-SENSEI?
YEAH, I'M NOT DONE YET TODAY.
WOW, REALLY? USUALLY YOU'RE GONE BY NOW.
YUP.
EXCUSE ME, SIR!!
RATTLE

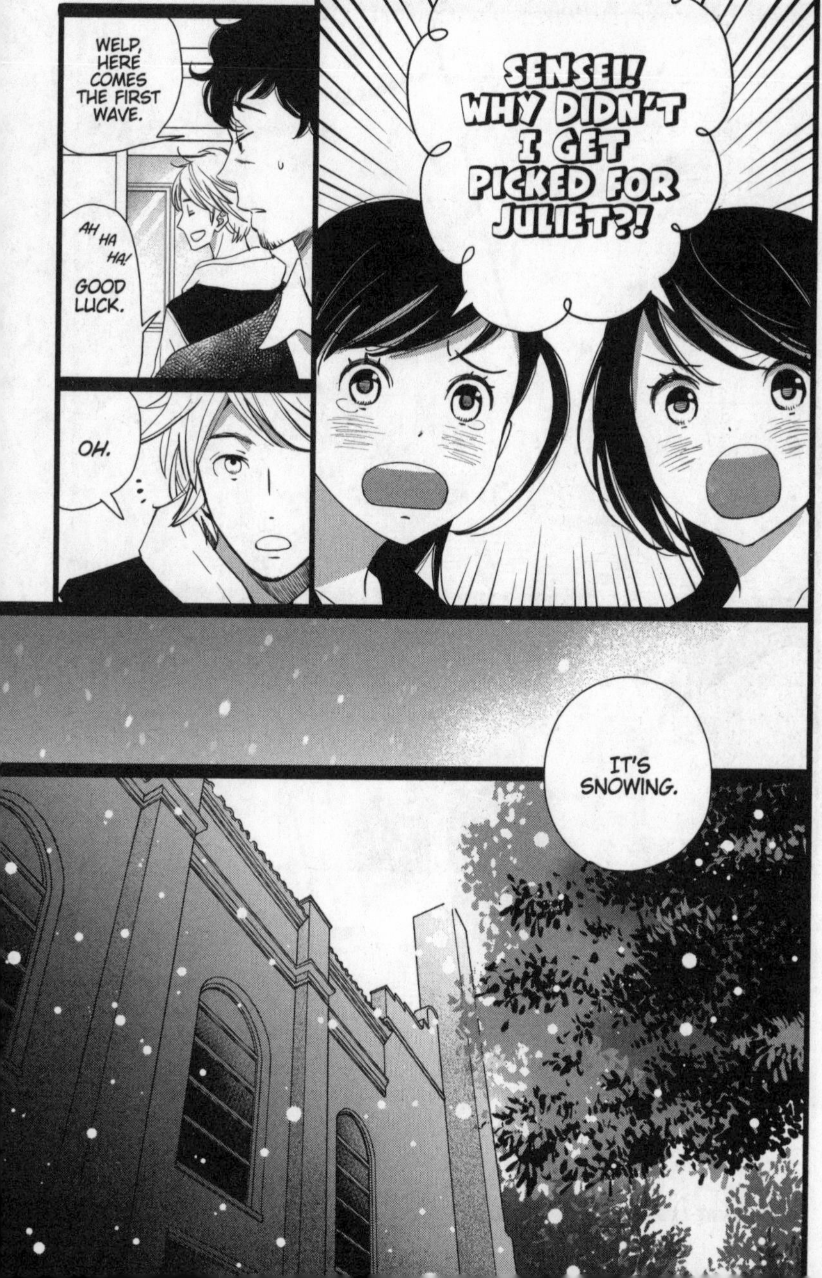
SENSEI! WHY DIDN'T I GET PICKED FOR JULIET?!
WELP, HERE COMES THE FIRST WAVE.
AH HA HA!
GOOD LUCK.
OH.
IT'S SNOWING.

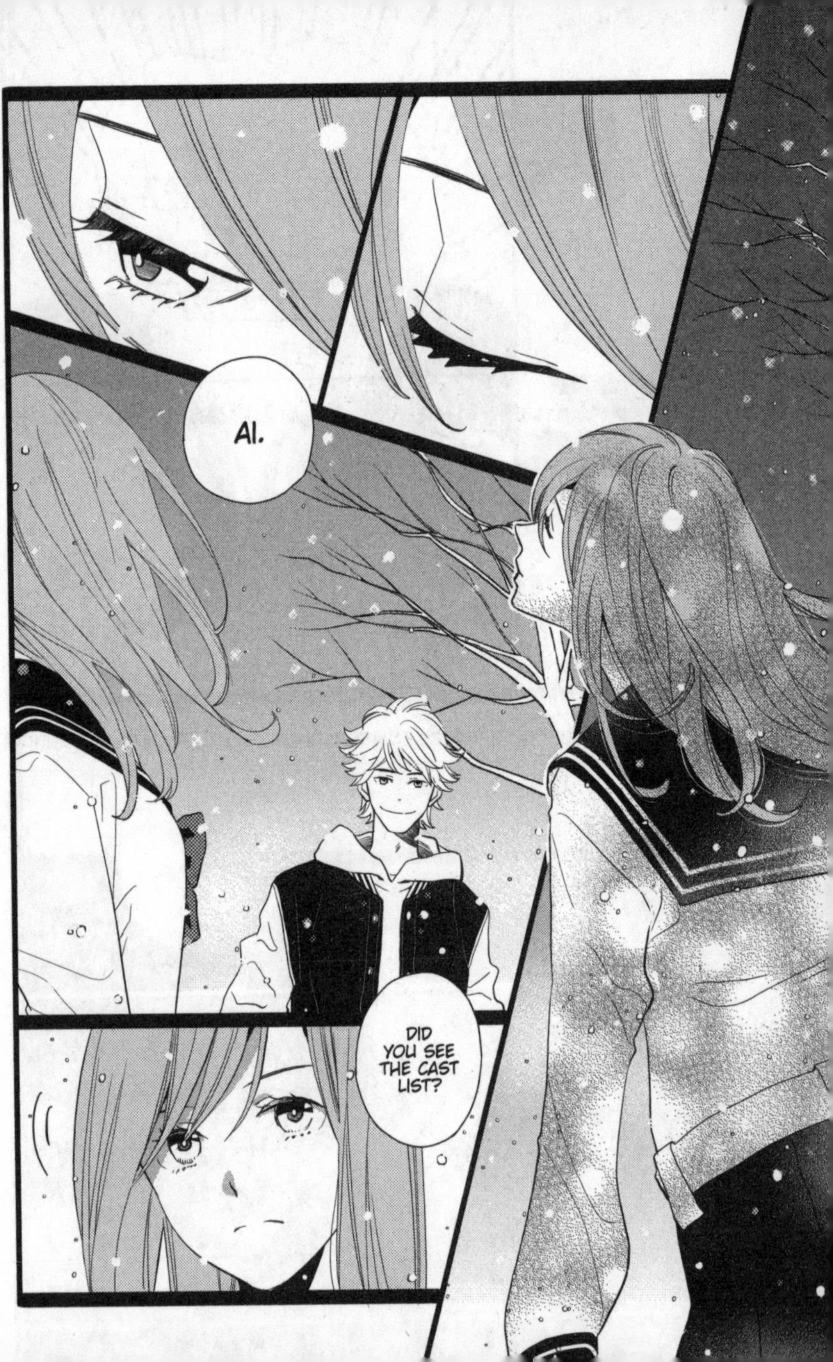
AI.
DID YOU SEE THE CAST LIST?

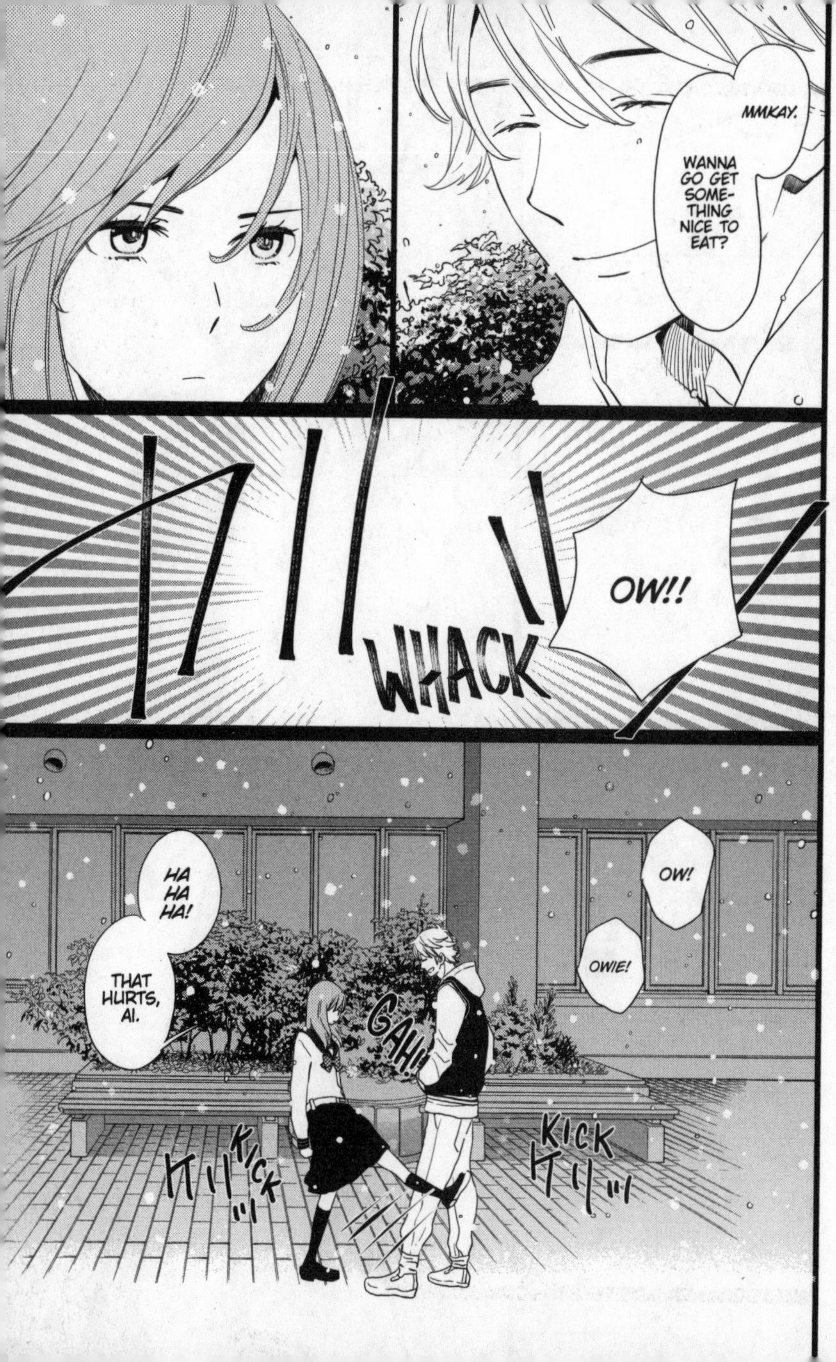
MMKAY.
WANNA GO GET SOME-THING NICE TO EAT?
OW!!
WHACK
OW!
OWIE!
KICK
GAH!!
KICK
HA HA HA!
THAT HURTS, AI.

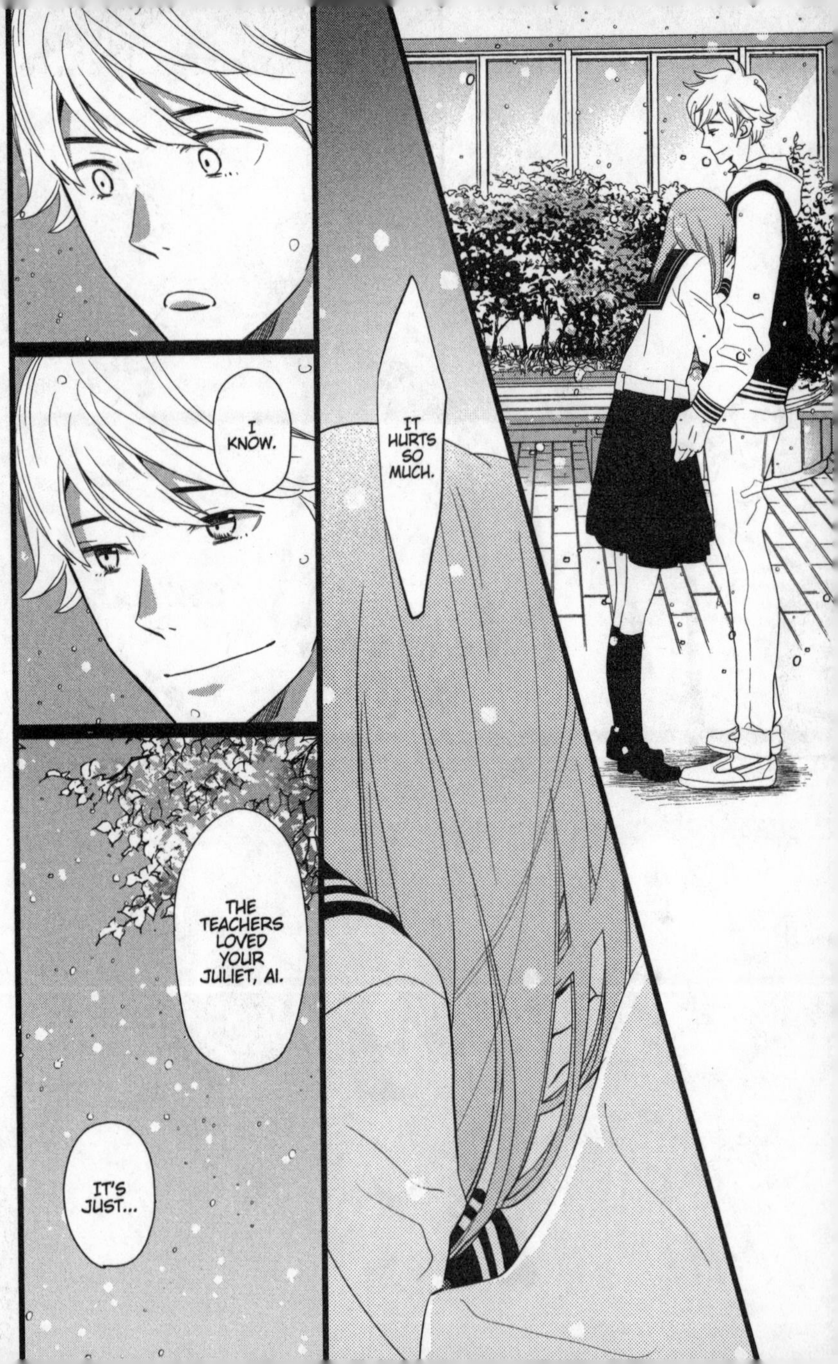
IT HURTS SO MUCH.
I KNOW.
THE TEACHERS LOVED YOUR JULIET, AI.
IT'S JUST...

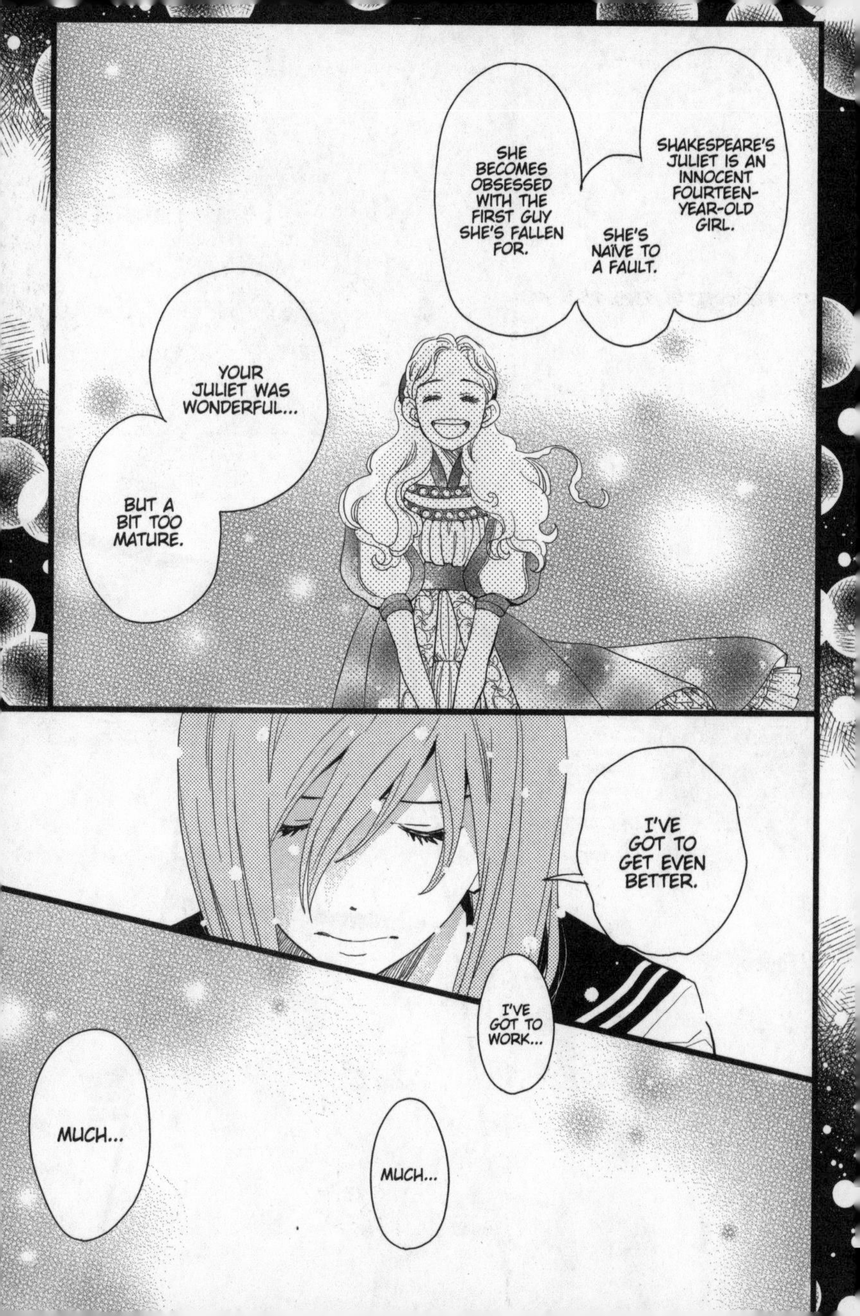
SHAKESPEARE'S JULIET IS AN INNOCENT FOURTEEN-YEAR-OLD GIRL.
SHE'S NAÏVE TO A FAULT.
SHE BECOMES OBSESSED WITH THE FIRST GUY SHE'S FALLEN FOR.
YOUR JULIET WAS WONDERFUL...
BUT A BIT TOO MATURE.
I'VE GOT TO GET EVEN BETTER.
I'VE GOT TO WORK...
MUCH...
MUCH...

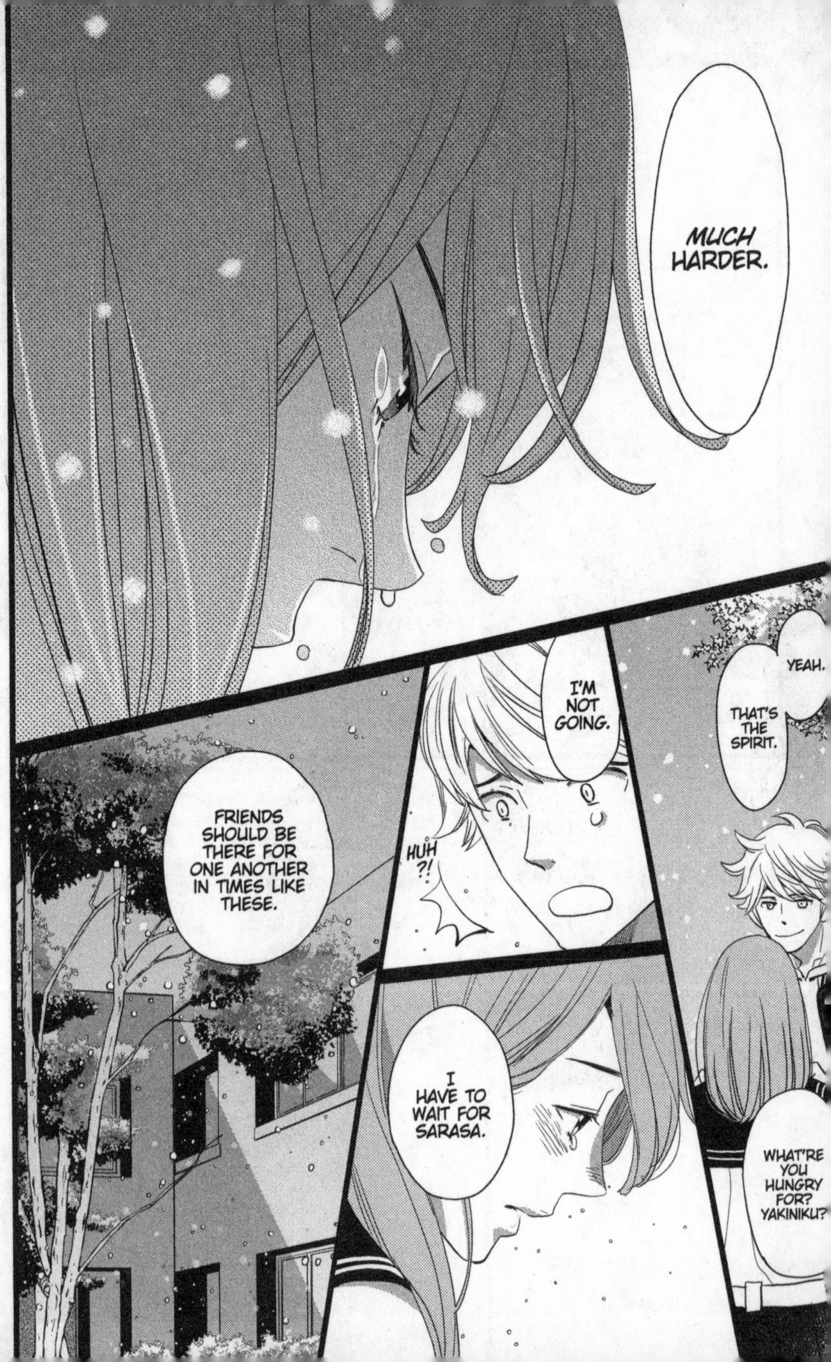
MUCH HARDER.
YEAH.
THAT'S THE SPIRIT.
WHAT'RE YOU HUNGRY FOR? YAKINIKU?
I'M NOT GOING.
HUH?!
I HAVE TO WAIT FOR SARASA.
FRIENDS SHOULD BE THERE FOR ONE ANOTHER IN TIMES LIKE THESE.

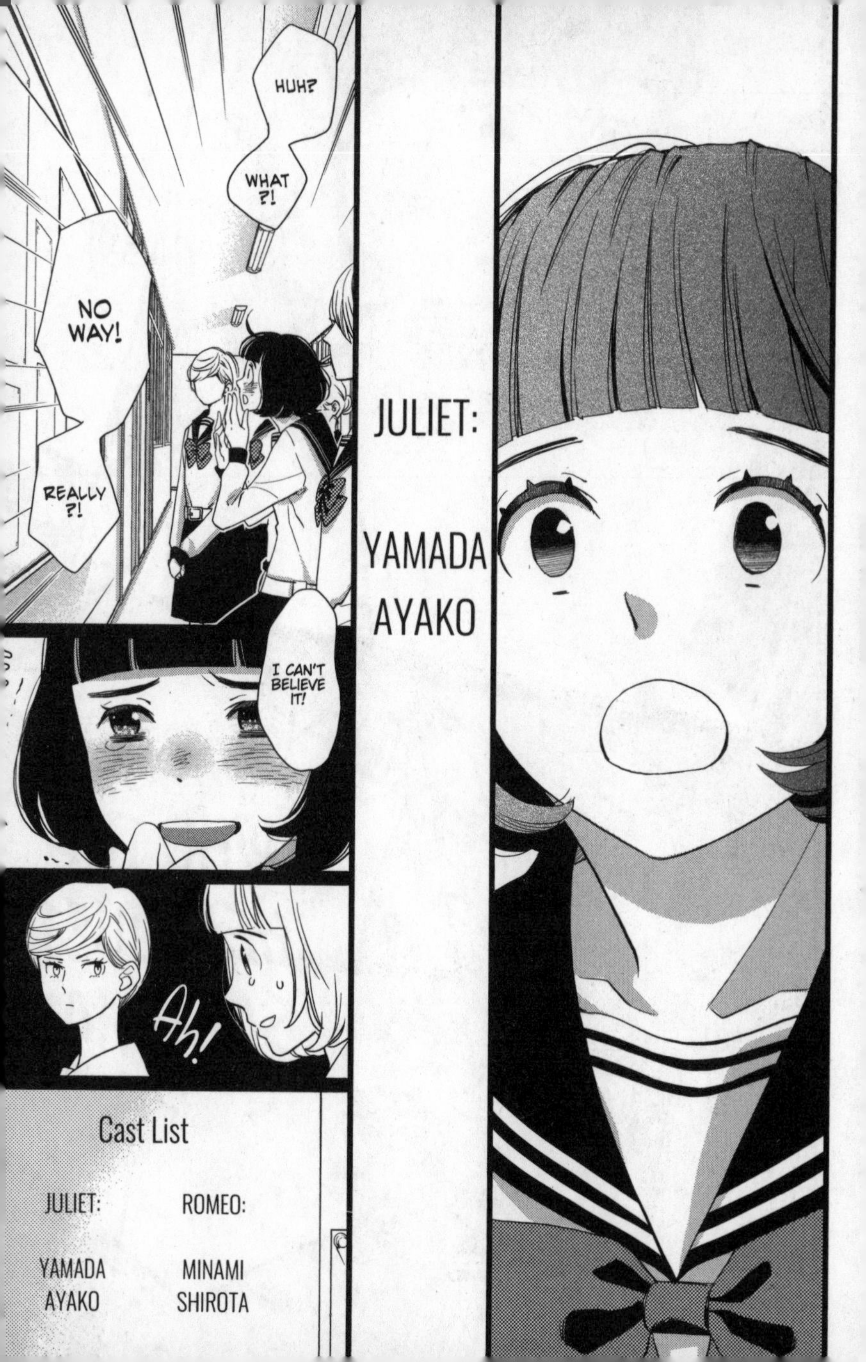
JULIET:
YAMADA AYAKO
HUH?
WHAT?!
NO WAY!
REALLY?!
I CAN'T BELIEVE IT!
Ah!
Cast List
JULIET:
YAMADA AYAKO
ROMEO:
MINAMI SHIROTA

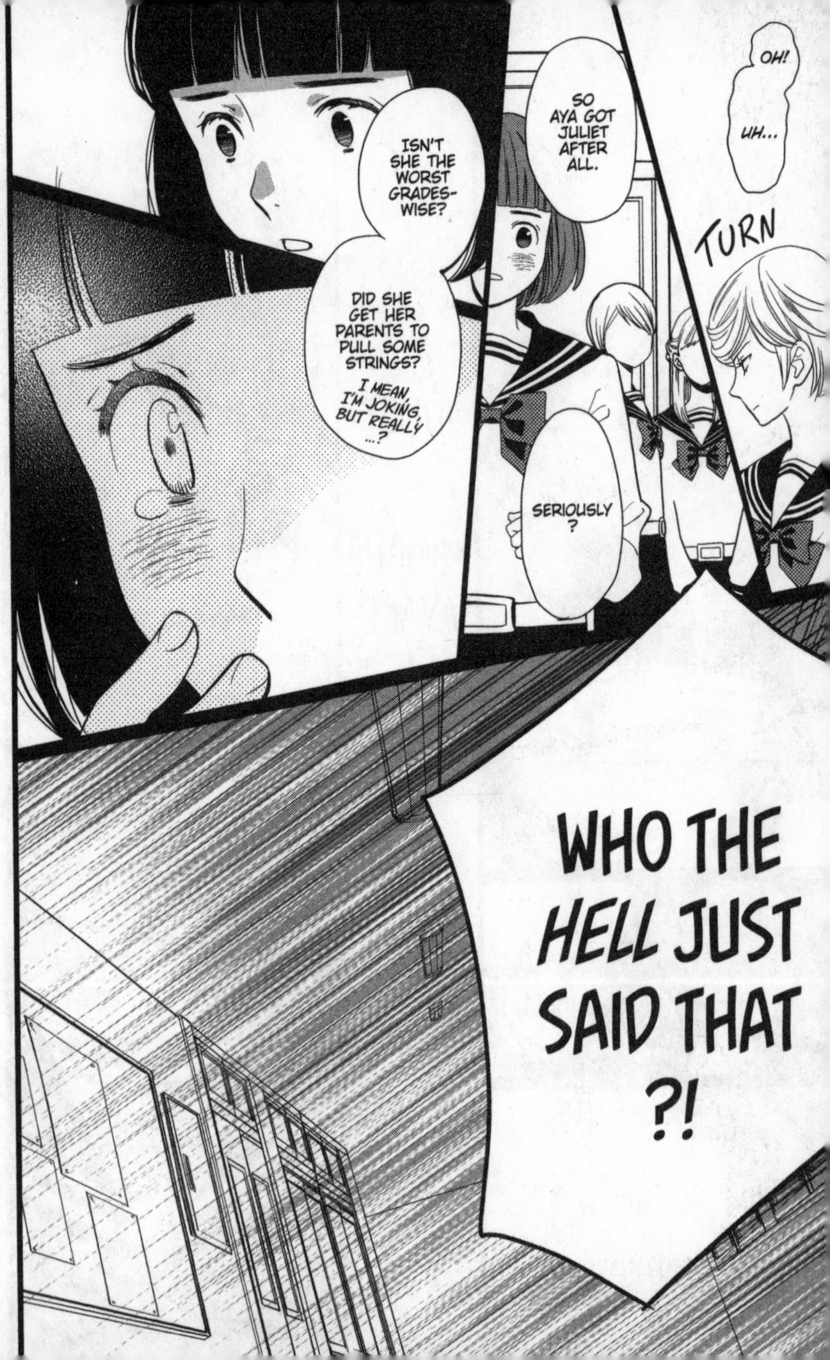
OH!
UH...
TURN
SO AYA GOT JULIET AFTER ALL.
SERIOUSLY?
ISN'T SHE THE WORST GRADES-WISE?
DID SHE GET HER PARENTS TO PULL SOME STRINGS?
I MEAN, I'M JOKING, BUT REALLY ...?
WHO THE *HELL* JUST SAID THAT?!

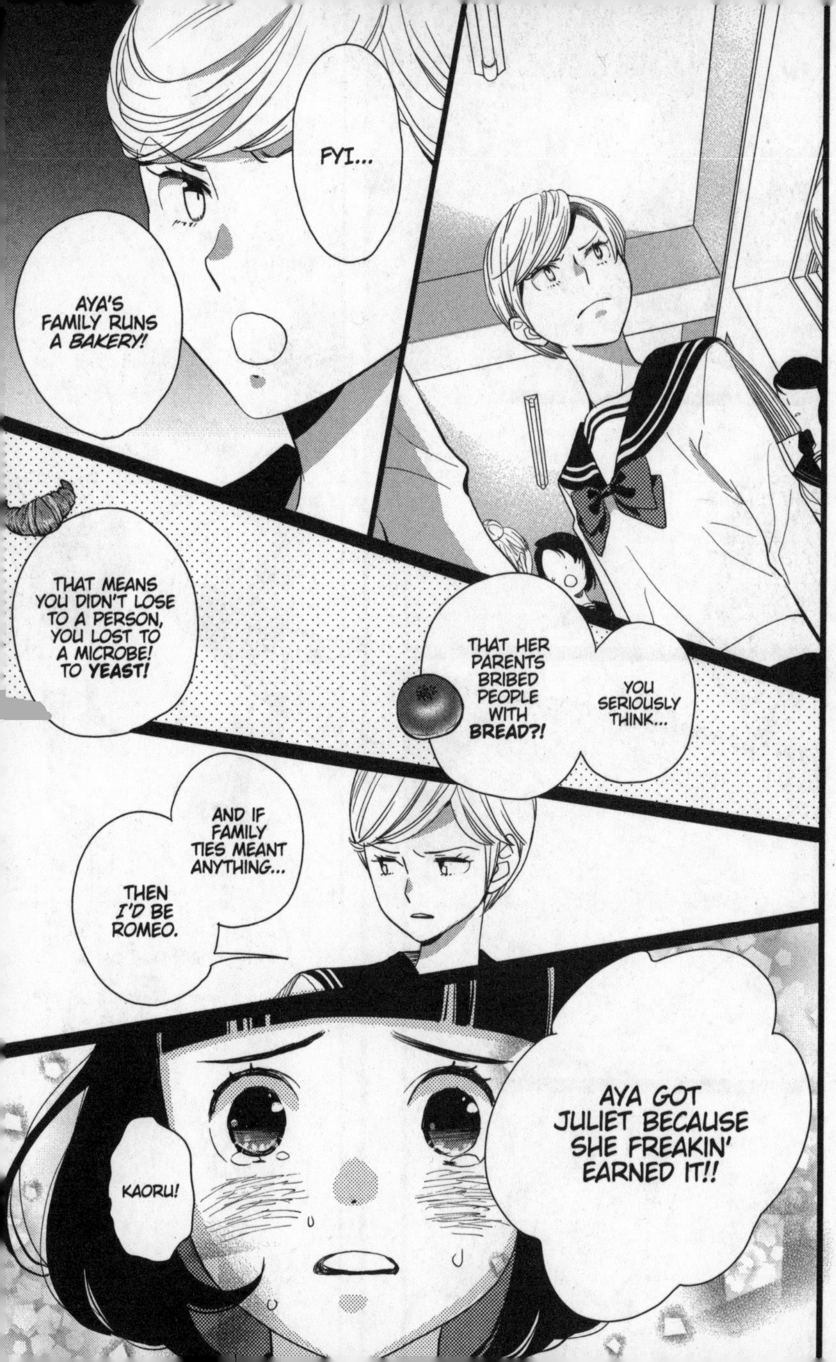
FYI...
AYA'S FAMILY RUNS A *BAKERY!*
YOU SERIOUSLY THINK...
THAT HER PARENTS BRIBED PEOPLE WITH **BREAD?!**
THAT MEANS YOU DIDN'T LOSE TO A PERSON, YOU LOST TO A MICROBE! TO **YEAST!**
AND IF FAMILY TIES MEANT ANYTHING...
THEN *I'D* BE ROMEO.
AYA GOT JULIET BECAUSE SHE FREAKIN' EARNED IT!!
KAORU!

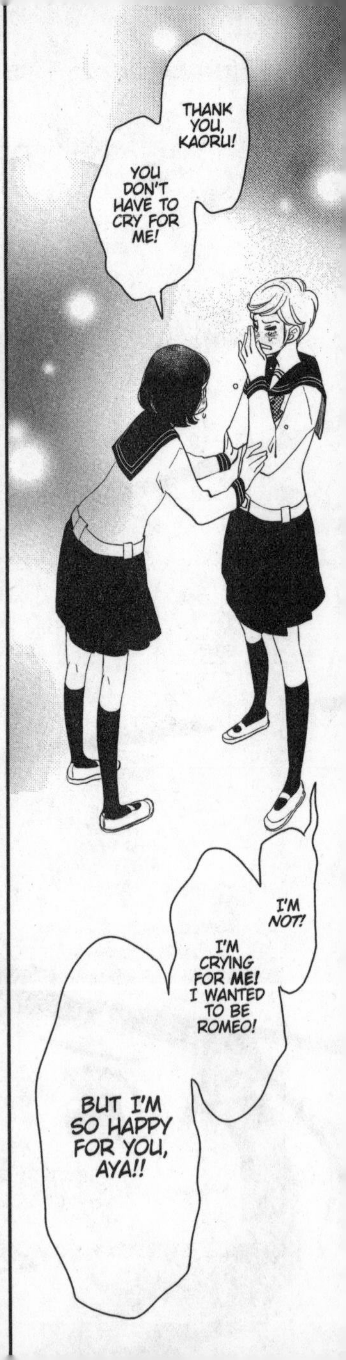
THANK YOU, KAORU!
YOU DON'T HAVE TO CRY FOR ME!
I'M NOT!
I'M CRYING FOR ME! I WANTED TO BE ROMEO!
BUT I'M SO HAPPY FOR YOU, AYA!!
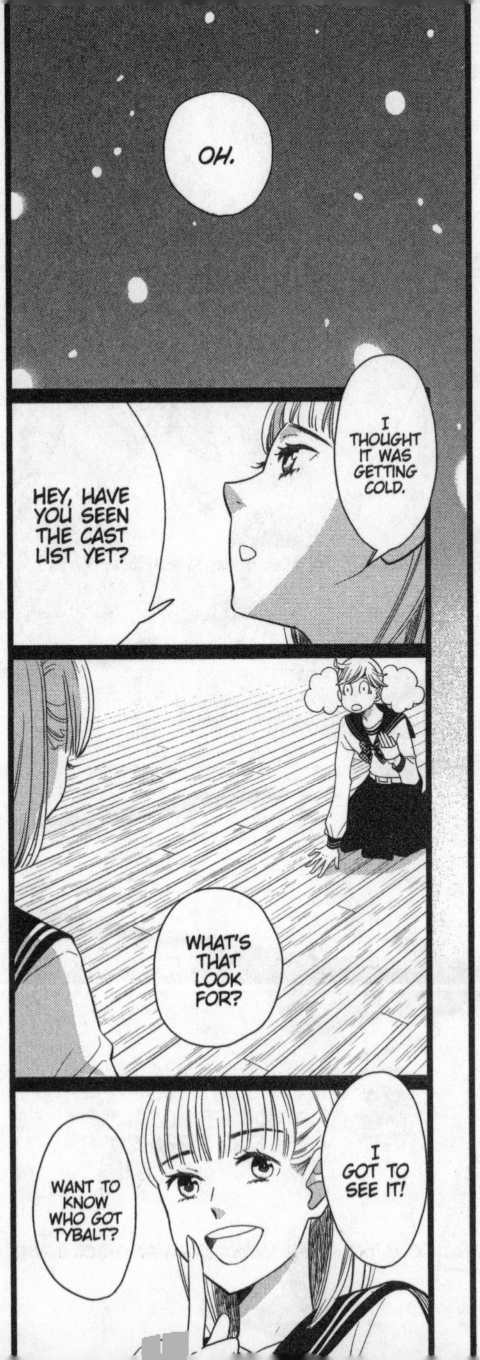
OH.
I THOUGHT IT WAS GETTING COLD.
HEY, HAVE YOU SEEN THE CAST LIST YET?
WHAT'S THAT LOOK FOR?
I GOT TO SEE IT!
WANT TO KNOW WHO GOT TYBALT?

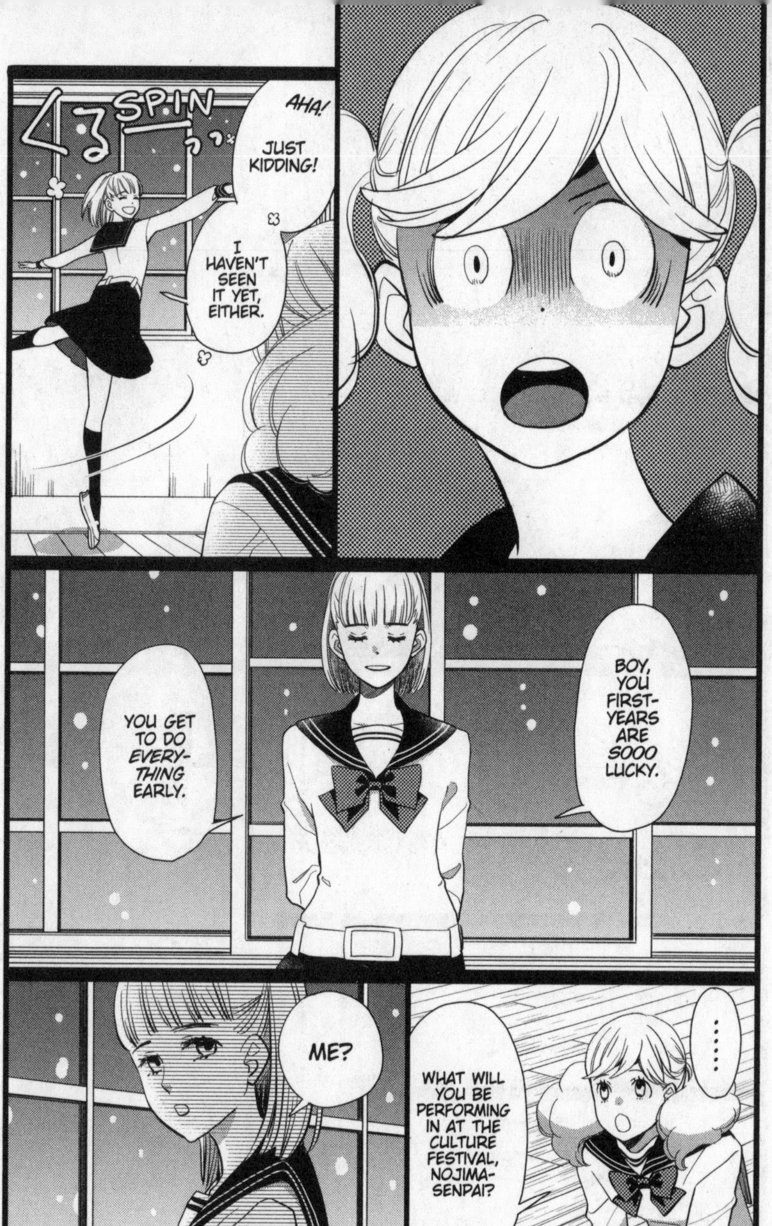
くる SPIN
AHA!
JUST KIDDING!
I HAVEN'T SEEN IT YET, EITHER.
BOY, YOU FIRST-YEARS ARE *SOOO* LUCKY.
YOU GET TO DO *EVERYTHING* EARLY.
......
WHAT WILL YOU BE PERFORMING IN AT THE CULTURE FESTIVAL, NOJIMA-SENPAI?
ME?

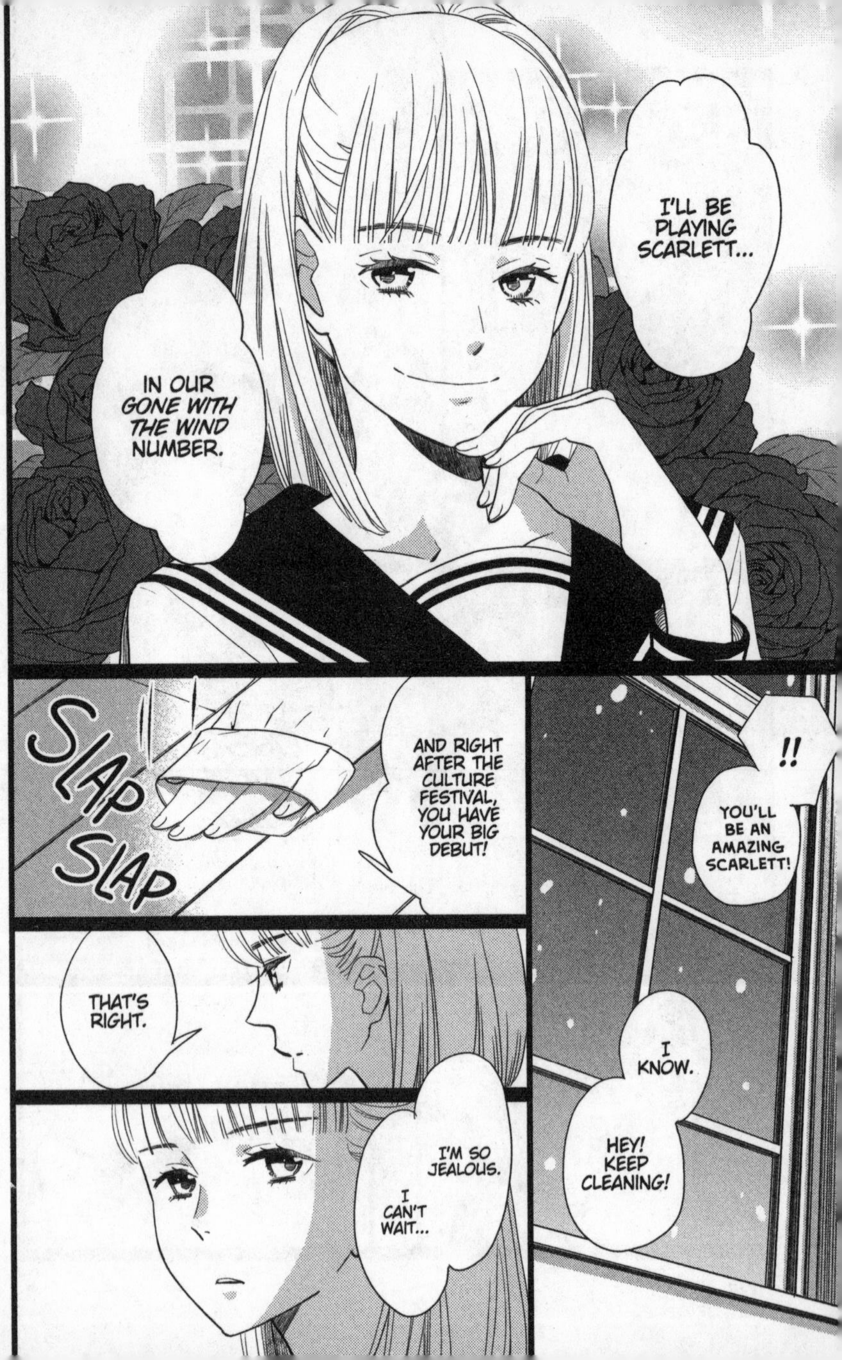
I'LL BE PLAYING SCARLETT...
IN OUR *GONE WITH THE WIND* NUMBER.
!!
YOU'LL BE AN AMAZING SCARLETT!
I KNOW.
HEY! KEEP CLEANING!
SLAP SLAP
AND RIGHT AFTER THE CULTURE FESTIVAL, YOU HAVE YOUR BIG DEBUT!
THAT'S RIGHT.
I'M SO JEALOUS.
I CAN'T WAIT...

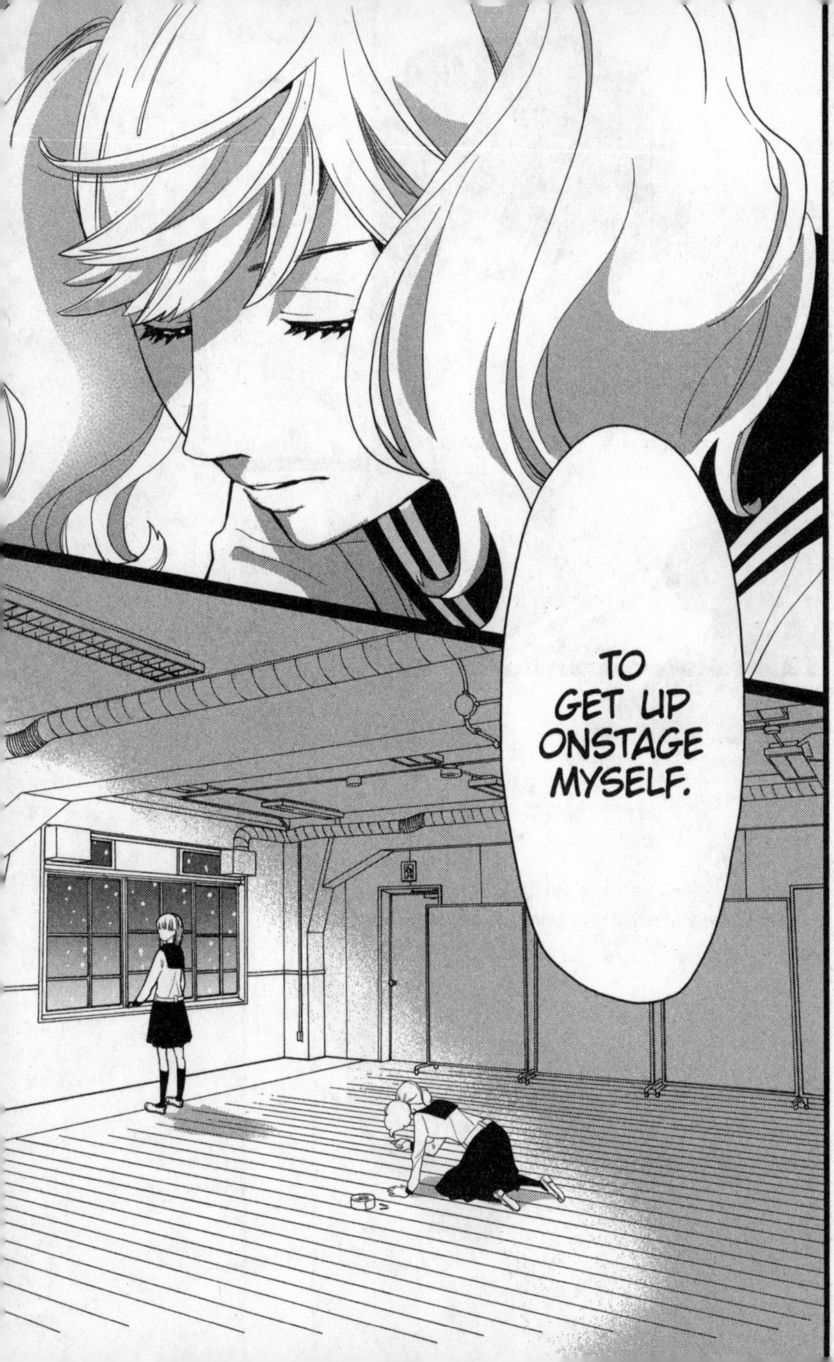
TO GET UP ONSTAGE MYSELF.

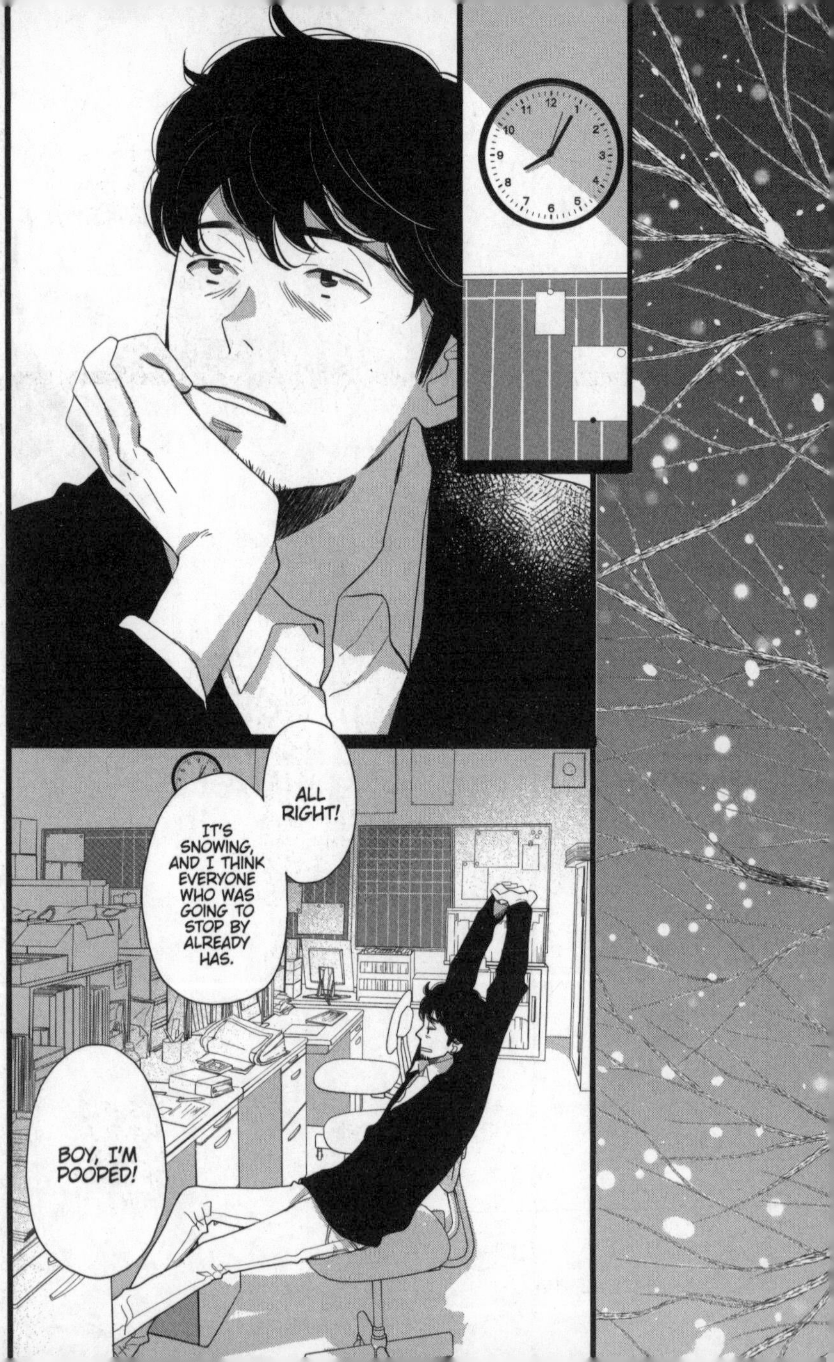
ALL RIGHT!
IT'S SNOWING, AND I THINK EVERYONE WHO WAS GOING TO STOP BY ALREADY HAS.
BOY, I'M POOPED!

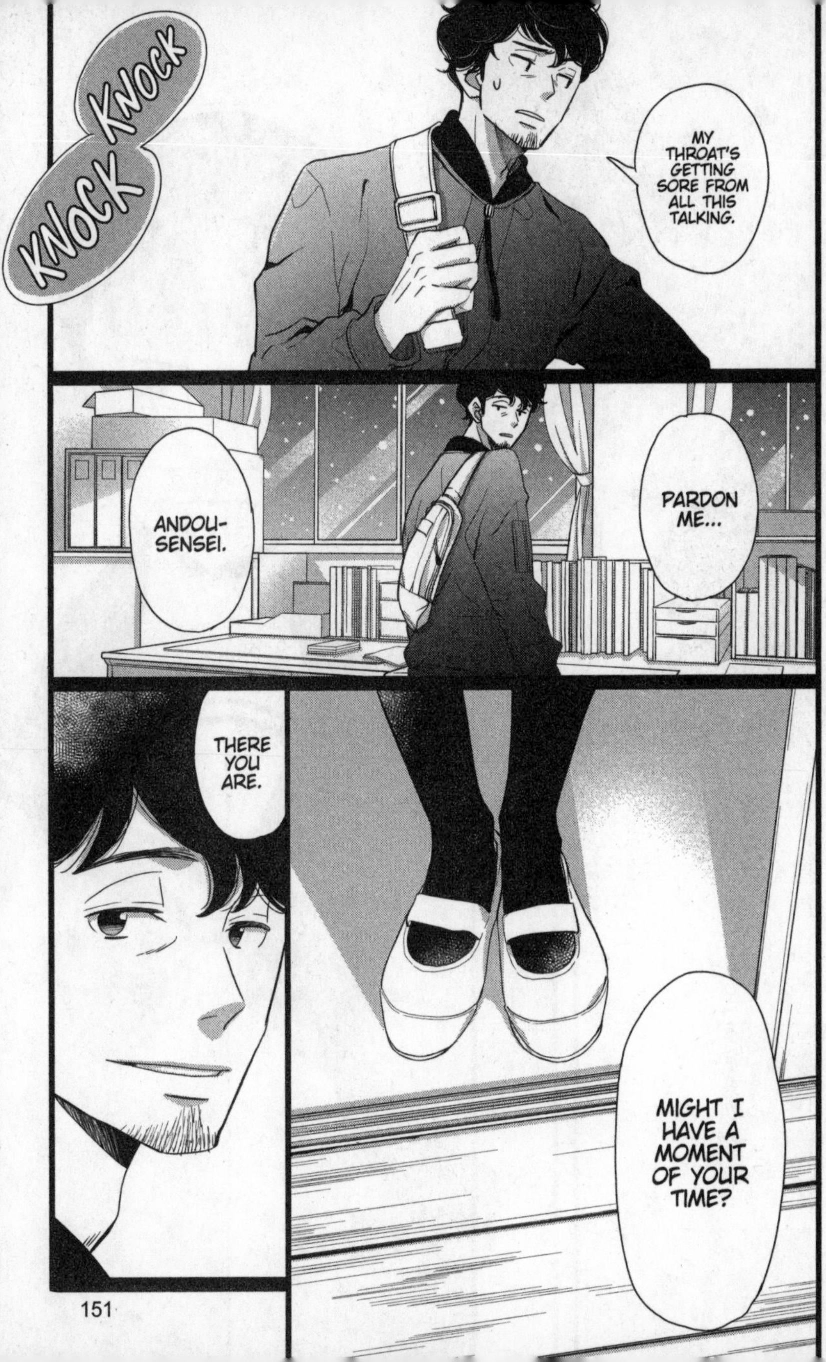
MY THROAT'S GETTING SORE FROM ALL THIS TALKING.
KNOCK KNOCK
PARDON ME...
ANDOU-SENSEI.
THERE YOU ARE.
MIGHT I HAVE A MOMENT OF YOUR TIME?

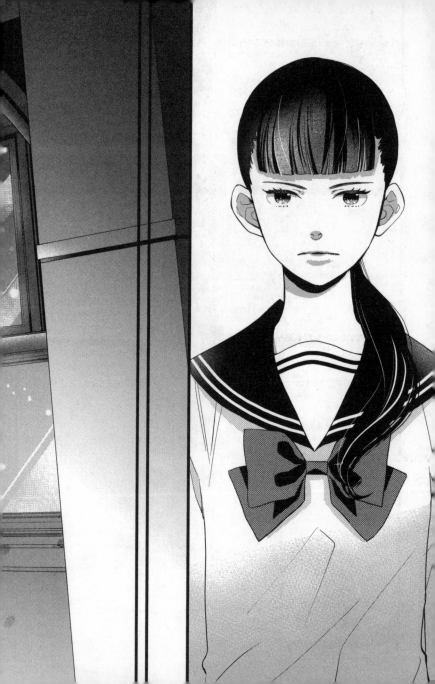

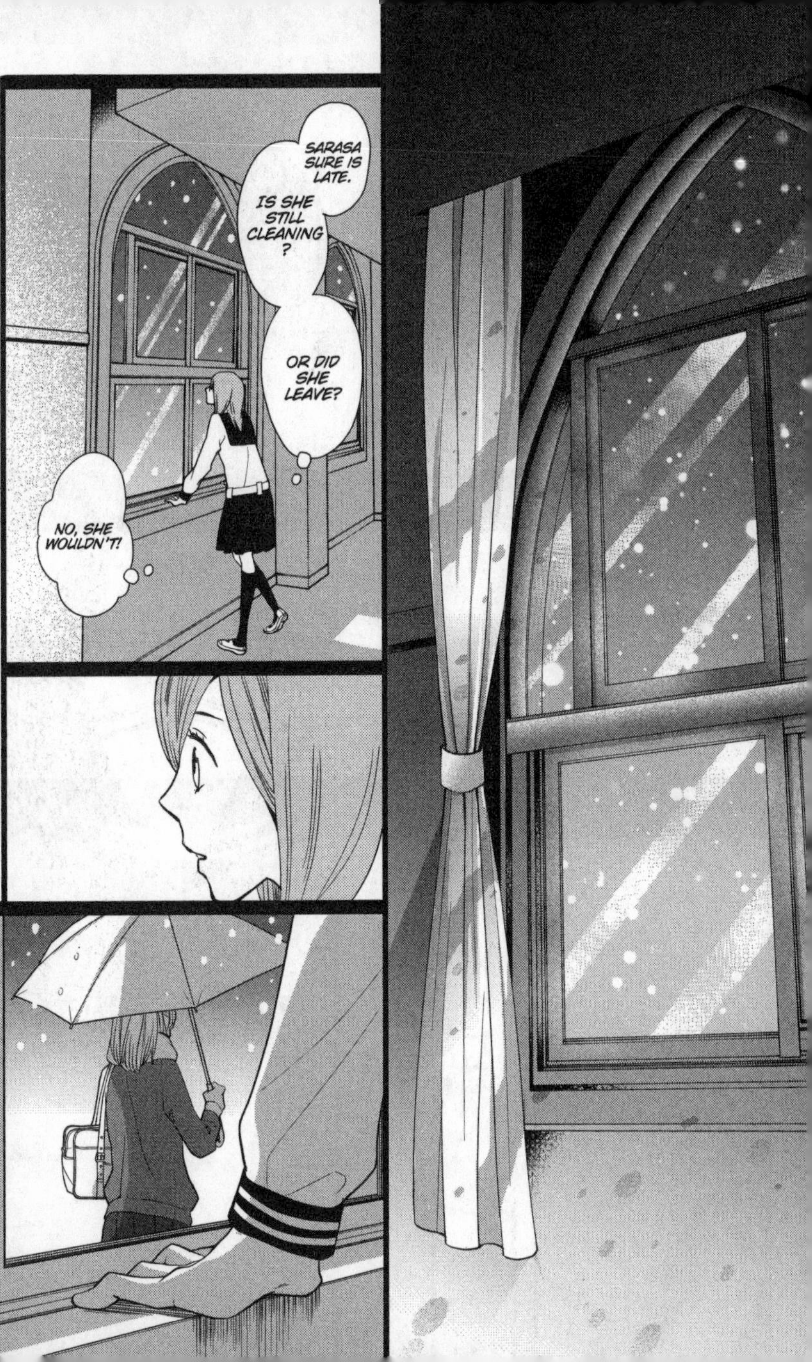
SARASA SURE IS LATE.
IS SHE STILL CLEANING?
OR DID SHE LEAVE?
NO, SHE WOULDN'T!

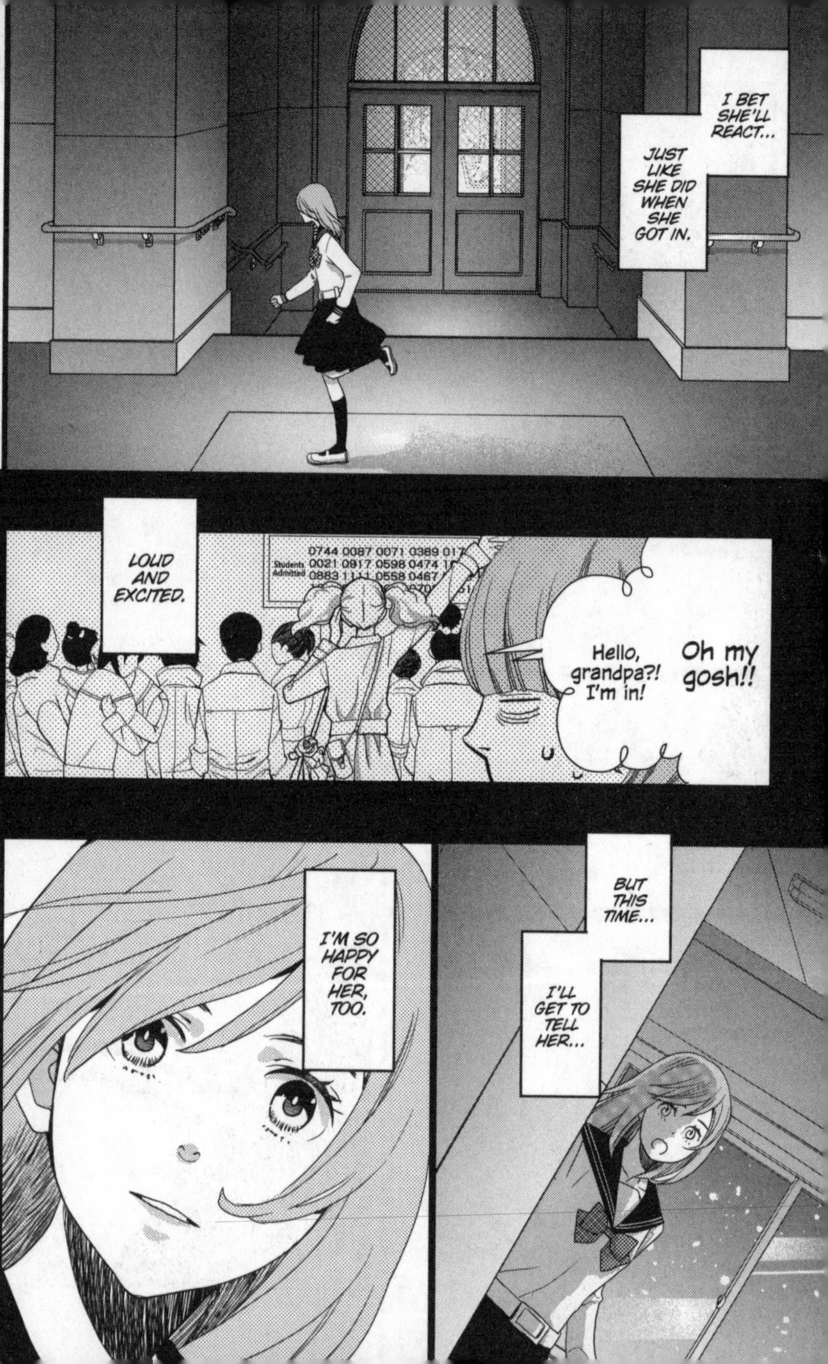
I BET SHE'LL REACT...
JUST LIKE SHE DID WHEN SHE GOT IN.
LOUD AND EXCITED.
Students Admitted
Hello, grandpa?! I'm in! Oh my gosh!!
BUT THIS TIME...
I'LL GET TO TELL HER...
I'M SO HAPPY FOR HER, TOO.

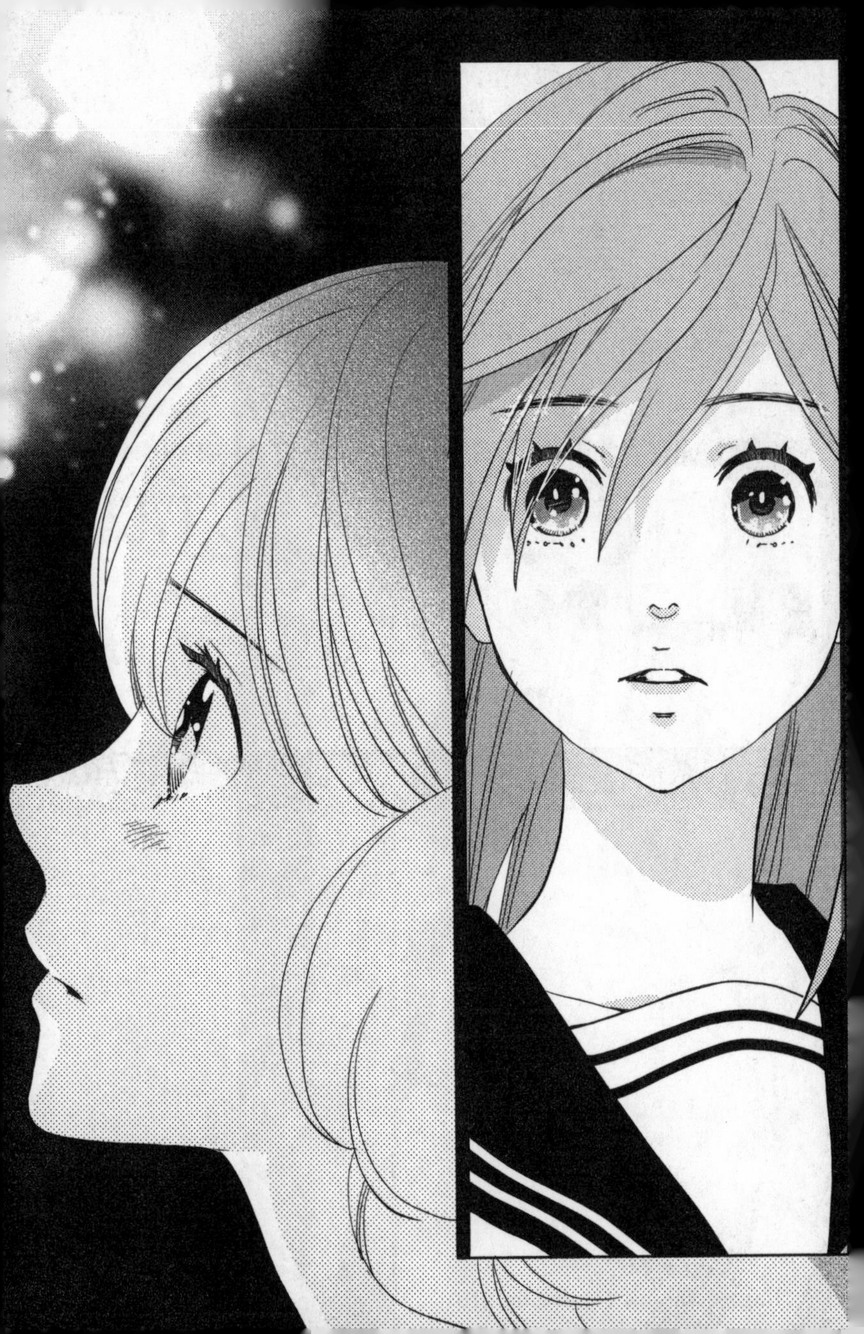

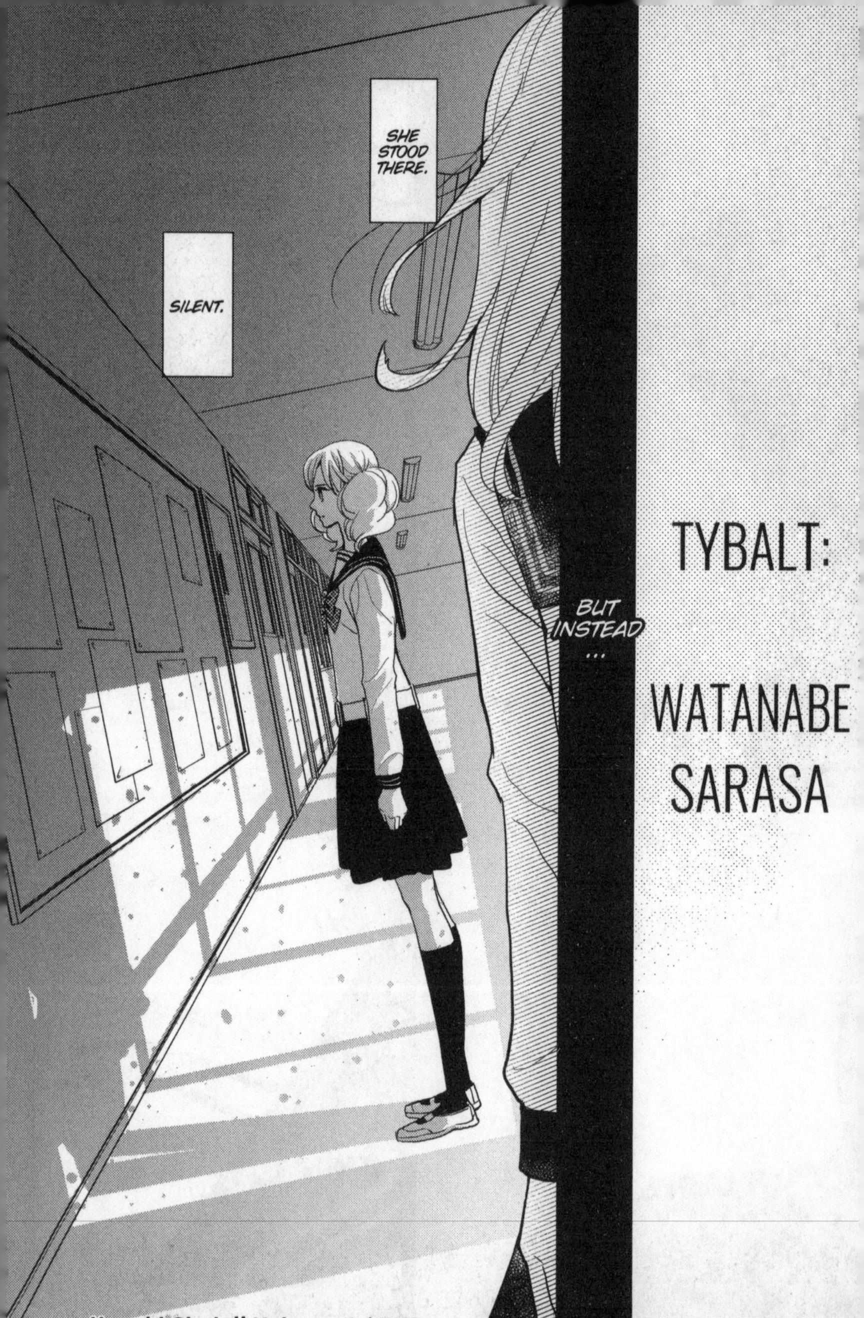
SHE STOOD THERE.
SILENT.
BUT INSTEAD ...
TYBALT:
WATANABE SARASA

Kageki Shojo!! Volume 6 / END

♡ Special Thanks ♡

Asai-san

Kazami-san

Karu-san

Momo-san

Nanami-san

Takisawa-san

Kuroki-san

Morita-san

Nono & Jill

&

all of

☙ my readers ❧

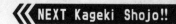

After missing out on the role, how will Class Rep Sugimoto handle the coming performance?

THE ROLES...

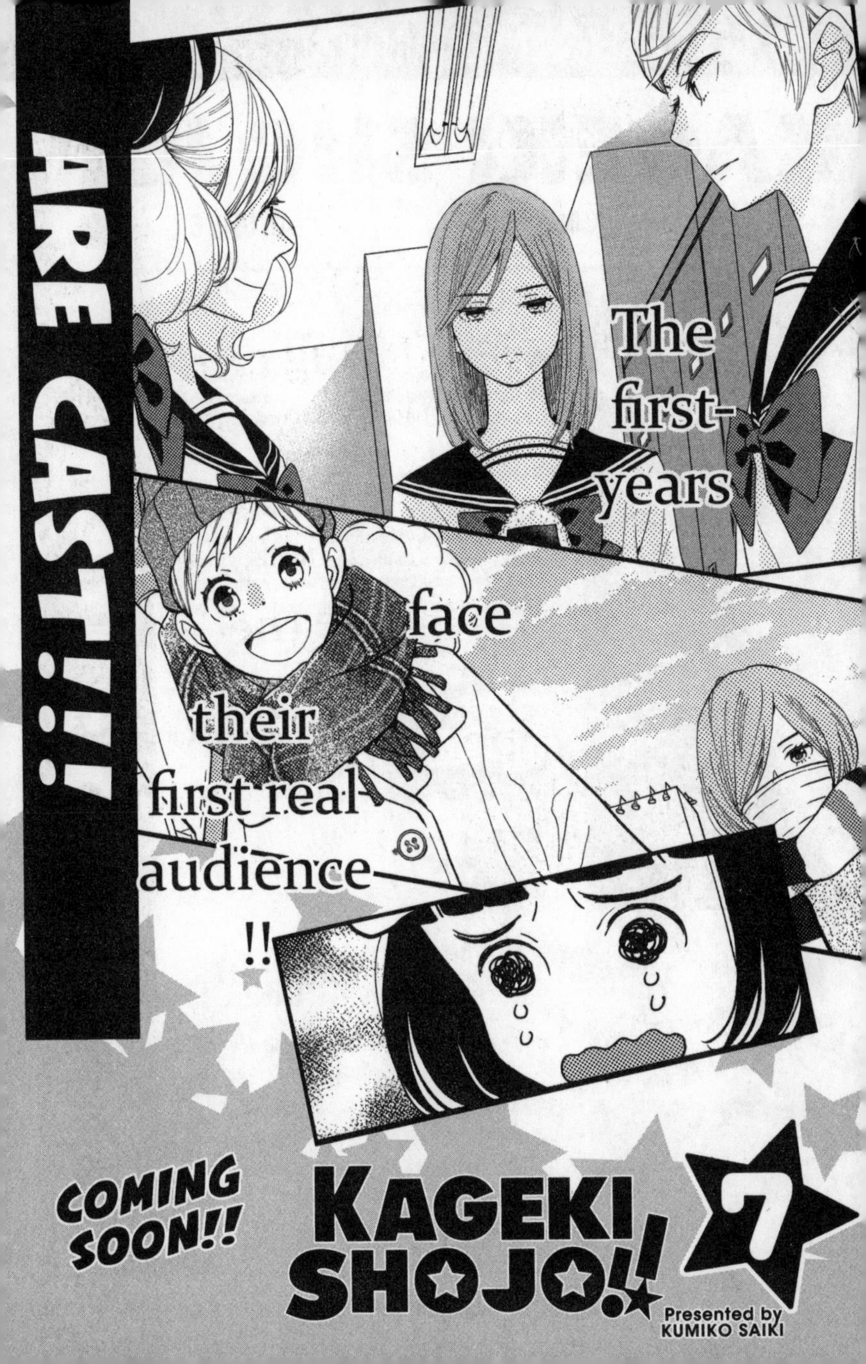
The first-years
face
their first real audience
!!
ARE CAST!!
COMING SOON!!
KAGEKI SHOJO!!
7
Presented by
KUMIKO SAIKI

SEVEN SEAS ENTERTAINMENT PRESENTS

KAGEKI SHOJO!!

story and art by **KUMIKO SAIKI** **VOLUME 6**

TRANSLATION
Katrina Leonoudakis

LETTERING
Aila Nagamine

COVER DESIGN
H. Qi

LOGO DESIGN
Courtney Williams

PROOFREADER
Alyssa Honsowetz

COPY EDITOR
B. Lillian Martin

SENIOR EDITOR
Shannon Fay

PRODUCTION DESIGNER
Christina McKenzie

PRODUCTION MANAGER
Lissa Pattillo

PREPRESS TECHNICIAN
Melanie Ujimori

PRINT MANAGER
Rhiannon Rasmussen-Silverstein

EDITOR-IN-CHIEF
Julie Davis

ASSOCIATE PUBLISHER
Adam Arnold

PUBLISHER
Jason DeAngelis

First published in Japan in 2018 by HAKUSENSHA, INC., Tokyo.
English language translation rights in U.S.A. arranged with HAKUSENSHA, INC., Tokyo through TOHAN CORPORATION, Tokyo.

Seven Seas press and purchase enquiries can be sent to Marketing Manager Lianne Sentar at press@gomanga.com. Information regarding the distribution and purchase of digital editions is available from Digital Manager CK Russell at digital@gomanga.com.

ISBN: 978-1-63858-306-6
Printed in Canada
First Printing: June 2022
10 9 8 7 6 5 4 3 2 1

READING DIRECTIONS

This book reads from ***right to left***, Japanese style. If this is your first time reading manga, you start reading from the top right panel on each page and take it from there. If you get lost, just follow the numbered diagram here. It may seem backwards at first, but you'll get the hang of it! Have fun!!

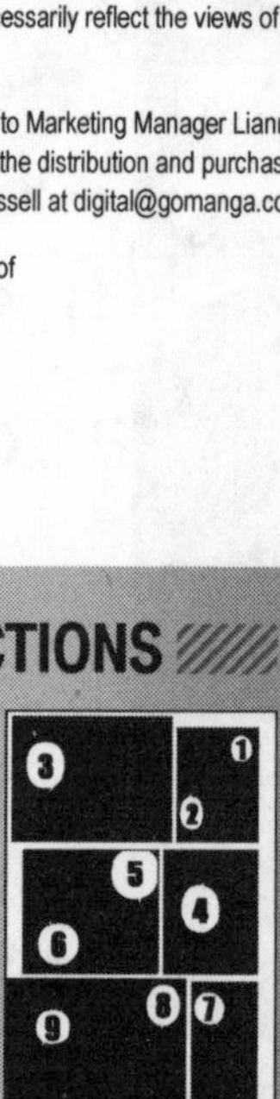
1
2
3
4
5
6
7
8
9

Follow us online: www.SevenSeasEntertainment.com